MW00477350

I & II CORINTHIANS

A Logion Press Commentary

Stanley M. Horton

Springfield, Missouri
02-0731

Logion Press books are published by Gospel Publishing House.

Library of Congress Cataloging-in-Publication Data
Horton, Stanley M.
1 & 2 Corinthians / Stanley M. Horton.
p. cm.
Includes bibliographical references and index.
ISBN 0-88243-731-3 (hc.)
1. Bible. N.T. Corinthians—Commentaries.
I. Title. II. Title: 1 and 2 Corinthians. III. Title: First & Second Corinthians.
IV. Title: First and Second Corinthians.
BS2675.3.H68 1999
227'.2077—dc21

Printed in the United States of America

CONTENTS

PREFACE

Because of Paul's concern that the gifts of the Spirit edify the Church, Pentecostals and charismatics have given special attention to his letters to the Corinthians. Paul, however, deals with many other practical problems in these letters. His inspired teaching, directions, and warnings are relevant today and need to be applied to our own congregations and to our individual lives. We all need to be open to what the Spirit has to say to us through God's holy Word.

In quoted Scripture, words I wish to emphasize are highlighted with italics.

For easier reading, Hebrew, Aramaic, and Greek words are all transliterated with English letters.

A few abbreviations have been used:

Gk.: Greek
Heb.: Hebrew
Lat.: Latin
KJV: King James Version
NASB: New American Standard Bible
NCV: New Century Version
NEB: The New English Bible
NKJV: New King James Version
RSV: Revised Standard Version

My special thanks go to Dr. Zenas Bicket and Dr. Rob Starner for reading the manuscript and making valuable suggestions. Special thanks also to Glen Ellard, Paul Zinter, and Leta Sapp at Gospel Publishing House and to all who assisted in preparing this book. Thanks also to my wife, Evelyn, for her encouragement.

FIRST CORINTHIANS

INTRODUCTION TO FIRST CORINTHIANS

CORINTH IN THE FIRST CENTURY

The splendid commercial city of Corinth was located just south of the ten-mile wide isthmus that connects central Greece with the Peloponnesus. It dominated the harbors of Lechaeum two miles on the west and Cenchreae six miles on the east (Acts 18:18; Rom. 16:1–2). To avoid a two-hundred-mile trip around the stormy Cape Malea, ships would dock at these harbors and have their cargoes transported across the isthmus and loaded on ships waiting on the other side. Small boats were also hauled across. Dominating this commerce made Corinth wealthy.

Though the site of Corinth was occupied as early as the Neolithic Period, Romans destroyed it about 146 B.C. and left it deserted until 44 B.C., when Julius Caesar rebuilt it as a Roman colony for freed slaves (mostly Syrians, Egyptians, and Jews). Though Latin was made the official language, Greek was the language spoken by the people, and the culture was definitely Greek. The people were proud of their culture and many were intellectually arrogant.

The emperor Augustus made Corinth the capital of Achaia, which was governed by a proconsul (Acts 18:12). Its situation and prosperity attracted a large population, possibly 250,000 citizens plus 400,000 slaves, with quite a number of Jews being found in both groups. It was also a host city to sailors and travelers coming on business or looking for pleasure.

Just southwest of the ancient city, Mount Acrocorinth rose to an elevation of 1,886 feet and had a temple of Aphrodite on its summit. A large marketplace (Gk. *agora*) in the center of the city was surrounded by shops. These would include the meat markets mentioned in 1 Corinthians 10:25. Archaeologists have found inscriptions, one mentioning Erastus, a friend of Paul, as the commissioner of public works (see Acts 19:22; Rom. 16:23; 2 Tim. 4:20), and another found in a residential district reading "Synagogue of the Hebrews" (Acts 18:4).[1]

[1]Jack Finegan, *Light From the Ancient Past*, 2d ed. (Princeton, N.J.: Princeton University Press, 1959), 361.

Corinth was famous for its art, architecture, bronze foundries, baths, temples, and law courts. But the morals of its pagan society were so corrupt that "to Corinthianize" came to mean to live a most dissolute life. There were thousands of priestesses in the temples (especially the temple of Aphrodite, the so-called goddess of love) who were slave girls used as prostitutes selling their bodies as a religious act to raise money for the temples. They also acted as entertainers in the night life of the city. Every kind of sin was common and open in the city.

Paul would also have been aware of the Isthmian games held every year about ten miles east of Corinth; it included footraces, chariot races, wrestling , jumping, discus and javelin throwing, and a combination of boxing and wrestling. In addition there were competitions in music, oratory, and drama. The victor's crown was a wreath of dried wild celery. No wonder Paul called it a crown that will not last (1 Cor. 9:25).

Paul's Ministry In Corinth

Paul must have recognized both the great need in Corinth as well as its strategic location for evangelism. He arrived there during his second missionary journey, probably in A.D. 50 or 51. Shortly after his arrival he met Aquila, a Jew born in the Roman province of Pontus in northern Asia Minor, and his wife, Priscilla (Acts 18:2; 1 Cor. 16:19). Since Aquila was a common slave name it may be that when the Romans invaded Pontus, they captured his family and sold or gave them as slaves in Rome. Later, many Romans considered it a religious thing to set slaves free and would even set them up in business. Because Priscilla (a diminutive form of Prisca) was a common name among high-class Romans, it may be that Aquila won her to the worship of the one true God, was set free, and married her.

In any case, Aquila and Priscilla were successful tentmakers in Corinth and Paul joined them, working daily at the tentmaking trade and preaching in the synagogue on the Sabbath. With great intensity he proclaimed Jesus as the Messiah, God's anointed Prophet, Priest, and King. Soon most of the unbelieving Jews took a strong stand against the gospel, even using abusive language against Paul. He shook his outer garments against them to show he rejected their blasphemy and called down their blood on their heads, thus warning them that they would be responsible for the judgment God would send on them (cf. Ezek. 3:16–21). Paul then went next door to the house of Titius

Justus, who was probably a Roman citizen. A number of Jews joined Paul, including Crispus, the ruler (elder) of the synagogue, and his household. A large number of Gentiles believed and were baptized.

In a night vision Jesus told Paul not to fear, that he should keep on proclaiming the Word, that the Lord would not let anyone harm him. Many then did come to Jesus, and no one harmed Paul, just as Jesus promised. But in the spring of A.D. 51 a new proconsul, Gallio, was appointed by the Roman Senate.[2] Probably thinking they could take advantage of Gallio's lack of knowledge of the situation, unbelieving Jews rose up against Paul and brought him before the proconsul's tribunal. They accused Paul of persuading people to worship God in a way contrary to Roman law. (Judaism was a legal religion, so they were saying Christianity was different from Judaism and therefore illegal.) Gallio saw that the case really involved only their Jewish law, and he had them driven from the tribunal. This pleased the (Greek) crowd, and they seized Sosthenes, the new ruler of the synagogue, and punched him with their fists. Paul continued to minister for a time in Corinth and even Sosthenes accepted the gospel (1 Cor. 1:1).

Authorship, Occasion Of Writing, and Date

Paul came to Ephesus during his third missionary journey.[3] He spoke freely in the synagogue for three months, then opposition arose. He then withdrew and for two years he taught and preached daily in the lecture hall of Tyrannus (Acts 19:8–10). Apollos taught in Corinth during part of this time. But when problems arose, the Corinthian believers sent Paul letters, to which he replied. The first brief reply (see 1 Cor. 5:9), which has not been preserved, counseled them to avoid fellowship with immoral people; they took this to mean immoral unbelievers, though Paul meant Christians who became immoral (5:10–11).[4] Then some Corinthians belonging to the household of Chloe reported disharmony to Paul. Following that, a letter (probably

---

[2]Inscriptions indicate Gallio arrived in Corinth as proconsul on July 1, A.D. 51, and continued to July 1, A.D. 52. Acts 18:12 records how the Jews dragged Paul before Gallio, probably early during that period.

[3]Ephesus in the province of Asia was across the Aegean Sea from Corinth. Paul traveled from Ephesus to Corinth by way of Troas and Macedonia.

[4]Some writers take 2 Cor. 6:14 through 7:1 to be part of this letter; however, that passage deals with relations to unbelievers rather than believers. See Everett F. Harrison, *Introduction to the New Testament*, rev. ed. (Grand Rapids: Wm. B. Eerdmans, 1984), 284.

brought by Stephanas, Fortunatus, and Achaicus; 16:17) raised several questions involving serious problems. Paul, inspired by the Holy Spirit, proceeded to deal with these matters in 1 Corinthians about A.D. 54 or 55. In addition to dealing with sins, he deals with marriage, public worship, the Holy Spirit's gifts and ministries, and an offering for the Jerusalem saints. Some commentators suppose Titus delivered the letter. Others think the brothers mentioned in 16:17 may have been the bearers.

First Corinthians was circulated and recognized very early as being from Paul. Clement of Rome referred to it in his first epistle to the Corinthians about A.D. 95.[5] The Muratorian Canon (about A.D. 170) put it at the head of the list of Paul's epistles. The Church as a whole, down through the centuries, has continued to recognize it as authored by Paul and as being a part of the inspired canon of Scripture.

[5]Clayton N. Jefford, *Reading the Apostolic Fathers* (Peabody, Mass.: Hendrickson Publishers, 1996), 108.

FIRST CORINTHIANS OUTLINE

I. Introduction 1:1–9

A. Greeting 1:1–3

B. Complimenting the Corinthians 1:4–9

II. Dissension in the Church 1:10–4:21

A. An appeal for unity 1:10–12

B. Reasons for unity 1:13–3:23

1. The message of the Cross 1:13–2:16
   a) Christ is not divided 1:13–17
   b) Salvation through the crucified Christ 1:18–25
   c) No one can boast before God 1:26–31
   d) Paul's preaching 2:1–5
   e) The wisdom of God 2:6–16
2. The Church is God's field, God's building 3:1–9
3. A judgment day is coming 3:10–15
4. The Church is God's temple 3:16–17
5. All things are yours 3:18–23

C. Paul's faithfulness 4:1–21

1. The Lord will judge 4:1–5
2. No reason for boasting 4:6–7
3. The apostles a spectacle to the universe 4:8–13
4. Paul their father through the gospel 4:14–17
5. Paul will deal with arrogant people 4:18–21

III. Sinning Christians must be judged 5:1–6:19

A. Sexual immorality ignored 5:1–13

1. The sinner needs to be dealt with 5:1–5
2. Get rid of the old yeast 5:6–8

3. Judge and expel sinning Christians 5:9–13

B. Let believers judge believers 6:1–8

C. The wicked will not inherit the kingdom of God 6:9–11

D. Flee sexual immorality 6:12–19

1. The body is meant for the Lord 6:12–17
2. The body is the temple of the Holy Spirit 6:18–19

IV. QUESTIONS ANSWERED 7:1–11:2

A. Marriage 7:1–40

1. Avoid immorality 7:1–7
2. Advice to the unmarried and widows 7:8–9
3. Divorce forbidden by the Lord 7:10–11
4. Living in peace with unbelieving spouses 7:12–16
5. Remaining in the situation God calls one to 7:17–24
6. Should virgins marry? 7:25–38
7. A widow is free to remarry 7:39–40

B. Food sacrificed to idols 8:1–13

1. Love builds up 8:1–3
2. Idols are nothing 8:4–6
3. Do not become a stumbling block to the weak 8:7–13

C. Paul's apostleship 9:1–27

1. Paul's claim to apostleship 9:1–2
2. The rights of preachers 9:3–14
3. Paul did not make use of his rights 9:15–18
4. Paul's servant leadership 9:19–22
5. Paul's self-discipline 9:23–27

D. Examples from Israel's history 10:1–13

1. God's displeasure with most who crossed the Red Sea 10:1–5
2. Reasons for God's displeasure 10:6–10
3. Warnings for us 10:11–13

E. Flee idolatry 10:14–22

F. Seek the good of others 10:23–11:2

V. Directions for worship 11:3–33

A. Propriety in prayer and prophecy 11:3–16

B. Propriety in the Lord's Supper 11:17–34
1. Divisions expressed 11:17–22
2. The Lord's directions 11:23–26
3. Partaking in an unworthy manner 11:27–34

VI. Spiritual gifts 12:1–14:40

A. A variety of gifts given and needed 12:1–31
1. Do not be ignorant of spiritual gifts 12:1–3
2. The work of the Trinity 12:4–6
3. Distributed by the Spirit for the common good 12:7–11
4. One body with many parts 12:12–20
5. Every part needed 12:21–26
6. A variety appointed in the Church 12:27–31

B. Gifts must be exercised with love 13:1–13
1. The necessity of love 13:1–3
2. The nature of love 13:4–7
3. The priority of love 13:8–13

C. The gifts of prophecy and tongues 14:1–40
1. Prophecy edifies the church 14:1–5
2. Tongues need interpretation 14:6–19
3. The effects of tongues and prophecy 14:20–25
4. Worship in an orderly way 14:26–40
   a) Contribution to worship by all 14:26
   b) Directions for tongues speakers 14:27–28
   c) Directions for prophets 14:29–33
   d) Directions for women 14:34–35
   e) The Lord's command 14:36–40

VII. Christ's resurrection and ours 15:1–58

A. The gospel Paul preached 15:1–11

B. The reality of resurrection of the dead 15:12–58

1. The resurrection is vital to our hope 15:12–19
2. Christ's resurrection and the final consummation 15:20–28
3. A challenge to believe in the resurrection 15:29–34
4. The resurrection body 15:35–54
5. Victory through Christ 15:55–58

VIII. Concluding instructions 16:1–24

A. The collection for God's people 16:1–4

B. Paul's expectation to come to Corinth 16:5–9

C. Concern for Timothy and Apollos 16:10–12

D. A challenge to faith, courage, and love 16:13–14

E. Recognition for the household of Stephanas 16:15–18

F. Concluding greetings and benediction 16:19–24

I. INTRODUCTION 1:1–9

A. Greeting 1:1–3

[1]Paul, called to be an apostle of Christ Jesus by the will of God, and our brother Sosthenes,

Paul, following the Greek custom in letters, identifies himself and then declares his authority as a called apostle ("sent one") of Christ (the Messiah, God's anointed Prophet, Priest, and King) Jesus. He was called and sent out by Jesus just as the other apostles were. His authority was confirmed further as being "by the will of God." It was not his own idea, nor did he desire to become an apostle when he was stopped on the Damascus road (Acts 9:1–30). Like the other apostles, he was chosen by Jesus (see Luke 6:12–13; John 15:16). Encouraged by Ananias and Barnabas, he began to minister boldly (Acts 9:20–22, 26–30; 11:22–26). Later, the apostles in Jerusalem recognized Paul's apostleship and ministry to the Gentiles and gave him the right hand of fellowship (Gal. 2:7–9). Even so, some, especially in Corinth, questioned and some rejected his apostleship. Because he was the last of the apostles to see the risen Christ, those who did accept it considered him "abnormally born" (1 Cor. 15:7–8). Because of this, some challenged his apostolic authority (1 Cor. 9:3; 2 Cor. 11:4–6,13). Thus, he was careful to declare his apostleship again and again as not "by man, but by Jesus Christ and God the Father" (Gal. 1:1; 2:8; cf. Rom. 1:1; 11:13; 1 Cor. 1:1; 9:1; 2 Cor. 1:1; 12:12; Eph. 1:1; Col. 1:1; 1 Tim. 1:1; 2:7; 2 Tim. 1:1,11).

A certain Sosthenes was the chief ruler of the Jewish synagogue in Corinth when the Jews dragged Paul before the judgment seat of the Roman proconsul Gallio. Gallio threw the case out of court and the crowd beat up Sosthenes (Acts 18:12–17).[1] Sosthenes was not a common name, so it is probable that the same Sosthenes became a Christian, joined Paul to learn more of the gospel in order to become a good minister of Christ, and is here identified as "Brother Sosthenes."[2] Nothing indicates that he had any part in writing the letter, however. He was with Paul and Paul included him in the saluta-

[1]For the identity and motive of the crowd see Introduction, 11.

[2]The Greek has "Sosthenes the brother," which is best taken as a title as in the *Jerusalem Bible.*

tion because he was well-known to the Corinthian church.[3]

> **[2]To the church of God in Corinth, to those sanctified in Christ Jesus and called to be holy, together with all those everywhere who call on the name of our Lord Jesus Christ—their Lord and ours: [3]Grace and peace to you from God our Father and the Lord Jesus Christ.**

God's church (Gk. *ekklēsia,* "assembly of citizens") "in its local expression"[4] in Corinth is identified as consisting of those who have been (and still are) sanctified or made holy in and by Christ Jesus.[5] This is the position they have in Him not because of their righteousness but because of His (Rom. 3:22; 4:11–12,23–24; Phil. 3:9). This righteousness by faith leads to true holiness (Rom. 6:19; Eph. 4:24). As believers they are the called ones. Old Testament prophets were called of God. Paul was called. All believers are called, for they have responded to God's call to salvation and holiness (Rom. 1:6–7; cf. Rom. 8:28; Jude 1; Rev. 17:14).[6] All believers are holy ones (separated ones), "saints by calling" (NASB), meaning that in and by Jesus Christ, offering of himself on the cross, they have been set apart for the worship and service of God (Heb. 10:10). That is, whatever they do (including secular work), they are to work at it with all their hearts, "as working for the Lord, not for men. . . . It is the Lord Christ you are serving" (Col. 3:23–24). He expects us to do all our work as well as our worship with excellence, enthusiasm, and good ethics. This practical confession of the lordship of Jesus is an important evidence of the work of the Holy Spirit in our lives.

We note that Paul calls them all holy ones or saints, even though some still had problems and some were doing wrong things. They were not yet perfect, but they were headed in the right direction. They

---

[3]As the use of the article in the Gk. implies. See Archibald Robertson and Alfred Plummer, *A Critical and Exegetical Commentary on the First Epistle of St. Paul to the Corinthians,* 2d ed. In The International Critical Commentary Series (Edinburgh: T. & T. Clark, 1914), 2.

[4]George Eldon Ladd, *A Theology of the New Testament* (Grand Rapids: Wm. B. Eerdmans, 1974), 537. Ladd points out that the "local church is not part of the church but is *the church* in its local expression," making all Christ's power available to it (italics in original).

[5]The Father (1 Thess. 5:23) and the Holy Spirit (Rom. 15:16) are also involved in our sanctification.

[6]Stanley M. Horton, ed. *Systematic Theology,* rev. ed. (Springfield, Mo.: Logion Press, 1995), 359, 533.

had turned their backs on the ways of the world to follow Jesus. Unfortunately, some human traditions have used the word "saint" for people who are supposed to have special merit. However, none of us can depend on our own merits. We must depend wholly on the merits of our crucified and risen Savior, Jesus. The Holy Spirit will help us put into practice the righteousness and holiness that is ours through Christ. The plural (i.e., "those") also indicates that we are to work and worship in fellowship with each other.

Then because Paul wanted the Corinthian believers to remember they were part of the larger body of Christ and because he expected this letter to be circulated to other churches, he includes all those who call on the name of our Lord Jesus Christ, that is, who are saved by Him, born again by the Holy Spirit, and who pray to Jesus. By calling Him "their Lord and ours" Paul emphasizes the unity of the Church under the lordship of Jesus Christ. This also extends the invitation to believers throughout time, including us, to read this letter and receive grace (unmerited favor) and peace (including health and well-being) that come from God, who is now our Father, and from Messiah ("Anointed One") Jesus, who is now our Lord—not just master, but divine Lord. He is the same Person who revealed himself as the Angel of the Lord and received worship in the Old Testament (Num. 22:31; et al.). He desires to pour out His gifts and blessings on all who believe, trust, love, and serve Him.

B. Complimenting The Corinthians 1:4–9

4I always thank God for you because of his grace given you in Christ Jesus. 5For in him you have been enriched in every way—in all your speaking and in all your knowledge—6because our testimony about Christ was confirmed in you.

During much of this letter Paul has to deal with problems and wrong teachings that arose among the Corinthian believers and caused many of them to oppose him. However, God deserves our thanks, so he begins on a positive note thanking God always for God's grace (Gk. *charis,* including both a state of grace which is theirs because of the redemptive work of Christ and also all the charismatic gifts[7]) given to

[7]Robertson and Plummer, *Commentary,* 5. Fred Fisher, *Commentary on 1 and 2 Corinthians* (Waco, Tex.: Word Books, 1975), 21.

them now that they are in Christ and are part of His Body, the Church, and in right relation to Him.[8] This grace was being manifest in two special ways, in their speaking (including tongues, interpretation, and prophecy) and in the rich knowledge (including the gift of the word [message] of knowledge) that their speaking revealed.[9] Verse 6 indicates their speaking and knowledge was about the Christ, the Messiah. Paul's testimony about Him came from the Old Testament Scriptures as well as from what he had learned from Jesus himself. It was confirmed among them by the work of the Holy Spirit as He guided and empowered their church. Hebrews 2:3–4 indicates it was "by signs, wonders and various miracles, and gifts of the Holy Spirit distributed according to his [God's] will." These supernatural manifestations demonstrated that Paul's testimony about Christ was confirmed in exactly the same way the other apostles' testimony about Christ was confirmed (Acts 2:43; 4:29–30; cf. 1 Cor. 9:2). The Spirit's witness also brought it home to their hearts (2:4–5; Gal. 4:6).

> **7Therefore you do not lack any spiritual gift as you eagerly wait for our Lord Jesus Christ to be revealed. 8He will keep you strong to the end, so that you will be blameless on the day of our Lord Jesus Christ. 9God, who has called you into fellowship with his Son Jesus Christ our Lord, is faithful.**

Because the Spirit confirmed Paul's witness to Christ and because the people responded in faith and obedience to the Spirit in His distribution of the gifts, all of the spiritual (charismatic) gifts[10] were present among them. This implies "a dynamic experience of the Spirit Himself."[11] This is something to keep in mind. Paul is writing to a

---

[8]Gordon Clark suggests that like Paul we should not only count our blessings, but our neighbor's as well to see what the Lord has done. Gordon H. Clark, *First Corinthians: A Contemporary Commentary* (Nutley, N.J.: Presbyterian & Reformed Publishing Co., 1975), 10.

[9]Speaking and knowledge were gifts highly prized by the Greeks. See Stanley M. Horton, *What the Bible Says About the Holy Spirit* (Springfield, Mo.: Gospel Publishing House, 1976), 197. See also Gordon D. Fee, *The First Epistle to the Corinthians* (Grand Rapids: Wm. B. Eerdmans, 1991), 39.

[10]Gk. forms of *charisma* occur seven times in 1 Corinthians (1:7; 7:7; 12:4,9, 28,30,31). Every *charisma* is a gift of *charis* (grace), graciously given by the Spirit. The Holy Spirit used Paul in many of these gifts (cf. 1 Cor 14:18).

[11]J. Rodman Williams, *Salvation, the Holy Spirit & Christian Living,* vol. 2 of *Renewal Theology* (Grand Rapids: Zondervan Publishing House, Acadamie Books, 1990), 2:325.

congregation who have all experienced the baptism in the Holy Spirit with the initial outward evidence of speaking in other tongues. Later (chap. 14), Paul addresses their overuse of the gift of tongues and directs the Corinthians in the proper use of the gifts for edifying the Church and reaching out to unbelievers. But the problem is with the Corinthians and their attitudes. There is nothing wrong with the gifts. Paul never wants them to stop responding to the Holy Spirit and His gifts. He wants them to know that the gifts of the Holy Spirit are the God-given means for edifying or building up the local church, both spiritually and numerically, as chapters 12 to 14 indicate. Though human effort and modern business methods can bring together a great crowd, the Lord wants every local church to be Spirit-filled, Spirit-empowered, Spirit-gifted, and Spirit-led.

The intensity and reality of the Corinthians' faith was evidenced also by their anticipation of the return of Jesus, when He will be revealed in power and glory, a power and glory He now has at the Father's throne. As faithful Christians they lived every day expecting that it might be the day of His return. The Book of Revelation was not yet written, but from Old Testament prophecies and from the teachings of Jesus, Paul must have recognized that there would be a complex of events in the end times, so there might be some time before that day comes. But the emphasis is on the personal return of Jesus himself and the consummation of our redemption, not on the complex of events before and during that day (cf. 1 Thess. 1:9–10; 4:13–17). "Their attention was to be on the Lord, not on the time."[12] Thus, Paul reminded the Corinthians that Christ[13] would confirm them in their faith so they would be above reproach, unimpeachable in the Day of Christ (which will include the judgment seat of Christ; see Rom. 14:10; 2 Cor. 5:10). Progressive sanctification and the continued cleansing of the blood are implied (1 John 1:7).

At this point all believers expected that Jesus could return in their own lifetime. Paul later realized he would not live to see that day come, but he still anticipated it and the crown of righteousness it would bring for him and for all who long for Christ's appearing (2 Tim. 4:8). We too need to keep that anticipation and that recognition of the

---

[12]Stanley M. Horton, *Our Destiny: Biblical Teachings on the Last Things* (Springfield, Mo.: Logion Press, 1996), 145.

[13]Or, Paul may mean God would keep them strong. See Fee, *First Epistle to the Corinthians,* 43–44.

immanence of His return. It is one of the most important incentives to holy living (see 1 John 3:2–3).

The Corinthians recognized that the charismatic gifts of the Spirit were by grace through faith. They also expected them to continue until Jesus comes. So may we, for the time of His coming is not revealed even yet (Acts 1:7; Mark 13:32–33; also see comments on 13:12).

Until He comes in person, Jesus is with us in spirit, for the Bible promises He will never desert us nor leave us alone (Heb. 13:5). He is with us to impart His strength, to confirm our faith, and to establish us so that we may be victorious in the battle against sin and stand blameless before Him when He comes. He died and shed His blood "to present you holy in his sight, without blemish and free from accusation—if you continue in your faith, established and firm, not moved from the hope held out in the gospel" (Col. 1:22–23). We can do this because God has called us into fellowship (and partnership) with Jesus and because God is faithful (cf. Deut. 7:9; 2 Cor. 1:18). We know He is faithful because we have experienced His faithfulness as we have responded to His call into fellowship with His anointed Son, Jesus—who has become our Lord. This was made possible because God was faithful to send Jesus to save us. He faithfully works through Jesus who is "the author and perfecter of our faith" (Heb. 12:2). He faithfully works through the Holy Spirit and His gifts to purify, sanctify, and promote growth and maturity. God's faithfulness is always there to help us to be faithful.

Study questions for this section may be found in appendix B.

II. DISSENSION IN THE CHURCH 1:10–4:21

A. An Appeal For Unity 1:10–12

10I appeal to you, brothers, in the name of our Lord Jesus Christ, that all of you agree with one another so that there may be no divisions among you and that you may be perfectly united in mind and thought. 11My brothers, some from Chloe's household have informed

me that there are quarrels among you. 12What I mean is this: One of you says, "I follow Paul"; another, "I follow Apollos"; another, "I follow Cephas"; still another, "I follow Christ."

After his opening greetings, Paul, quickly turns to situations in the Corinthian assembly that need correction. He calls them brothers, recognizing them as fellow members of the family of God. (Paul's use of the term "brothers" throughout includes "sisters.") Then, speaking in the name and authority of Jesus Christ, he deals with a basic and most pressing problem. Solemnly, but gently, he urges them to make a change from dissension to unity—not organizational unity, but spiritual unity, a unity where they would be (by a process of gentle restoration) perfectly united[1] in mind and thought. Because Paul received the gospel directly from Jesus himself (Gal. 1:11–12), he must have known of Jesus' prayer for the unity of believers, a unity of love, and for a unity of relationship to Him and the Father, a unity of desire that the world might see the glory of Jesus and realize God the Father sent Him (John 17:20–26). Jesus wanted this unity so the witness of believers would be effective in a divided world. Consequently, Paul wanted them to give up any kind of party spirit. (As Paul later brings out in chapter 12, this does not mean unison or uniformity, but variety that operates in harmony.)

Paul knew there was a need for this exhortation to unity because some trusted friends from Chloe's household (who probably lived in Ephesus) visited Corinth and reported that there was a danger that factions might develop among them.[2] In fact, they were already arguing among themselves. Instead of seeking the unity of the Spirit under the headship of Christ, many of them were focusing on human leaders. Paul later indicates they were reasoning from a human standpoint. That is, they thought they had logical reasons for exalting human leaders.

Some were saying they were followers of Paul, probably because they felt they should be loyal to him as the founder of the assembly and the first one to give them the true gospel. Others were followers

---

[1]The Greek word means "knit together," used of preparing or mending nets (Matt. 4:21; Mark 1:19) and of restoring or rebuilding the temple (Ez. 4:12, 13,16; 5:3,9–11) as well as restoring erring brothers and sisters (Gal. 6:1).

[2]The Greek present subjunctive ("that there may be" v. 10) indicates that the church was not yet divided but the tendency was in that direction.

of Apollos, who was a fervent preacher as well as "a great help to those who by grace had believed. For he vigorously refuted the Jews in public debate, proving from the Scriptures that Jesus was the Christ" (Acts 18:28). He had done much to further establish the believers. Still others claimed to be followers of Cephas, that is, Peter (John 1:42), possibly because they knew of his anointed leadership since the Day of Pentecost and because he was one of the original apostles who had been with Jesus during His earthly ministry.[3]

But some said they were followers of Christ, possibly taking a superior attitude, as if they were more spiritual because of this claim. They may have implied that Christ belonged to them and not to the others.[4] It seems they are the ones Paul referred to as claiming a superior wisdom and knowledge (8:1) that made them free from restraints and moral demands (5:1–2; 6:12; 10:23). They distorted the gospel and were joining in the arguments with the same spirit of contention (2 Cor. 10:7, 10,11; 11:4, 20,21,23). Most of the problems Paul had to deal with in this letter probably came from their influence. Paul considered them false teachers, who were his enemies (4:18–19). Paul does not mention Peter again and he certainly would not be among the false teachers (cf. Gal. 2:7–8). Luke speaks favorably of the ministry of Apollos (Acts 18:27–28), as does Paul later (3:5–6; 16:12; Titus 3:13).

It is important today that we avoid becoming so attached to a pastor or evangelist that we trust that person more than we trust Christ. "We must always be careful to center our love, devotion, and loyalty upon God and His Word, not on any minister or person."[5]

B. Reasons For Unity 1:13–3:23

1. The Message Of The Cross 1:13–2:16

a) Christ Is Not Divided 1:13–17

13Is Christ divided? Was Paul crucified for you? Were you baptized into the name of Paul? 14I am thankful that I did not baptize any of you except Crispus and Gaius, 15so no one can say that you were baptized into my

---

[3]These may have been Jewish believers who had come to Corinth from Judea and knew Peter by his Aramaic name, Cephas.

[4]Robertson and Plummer, *Commentary,* 13.

[5]Donald Stamps, ed., *Full Life Study Bible* (Grand Rapids: Zondervan Publishing House, 1992), 1768.

name. 16(Yes, I also baptized the household of Stephanas; beyond that, I don't remember if I baptized anyone else.) 17For Christ did not send me to baptize, but to preach the gospel—not with words of human wisdom, lest the cross of Christ be emptied of its power.

Now Paul raises questions meant to refute the dissension and party spirit. Each group thought they had logic on their side. But they were reasoning in the same way Peter had when he wanted to put up three shelters on the Mount of Transfiguration. Like him, they needed a new vision of Jesus, of whom the Father said, "'This is my Son, whom I love; with him I am well pleased. Listen to him!'" (Matt. 17:5; cf. 1 Cor. 1:24). So Paul asks first if Christ is divided or separated into parts.[6] He later (chap. 12) recognizes the local assembly of believers as the Body of Christ, with parts that have different gifts, different functions, but still united and needing each other. So the emphasis here is on *wrongful* separation. The local assembly is one body and should not have parts divided against each other (cf. 12:25).

Instead of dealing with the other parties, Paul deals with those who claim to follow him in this wrongful way. His intention is to show how wrong that is, with the implication that they should apply the same arguments to the wrongfulness of following the others in a partisan way. To do this, Paul begins by giving reasons why they should not consider themselves his followers. Later, he does tell them to imitate him (4:16) and to follow his example as he followed the example of Christ (11:1). But they were not doing this. They were exalting themselves, probably not as a special party, but attaching themselves to his name, thinking themselves better than the rest of the church, drawing attention to themselves instead of to Christ. But all of these Corinthians were failing to take in the full meaning of the Cross. That is, they were looking at spiritual things from the standpoint of human reason instead of from the standpoint of what God did in Christ's death and resurrection.

Paul was not crucified for them. Focusing on Paul takes away glory from the One who died for them all, including Paul. Paul's name was not used when they were baptized into the name of the Father and the Son and the Holy Spirit. (Note that "into the name" [Gk., *eis to onoma*] is the same in Greek here as in Matthew 28:19, meaning "into

---

[6]Or, this may mean "is Christ apportioned out as only one among many . . . so that only one group has him?" Fee, *First Epistle to the Corinthians*, 60.

the fellowship, worship and service," but Acts 2:38 uses a different wording that could be translated "upon the name" [Gk., *epi to onomati*], meaning "upon the authority," and the authority is given by Jesus in Matthew 28:19).[7]

Since water baptism signifies the identification of the believer with Christ and indicates coming under the realm of His lordship and authority, Paul is very concerned that they do not suppose it had anything to do with their relationship to him. The Corinthian congregation was founded in the name of Jesus, not in Paul's name. Paul was not seeking their allegiance. There was certainly no grounds for belonging to a "Pauline" party. He was not a rival of Christ.[8] To be sure they understood this, he expresses thankfulness that he baptized only Crispus (the synagogue ruler, Acts 18:8) and Gaius (the wealthy man who hosted Paul and the church, Rom. 16:23) and the household of Stephanas (Paul's first converts in the province, 1 Cor. 16:15–17). Apparently, once Paul baptized a few Christians, he delegated them to take over the responsibility and privilege of baptizing new converts and thus welcoming them into the fellowship of the church. In this he was following the examples of Christ (John 4:1–2) and Peter (Acts 10:48).

Paul, however, was not minimizing the importance of water baptism (cf. Rom. 6:3–7). Rather, he was recognizing what his ministry was. He was sent (made a sent one, an apostle) to preach the gospel: the good news of salvation through Jesus Christ, salvation that would bring people into fellowship with God and Christ in the Holy Spirit, salvation that will be complete when Jesus comes again. The Corinthians were saved by grace through faith apart from water baptism (Eph. 2:8–9). Baptism came as a testimony to their faith after they believed and were brought into fellowship with God through the blood of Jesus. Paul certainly did nothing that would give reason for the factions that were in danger of developing in the church at Corinth.

To explain his ministry further, Paul goes on to say that his preaching was not a matter of explaining the truth in words of human wisdom, that is, in the manner of the clever Greek orators the Corinthians must have often heard. Nor did he let the human wisdom of the Greek philosophers influence his concept of the gospel and the teachings, ministry, and work of Christ—as was probably the case with some of them. "The gospel is not a philosophy but a message."[9]

---

[7]Horton, *Systematic Theology,* 175–76.
[8]Robertson and Plummer, *Commentary,* 13.
[9]Fisher, *1 and 2 Corinthians,* 28.

b) Salvation Through The Crucified Christ 1:18–25

18For the message of the cross is foolishness to those who are perishing, but to us who are being saved it is the power of God.

To those who are perishing—on their way to hell, spiritually dead and thus controlled by the sinful nature (Rom. 8:8), blinded by Satan (2 Cor. 4:4)—the message of the cross (and therefore, the whole doctrine of the atonement)[10] is absurd. They think it foolish to believe that the Roman execution of one declared to be a guilty criminal and enemy of the state could be used by God to bring salvation. But to those who are being saved—who have accepted Christ as Savior and Lord, who have a present relationship with God, who are living for Him, and who are on their way to heaven—the message of the Cross, the message that has at its center the death of Jesus on the cross and the shedding of His blood, is the power of God. They know it is, because they have experienced its power to save them. God's power is still necessary not only for salvation, but for sanctification, peace, spiritual blessing, and hope (cf. Rom. 15:13). His power is available also for healing and casting out demons.

The cross of Christ is full of God's power, for it was the means by which Jesus accomplished our salvation when He shed His blood and died for us. To try to explain the Cross or deduce its importance in terms of human wisdom and philosophy would rob it of its power, that is, of its ability to transform sinners into saints. That is exactly what liberal theologians are doing today. But Paul proclaimed its power to save, to deliver from sin and Satan, to heal, to restore fellowship with God—and so must we. The Holy Spirit will make the Cross and its power real to hungry hearts (cf. Rom. 1:16).

19For it is written: "I will destroy wisdom of the wise; the intelligence of the intelligent I will frustrate."
20Where is the wise man? Where is the scholar? Where is the philosopher of this age? Has not God made foolish the wisdom of the world? 21For since in the wisdom of God the world through its wisdom did not know him, God was pleased through the foolishness of what was preached to save those who believe.

Probably because Paul recognizes that the divisions in the church

[10]Clark, *First Corinthians,* 20.

are the result of human thinking and human wisdom, he goes on to make a strong contrast between God's wisdom ("it is written")[11] and human wisdom, the latter of which we might call "worldly common sense."[12] Most of this comes from human philosophies that take God off the throne and put self or human reason on the throne. Then because human wisdom has treated the Cross as something absurd, Paul refers to Isaiah 29:14 where God declares His purpose to destroy the "wisdom of the wise" and frustrate or set aside the "intelligence of the intelligent," causing it to vanish in the light of divine truth.

When Paul asks where is the wise man, the scholar (the expert teacher of the law of Moses),[13] or the philosopher of this age, he is emphasizing the futility of human wisdom. It has no ability to meet the real needs of people or to help them find God and salvation. We can see this in the writings of the ancient Greek philosophers that Paul must have read, since he was educated as a Roman citizen before he came under Gamaliel. (Gamaliel did not forbid the reading of Greek authors, and Paul refers to Greek writers in Acts 17:28.)

The same thing is true of most modern philosophies, especially the humanism and the atheistic existentialism that dominates much of education today. They portray the universe "as totally lacking purpose and ultimate destiny,"[14] and therefore without room for God or for any meaning or hope. They all end up on a dead-end street. Their naturalistic philosophies are truly foolish, truly absurd. We must avoid them and the secular worldview that depends on them.

God, however, knows that human wisdom could not know Him. Therefore, in His wisdom, He was pleased to use the preaching of what the world called foolishness in order to save those who believe.[15] The preaching of the Cross, along with the declaration that the crucified and resurrected Jesus is Lord and Savior, is still the power of God for the salvation of everyone who believes, that is, who keeps on believing and obeying the gospel (Rom. 1:16).

---

[11]That is, written in the Old Testament.

[12]Robertson and Plummer, *Commentary*, 19

[13]Fee, *First Epistle to the Corinthians*, 71.

[14]Michael D. Palmer, comp. and ed., *Elements of a Christian Worldview* (Springfield, Mo.: Logion Press, 1998), 35.

[15]The present active participle in the Greek indicates that they keep on believing and their faith keeps appropriating salvation. It is not enough to have believed once.

22Jews demand miraculous signs and Greeks look for wisdom, 23but we preach Christ crucified: a stumbling block to Jews and foolishness to Gentiles, 24but to those whom God has called, both Jews and Greeks, Christ the power of God and the wisdom of God. 25For the foolishness of God is wiser than man's wisdom, and the weakness of God is stronger than man's strength.

Paul knew the Jews came to Jesus demanding a miraculous sign from heaven (Luke 11:16, 29–30). This was characteristic of them. They knew from the Law and the Prophets that God is a miracle-working God. But they were not convinced by the miracles of Jesus. Jesus told them that the only sign that would save them would be the sign of the prophet Jonah—fulfilled in His death and resurrection. But even this sign would fail to convince them if they did not accept Jesus as the fulfillment of the prophetic Word (cf. what Abraham told the rich man in hell: "'If they [the rich man's brothers] do not listen to Moses and the Prophets, they will not be convinced even if someone rises from the dead'" [Luke 16:31]).

The Greeks, on the other hand, were not concerned about miracles. They loved to speculate and wanted to satisfy their intellectual curiosity. They exalted their philosophers and kept seeking human wisdom, exalting themselves and their own human reason as they did so. The only wisdom that could save them was a faith that accepts God's judgment on human wisdom and accepts the apparent foolishness (nonsense, stupidity, crazy idea) of the Cross as truly wise.

Paul kept preaching Christ as the crucified One even in the face of the opposition of Jews and Greeks, for those who respond to God's call, whether Jew or Gentile, find in Christ the power and wisdom of God. What the Gentiles thought was the crazy foolishness of God, that is, the Cross, proves to be wiser than any human wisdom. What the Jews thought was weakness when they saw Jesus hanging on the cross and dying proved to be stronger than any human strength. No human wisdom has been able to transform lives the way people are transformed when they come to the Cross. No human power has been able to raise the dead and give a new life to believers. Human wisdom cannot help us to know God. But we can all receive the answer to Paul's prayer that "the God of our Lord Jesus Christ, the glorious Father, may give you the Spirit of wisdom and revelation, so that you may know him better" (Eph. 1:17; cf. James 1:5).

c) No One Can Boast Before God 1:26–31

26Brothers, think of what you were when you were called. Not many of you were wise by human standards; not many were influential; not many were of noble birth. 27But God chose the foolish things of the world to shame the wise; God chose the weak things of the world to shame the strong. 28He chose the lowly things of this world and the despised things—and the things that are not—to nullify the things that are, 29so that no one may boast before him.

By calling them brothers, Paul wants them to know that he loves them in spite of what he must say to them. Apparently many of the Corinthians were taking pride in their Greek heritage and were beginning to take the superior attitude fostered by human wisdom. It may be that others boasted because of their spiritual gifts.[16] Paul calls them to face the facts of what they were at the time they accepted God's call to salvation (a call to whoever will believe, John 3:36). A few may have been wise, but only by human standards. Their wisdom was irrelevant in the light of God's wisdom. Crispus, the former synagogue ruler (Acts 18:8), and Gaius (Rom. 16:23) may have been wealthy. Erastus had a good position as the city's director of public works (Rom. 16:23). But their wealth and position were only by human standards and were irrelevant in the light of our position in Christ.

The great majority of the believers had no reputation as wise philosophers, influential teachers, or statesmen, nor were they members of the upper class of society.[17] As in so many cases in history, the gospel spread first among the poor and the downtrodden, those Jesus had great concern for and preached to (Matt. 11:4–5; 25:34–36).

They, in the eyes of the world, were not even persons: They were "foolish things." Yet God chose to use them to put to shame the wise. The world called them "weak things," but God used them to put to shame everything the world called strong. The world called them "low-born" or ignoble, despised things, and ignored them as if they had no existence—walked by them as if they were not there. But God used them to nullify the things that the world thought existed or treated as having being. He will ultimately bring down all worldly systems.

---

[16]Williams, *Renewal Theology,* 2:435.

[17]Roman and Greek society had practically no middle class. So Paul makes the contrast between the upper and lower classes.

Though these verses deal with the persons of verse 26, it is also true that God chose to show His power and bring His salvation through what the world called foolish things (especially the cross) to put to shame the wise, because their wisdom could not produce such a wonderful salvation. The same weak things put to shame the strong, for they could not change lives.

The Romans crucified thousands. As far as the world was concerned, the cross and Jesus on it would be just one more execution, an insignificant, even despised event. But God takes things that do not exist to nullify, or make of no effect, things that actually exist. That is, by His power as Creator and Redeemer He brings into existence events (the death and resurrection of Jesus) that will eventually bring worldly systems to an end.

From this we see that God's ways, standards, and values are different from the world's. We receive true wisdom only from Him, and when we see the foolishness of human wisdom and realize our inability to save ourselves, we cannot boast before Him, nor can any human being. We can only humble ourselves and recognize His greatness and power.

30It is because of him that you are in Christ Jesus, who has become for us wisdom from God—that is, our righteousness, holiness and redemption. 31Therefore, as it is written: "Let him who boasts boast in the Lord."

Not because of ourselves, but because of what God did through the death and resurrection of Jesus we are now in Christ, in right relation to Him, part of His body, the Church. Christ, who is the eternal wisdom of God (cf. Prov. 8), became wisdom for us from God. His wisdom that we have in Him and that He imparts to us includes His being our righteousness (cf. Rom. 4:24–25; Phil. 3:8–9), our holiness, including the sanctifying work of the Spirit whom Jesus promised to send (2 Thess. 2:13), and our redemption (Rom. 3:24; Eph. 1:7). Because of His redemption we who believe are delivered from the penalty and power of sin. Because of His righteousness being imputed to us, God looks at us just as if we had never sinned.[18]

Since Christ Jesus is the source of these things, and because they are the result of His sacrificial death on the cross (Heb. 10:10), we should not boast in them or in ourselves as possessing them. We can only fol-

---

[18]Horton, *Systematic Theology*, 366.

low Jeremiah's injunction to "boast in the Lord," which Paul states briefly; Paul undoubtedly means we should read the whole of Jeremiah 9:23–24, for he clearly had it in mind. For the Corinthian church, boasting in their human leaders was really a way of boasting about themselves, a way of exalting themselves. Any boasting or bragging can only bring harm to the church, but boasting in the Lord means we put our trust in Him and in Him alone.

In this chapter Paul develops what he has said about the superiority of God's power and wisdom and applies it to himself and his ministry.

d) Paul's Preaching 2:1–5

> **1When I came to you, brothers, I did not come with eloquence or superior wisdom as I proclaimed to you the testimony about God. 2For I resolved to know nothing while I was with you except Jesus Christ and him crucified.**

By calling them "brothers" Paul is acknowledging that he and all the believers in Corinth were members of the family of God. They are part of the family because Paul came not with the eloquence of Greek orators nor with the "superior" wisdom that was, like liberal theologies today, more philosophy than Bible. Unlike the philosophers, Paul did not desire to display the breadth of his knowledge or impress them with the extent of his vocabulary. He was concerned about only the content of his testimony about God, Christ, and salvation. So he proclaimed it in plain, simple language. When he said he resolved to know nothing "except Jesus Christ and Him crucified," he would spend no time proclaiming or even showing an interest in other subjects so that his hearers might experience the One he had come to know, the crucified Christ, and would thus come to experience "the testimony about God" in a positive relationship with Him.[19] He always stressed this when he came to a new place (see Acts 13:26–31). Nothing was more important than getting people to receive redemption through Christ.

---

[19]Some think Paul made this determination because of poor reception of the gospel in Athens. However, nothing is said to indicate that the synagogue in Athens rejected him. Apparently, they accepted him, and there were important converts at the Areopagus (Acts 17:17,34). It may be rather that he made this determination because he was concerned about the terrible wickedness and idolatry in Corinth.

[3]I came to you in weakness and fear, and with much trembling. [4]My message and my preaching were not with wise and persuasive words, but with a demonstration of the Spirit's power, [5]so that your faith might not rest on men's wisdom, but on God's power.

Paul includes himself among the weak things of the world that God is using. He came to Corinth "in weakness" (not sickness or illness, as the word sometimes means),[20] without worldly influence and without economic power or wealth. His "fear, and . . . trembling" were not a matter of timidity or cowardice, however. He recognized the awesomeness of God and of his responsibility to do the work God gave him to do. (See Ps. 2:11, where the kings of the nations were commanded to serve the Lord with reverence and rejoice in their awe, recognizing His powerful presence. See also 2 Tim. 1:7, "God did not give us a spirit of timidity, but a spirit of power, of love and of self-discipline.")

Paul refused to use the type of wise and persuasive words that characterized the Greek philosophers and orators because he knew that "like the word of the cross (1:18), the gifts of the Spirit are incomprehensible to the mind shaped by the world (2:4). It is precisely the work of the Spirit to reveal what this world cannot grasp on its own terms, namely that the power of God for salvation is to be found in the crucifixion of the Lord of glory (2:8–10; 2:2; 1:23–24)."[21] Paul understood, too, that when the Spirit gives power to witness (Acts 1:8), the witness is not just words but miracles, signs, and wonders that demonstrate the Spirit's power (Acts 2:32–33; 4:29–31; 5:12; 8:5–6; 14:3; Rom. 15:19; 1 Thess. 1:5; 2:13; Heb. 2:4). These demonstrations, including the baptism in the Holy Spirit with the initial evidence of speaking in tongues, give undeniable visible proof of God's desire to save, heal, restore, and give new direction to our lives.

God still wants our faith to rest on the power of the Holy Spirit, rather than depend on human wisdom. When we look at the wisdom of this world's wise men and philosophers, we see many of them contradicting each other. Their clever arguments are torn apart by other clever arguments. None of them knows all the facts or all the truth. All of them ignore or suppress everything that disagrees with their

---

[20]Some refer this to his "thorn in the flesh"; however, it may not have been a physical illness. See comments on 2 Cor. 12:7.

[21]Michael Duggan, "The Cross and the Holy Spirit in Paul," *Pneuma* 7, no. 2 (fall 1985): 137.

own thinking. They are all going down dead-end streets. But we can still receive the baptism in the Holy Spirit and step out in the same mighty power and gifts of the Holy Spirit that Paul and the apostles experienced. When the gospel is preached in the power and demonstration of the Spirit, lives are changed: People are delivered from slavery to sin and Satan, baptized in the Holy Spirit, and become faithful followers of the Lord as they learn to obey His righteous standards (Matt. 28:19–20).

e) The Wisdom Of God 2:6–16

**6 We do, however, speak a message of wisdom
among the mature, but not the wisdom of this age or
of the rulers of this age, who are coming to nothing.
7 No, we speak of God's secret wisdom, a wisdom that
has been hidden and that God destined for our glory
before time began. 8 None of the rulers of this age
understood it, for if they had, they would not have crucified the Lord of glory.**

Paul now uses the first person plural, probably to emphasize that he is speaking what is given him by Jesus through the inspiration of the Holy Spirit.

Though Paul did not use words of human wisdom, that does not mean he was ignorant or stupid or that the gospel is nonsense. He knew and proclaimed a higher wisdom, a better wisdom, than all the wisdom of this age, including that of the human rulers of this age. They may build great empires, but they are destined to come to nothing, doomed to perish. Paul made this better wisdom, this true wisdom (including all the fullness of the gospel with all of God's purpose and plan), available to mature believers. He implies, however, that many of the Corinthian believers were not yet mature, even though they thought they were (cf. 3:1; 14:20). They were still spiritual babies (see 3:1).

Though the wisdom Paul speaks is not worldly wisdom, neither is it the wisdom of the Old Testament. That wisdom, seen in the Book of Proverbs for example, was practical and often had to do with skills or with living well or with handling relationships. Paul calls the wisdom he taught "secret," or a mystery, because it was not fully revealed in Old Testament times and was never understood by the rulers of the age that began with Christ's first coming (cf. Luke 10:23–24). This wisdom is emphatically God's wisdom.[22] He destined it for our glory. Before time began God planned a salvation through Christ that would make it possible for us to share in His eternal glory. Paul brings this out in Romans, where he shows the gospel means justification by faith (chap. 4), assurance (chap. 5), victory over sin (chaps. 6,7), and our sharing in the glory of God and Christ (chap. 8). All this is included in the full, free salvation God prepared for us and made available through the Cross. We have a first installment of the glory now through the gift of the Holy Spirit (2 Cor. 1:22; 5:5; Eph. 1:14; 3:8,10). This assures us of what will be ours in the final state of the redeemed.

The rulers of this age who did not understand this include the Jewish leaders, the high priest, and the Romans, especially Pilate. What a contrast Paul sees between the weak, bleeding Jesus hanging on the cross and the reality of who He was and is, the Lord of glory[23] who reigns in majesty at the Father's throne—still bearing the marks of having been slain (Rev. 5:6).

> **9However, as it is written: "No eye has seen, no ear has heard, no mind has conceived what God has prepared for those who love him"—10abut God has revealed it to us by his Spirit.**

Paul explains this further by a free paraphrase condensed from Isaiah 64:4 and 65:17 in the light of Isaiah 52:15. What God has prepared is "not primarily the glories of heaven but the glories of the Cross and all it means in the plan of God."[24] These glorious truths of the gospel and the wonder of the Cross and the fullness of the salvation God has provided were not understood before God revealed them, beginning at the Day of Pentecost. "Mind" is the Greek *kardia,* usually translated "heart," but here it speaks of the inner mind, the deepest thoughts, and even includes the imagination. It is true Jesus opened the minds of the disciples after His resurrection (Luke 24: 45–47). However, the good news was not declared and spread until they received the promise of the Father, the gift of the Spirit (Luke

---

[22]Archibald Robertson and Alfred Plummer, *A Critical and Exegetical Commentary on the First Epistle of St. Paul to the Corinthians,* 2d ed. In The International Critical Commentary Series (Edinburgh: T. & T. Clark, 1914), 37.

[23]Divine glory, cf. Exod. 15:11; Ps. 24:7–10; Isa. 42:8; Matt. 16:27; John 17:24; Acts 7:2; Eph. 1:17.

[24]Stanley M. Horton, *What the Bible Says About the Holy Spirit* (Springfield, Mo.: Gospel Publishing House, 1976), 199.

24:49; Acts 1:4–5). Then the Spirit took the preaching of Peter and the other apostles and revealed the truth to the hearts and minds of those who heard and believed. Because they believed, because they saw what Jesus purchased on the cross, their hearts were filled with love for the God who so loved the world (John 3:16). So we too, through the Spirit, can now enjoy what God has prepared for us. Then, indeed, we shall share eternal fellowship with Jesus—which "will be wonderful beyond our present ability to imagine."[25]

The Spirit makes these truths available to all Christians. The word "us" is emphatic, contrasting with only a select few being able to attain wisdom, as worldly thinkers and philosophers taught. But the fact that the Spirit is the Revealer shows that we all need His illumination if we are to understand the Scriptures. As Jesus did for His disciples, so the Holy Spirit will do for us; for according to Jesus, the Holy Spirit is another Paraclete or Helper, just like Him (Luke 24:45; cf. Acts 15:28).

> **[10b]The Spirit searches all things, even the deep things of God. [11]For who among men knows the thoughts of a man except the man's spirit within him? In the same way no one knows the thoughts of God except the Spirit of God.**

We can depend on the Spirit's revelation of truth to us because He "searches, [or penetrates] all things," that is, He sheds light on them. Because He is deity, nothing is hidden from Him.[26] So He can and does shed light on the deep things of God, the profound truths that no human thinking, even of the most brilliant philosophers, has ever probed. They cannot for they do not have the Spirit.

Verse 11 confirms and explains further the fact that the Spirit knows and therefore correctly reveals "the deep things of God." We, as human beings, have secrets no one knows or perceives, but our spirit within us knows them. Even so the Spirit of God alone knows the thoughts of God. This does not mean we cannot know them. Rather, we know them as the Spirit reveals them (cf. John 14:9–11; 15:26; 16:13–15 which indicate that Jesus reveals the Father and the Holy Spirit reveals the Father and the Son).

---

[25]Stanley M. Horton, *Our Destiny: Biblical Teachings on the Last Things* (Springfield, Mo.: Logion Press, 1996), 258.

[26]Stanley M. Horton, ed., *Systematic Theology*, rev. ed. (Springfield, Mo.: Logion Press, 1995), 151.

[12]We have not received the spirit of the world but the Spirit who is from God, that we may understand what God has freely given us. [13]This is what we speak, not in words taught us by human wisdom but in words taught by the Spirit, expressing spiritual truths in spiritual words.

The "Spirit" we receive as Christians is very different from the "spirit of the world." That spirit is the spirit of human wisdom, the spirit that dominates a world alienated from God. Some take this spirit of the world to be Satan.[27] However, Paul does not seem to have Satan in mind here. Rather, it is the spirit of a world ruled by sin and by the sinful nature of unregenerate people. We have received the Spirit who is "from" God. Paul is talking here about the gift of the Spirit received in a specific, definite experience (as the Greek aorist tense indicates). In other words, Paul recognizes that he and all the Corinthian Christians received the promised gift of the Spirit. (He does not mention the initial outward evidence of speaking in other tongues here, for that was not an issue. Later he implies that all spoke in tongues, though all did not exercise the gift of tongues in the public meeting; see 12:30; 14:23.)

We have seen that one purpose of the gift of the Spirit is to give us power for witnessing (Acts 1:8). Now we see another purpose—to give us understanding of all that God has freely given us. The Spirit also witnesses to us that He indeed inspired the written Word of God, not in a mechanical way, of course, but by preparing the writers so that He could use their vocabulary and style to bring out the truth the way God wanted us to have it.

The understanding the Spirit gives includes understanding both salvation and the gifts that Paul speaks about. He did not begin his argument with methods of human wisdom and try to move toward the spiritual. He presented only what the Holy Spirit teaches, including what the Holy Spirit brought out from both the Old Testament and the teachings of Jesus.[28] He proclaimed them not with the words human wisdom uses to teach but with the words of the Spirit, explaining "spiritual truths in spiritual words."[29] Our vocabulary comes out

---

[27]Robertson and Plummer, *Commentary*, 45.

[28]See Acts 13:17–42 for an example of how the Holy Spirit used the Old Testament. Note also the promise of Jesus (John 14:26; 16:13–15).

[29]See Horton, *Systematic Theology*, 109.

of common experience. People who have not experienced the Spirit may borrow "spiritual words" from the Bible but cannot use them with their true meaning, for they have no understanding of spiritual things.

> **14The man without the Spirit does not accept the things that come from the Spirit of God, for they are foolishness to him, and he cannot understand them, because they are spiritually discerned. 15The spiritual man makes judgments about all things, but he himself is not subject to any man's judgment: 16"For who has known the mind of the Lord that he may instruct him?" But we have the mind of Christ.**

Paul emphasizes this further. "The man without the Spirit" is the *psuchikos anthrōpos,* "the natural or sensual human being," who relies only on what the physical senses relay and is thus concerned only with human aspirations and needs.

James adds that such wisdom "does not come down from heaven but is earthly, unspiritual [*psuchikē*], of the devil [*daimoniōdēs,* demonic in its nature or origin]" (James 3:15). Such people do not welcome the truths the Holy Spirit gives us. They reject them as silly or as so much stupidness. They are not able to understand or comprehend their truth. They have no way to evaluate spiritual truths, the truths of the gospel, for such things are "spiritually discerned." That is, they must be examined and evaluated in a manner consistent with the Holy Spirit. Only a person filled with the Spirit can do that.

For example, Israel was in an unspiritual condition in Isaiah's day. God told Isaiah that the very proclamation of the truth would "'make the heart of this people calloused; make their ears dull and close their eyes. Otherwise they might see with their eyes, hear with their ears, understand with their hearts, and turn and be healed'" (Isa. 6:10). John applies this verse to the people who would not believe in Jesus (John 12:37–41). Paul's preaching had the same effect (see 2 Cor. 2:14–16). (This does not mean that the Holy Spirit cannot use the Scriptures to lead "natural" or "sensual" human beings to faith in Christ and thus to salvation. It just means they cannot use their human reason or "common sense" to make a correct evaluation of the truth of the gospel.)

In contrast to the person who does not have the Spirit and does not have the ability to evaluate the Spirit's truths, the spiritual person, the person who has the Spirit and whose thinking is guided by the Holy

Spirit, is able to discern, examine, evaluate, understand, and make judgments about all "the" things. Though the Holy Spirit does help us discern what is going on in the world and will help us understand many things, the Greek article "the" indicates Paul means the specific things he has been talking about, the things of the Spirit, the truths about Christ and the Cross. When we, by the Holy Spirit, see these things in proper perspective, everything else is illuminated and we look at everything in a different light than the wise ones of the world do.

Besides the unbeliever having no ability to discern, examine, and evaluate spiritual truths, no unbeliever[30] is able to discern, evaluate, make judgments about, or understand the believer, who has the Holy Spirit, nor the believer's motives, lifestyle, or points of view.

To explain further why believers can make judgments, Paul quotes freely from Isaiah 40:13, where the point is that no one can regulate the Lord or tell Him what to do. He has all wisdom and needs no one to teach Him.[31] Then Paul identifies Christ with the Lord (for Jesus is God) and declares that we have the "mind of Christ" (cf. 1:30; Col. 2:3). We can know His will, His plan, His purpose. We can love the way He loves and evaluate things in the way He evaluates them. We can ask, "What would Jesus do?" and be able to give ourselves a correct answer.

This also gives another reason why the unbeliever cannot understand biblical truths or Spirit-filled people. Only when minds are joined with the mind of Christ through the activity of the Holy Spirit are such knowledge and understanding possible.[32] Gordon Fee notes that the contrast in this passage is between believer and unbeliever, not between elite Christians and "lesser" Christians who are living below their privileges. There are no grounds for elitism in the Bible.[33]

---

[30]Gordon H. Clark, *First Corinthians: A Contemporary Commentary* (Nutley, N.J.: Presbyterian & Reformed Publishing Co., 1975), 44. Clark points out that Paul did evaluate the Corinthian Christians and expected them to evaluate him, but "unbelievers do not have the mind of the Lord."

[31]Stanley M. Horton, *Isaiah*, vol. 12 of *The Complete Biblical Library: The Old Testament.* (Springfield, Mo.: World Library Press, 1995), 311.

[32]Howard M. Ervin, "Hermeneutics: A Pentecostal Option," *Pneuma* 3, no. 2 (fall, 1981): 18.

[33]Gordon D. Fee, *The First Epistle to the Corinthians* (Grand Rapids: Wm. B. Eerdmans, 1991), 120.

2. The Church Is God's Field, God's Building 3:1–9

[1]Brothers, I could not address you as spiritual but as worldly—mere infants in Christ. [2]I gave you milk, not solid food, for you were not yet ready for it. Indeed, you are still not ready.

In his first visit Paul could not teach the Corinthian believers true spiritual wisdom.[34] Though they were baptized in the Spirit and exercised gifts of the Spirit, Paul could not address them "as spiritual," that is, as wholly possessed and directed by the Spirit. Like ordinary people, they were still too worldly (Gk. *sarkinois,* "fleshly"), dominated by desires of the human flesh and mind.[35] They were acting like spiritual babies who had not grown in the things of Christ.[36] They had not grown spiritually to the point where they could understand the true wisdom he wanted to teach them.

Hebrews 5:13–14 identifies spiritual babies who live on milk as "not acquainted with the teaching about righteousness." They have not reached a maturity where they have "trained themselves to distinguish good from evil." They are familiar with "the elementary teachings about Christ . . . the foundation of repentance from acts that lead to death, and of faith in God, instruction about baptisms, the laying on of hands, the resurrection of the dead, and eternal judgment" (Heb. 6:1–2). These doctrines are important. However, the Corinthians needed to go on to the solid food of the most profound teachings of the Bible, teachings that have to do with righteousness and holiness.

[3]You are still worldly. For since there is jealousy and quarreling among you, are you not worldly? Are you

---

[34]This seems to imply that Paul had visited Corinth only once. "The second visit of painful character, which seems to be implied in 2 Cor. 13, may have been paid after this letter was written." Archibald Robertson and Alfred Plummer, *A Critical and Exegetical Commentary on the First Epistle of St. Paul to the Corinthians,* 2d ed. In The International Critical Commentary Series (Edinburgh: T & T. Clark, 1914), 53.

[35]See 1 John 2:16 for the Bible's definition of worldliness.

[36]Some see evidence here of a perpetual struggle between the old, carnal person and the new, spiritual one. John W. McKay, "The Experiences of Dereliction and of God's Presence in the Psalms: An Exercise in Old Testament Exegesis in the Light of Renewal Theology," in *Faces of Renewal,* ed. Paul Elbert (Peabody, Mass.: Hendrickson Publishers, 1988), 18.

not acting like mere men? [4]For when one says, "I follow Paul," and another, "I follow Apollos," are you not mere men?

The jealousy and quarreling (implying rivalry) among the Corinthian believers proved they were still worldly (Gk. *sarkikoi,* "fleshly"), dominated by the desires of the flesh and the mind, just like unbelievers (cf. 1 John 2:16).[37] They were acting like "mere men"—like ordinary, self-centered, unrenewed human beings, without a relationship with God—rather than like people who are truly led by the Spirit of God. Furthermore, the fact that they focused on men, arguing about whether they should follow Paul or Apollos, "indicated that there was confusion over the central message of the gospel."[38] They did not see the importance of the Cross in God's plan. Apparently, also, not many were following Paul, as the general tone of 1 Corinthians indicates. From chapter 5 on, Paul says no more about the arguments over human leaders and deals with the Corinthian assembly as a whole, most of whom had turned away from him.[39]

[5]What, after all, is Apollos? And what is Paul? Only servants, through whom you came to believe—as the Lord has assigned to each his task. [6]I planted the seed, Apollos watered it, but God made it grow. [7]So neither he who plants nor he who waters is anything, but only God, who makes things grow.

Paul here is talking about the work of preaching and teaching ministries. He and Apollos, like all who believe, are servants (see Luke 22:25–27). When people come to believe through the message, it is only because God's servants have been faithful to their assigned task. "Each" in KJV is translated "every man," referring back to Paul and Apollos, and means "every man who ministers," or better, each one (man or woman) who is assigned by the Lord to minister and through whom sinners come to believe.

---

[37]See Donald Stamps, ed., *The Full Life Study Bible* (Grand Rapids: Zondervan Publishing House, 1992), 1754–55, 1772–73, for a good discussion of the contrast between the spiritual person and "the unregenerated or fleshly person."

[38]Michael Duggan "The Cross and the Holy Spirit in Paul: Implications for Baptism in the Holy Spirit," *Pneuma* 7, no.2 (fall 1985): 136.

[39]Gordon D. Fee, "Tongues—Least of the Gifts? Some Exegetical Observations on I Corinthians 12–14," *Pneuma* 2, no. 2 (fall, 1980): 5.

No one has the right to choose which ministry he or she would like to perform. When Jesus told the apostles "'You did not choose me, but I chose you and appointed you to go and bear fruit—fruit that will last'" (John 15:16), He was not talking about salvation, but ministry. He was referring to the time when He spent a night in prayer and then, out of a large number of disciples, chose twelve to be with Him, to receive special training, and to be a special group of apostles (Luke 6:12–16). He does have a plan and a ministry for every believer but the choice is His, not ours.

In God's providence, Paul planted the seed of God's Word to establish the assembly at Corinth (Acts 18:1–17). Then Apollos watered it and cared for it, encouraging the assembly's spiritual development. But all the while Paul was planting and all the while Apollos was watering, God was making it grow. Thus, Paul and Apollos are really nothing. The attention of the assembly should not be on them, as if they were the important ones, but on God who alone makes possible salvation, spiritual growth, and growth in numbers (cf. Acts 2:47).

> **8The man who plants and the man who waters have one purpose, and each will be rewarded according to his own labor. 9For we are God's fellow workers; you are God's field, God's building.**

Those who spread the gospel and those who continue the work of building by edifying the believers are not rivals, though they are individually distinct. Both will be rewarded, and the rewards will differ, depending on how each one labors. Paul does not reveal the nature of the reward here. Probably we can refer back to the parables of Jesus concerning the talents (Matt. 25:14–30) and the minas (Luke 19:12–27).

Paul expected their labor to be "prompted by love" (1 Thess. 1:3). "Labor" (Gk. *kopon*) also implies working hard, toiling through difficulties, enduring hardships.

We must be diligent, responsible workers, and we must also be "workers *together* for God" (NCV)—not working "with" God, but working together under God—workers who cooperate with each other as we serve the Lord and build up the assembly of believers. We belong to God, and the assembly belongs to God. The assembly is His "field" (where He causes growth), His "building" (His temple where the Holy Spirit dwells). We are all His servants.

3. A Judgment Day Is Coming 3:10–15

[10]By the grace God has given me, I laid a foundation as an expert builder, and someone else is building on it. But each one should be careful how he builds. [11]For no one can lay any foundation other than the one already laid, which is Jesus Christ.

The grace by which Paul laid the foundation of the assembly in Corinth not only included unmerited favor but gracious gifts. These gifts, not his own intelligence and skill, made him the expert builder.

"Someone else," probably one or more of the current leaders of the Corinthian assembly, was building on that foundation. Apollos was probably not in mind here.[40] Acts shows Apollos was indeed careful how he built, for he too emphasized that Jesus was (and is) the Christ, God's anointed Prophet, Priest, and King (Acts 18:27–28).

Now others would need to be careful how they built always keeping the same foundation in mind. We, today, need to be careful that the one we focus our attention on, as we build up and edify our local assemblies, is the same Jesus revealed in the Scriptures, both in the Old and the New Testaments.

That foundation has been laid in the historical ministry, death, resurrection, and ascension of Jesus. No other foundation can be laid for God's *ekklēsia,* God's church, God's building.[41] This implies that if anyone introduces any other book than the Bible as the authority or any other doctrines than are found in the Bible, whatever they are building is not the Church.

[12]If any man builds on this foundation using gold, silver, costly stones, wood, hay or straw, [13]his work will be shown for what it is, because the Day will bring it to light. It will be revealed with fire, and the fire will test the quality of each man's work. [14]If what he has

---

[40]Gordon D. Fee, *The First Epistle to the Corinthians* (Grand Rapids: Wm. B. Eerdmans, 1991), 138.

[41]In Eph. 2:20 Paul does suggest that the Church is "built on the foundation of the apostles and prophets." "Perhaps this means that these early leaders were uniquely used by the Lord to establish and undergird the temple of the Spirit with the teachings and practices they had learned from Christ, which continue to be communicated to believers today through Scripture." Michael Dusing, "The New Testament Church," in *Systematic Theology,* ed. Stanley M. Horton, rev. ed. (Springfield, Mo.: Logion Press, 1995), 536.

built survives, he will receive his reward. 15If it is burned up, he will suffer loss; he himself will be saved, but only as one escaping through the flames.

Because of the Corinthians wrong attitudes they needed to be reminded that there is a judgment day coming. Then "the quality" (not the quantity) of every person's work will be tested for rewards. Paul has in mind here primarily the leaders of the Church. However, the testing of the Day of the Lord, that is, at the judgment seat of Christ, will surely involve the work of all believers (cf. 2 Cor. 5:10 which refers to all Christians). Some suppose Paul had in mind testing during persecution, others see it as a basis for purgatory, but "the Day" refers to a future day of judgment at the end of the age.[42]

"Gold, silver, [and] costly stones" speak of building up the assembly of believers with scriptural truth that enables them to live lives that bring glory to God before the world around them. "Wood, hay [and] straw" speak of inferior teaching coming from mere human wisdom or wrong motives, such as that which was bringing division and argumentation among the Corinthian believers.

Motives are also a consideration here. As 1 Corinthians 13:3 says, if I "have not love, I gain nothing," that is, I will have no reward. Thus, without love, any work we do for the Lord and for the church will turn out to be wood, hay, or straw, and will be burned up. Faithfulness, too, is important (Matt 25:21–23; Luke 12:42–43; Col. 3:23–24; Heb. 6: 10–11).[43] Paul, again, is primarily referring to leaders. They will not lose their salvation, but they will suffer loss of any reward. This will certainly make them feel ashamed (2 Tim. 2:15; 1 John 2:28), for they will not receive the glory and honor God wants to give them (Rom. 2:7–11).

4. The Church Is God's Temple 3:16–17

16Don't you know that you yourselves are God's temple and that God's Spirit lives in you? 17If anyone destroys God's temple, God will destroy him; for God's temple is sacred, and you are that temple.

42"The purpose of the 'fire' is not to *purge* but to *test* for reward. . . . No punishment is in view." James E Rosscup, "A New Look at 1 Corinthians 3:12—'Gold, Silver, Precious Stones,'" *The Master's Seminary Journal.* 1,no.1 (spring, 1990): 37n. 14.

43Stanley M. Horton, *Our Destiny: Biblical Teachings on the Last Things* (Springfield, Mo.: Logion Press, 1996), 85.

To emphasize the seriousness of the judgment (especially on wrong motives, wrong attitudes, and worldly wisdom, as well as works of the sinful flesh) Paul reminds the Corinthian believers that they are "God's temple," indwelt by the Holy Spirit. "You" in this passage is plural and refers to the local assembly of believers, who have fellowship "with the Father and with his Son, Jesus Christ" (1 John 1:3), because the Holy Spirit dwells in their midst (2 Cor. 13:14).[44] The Greek has two words for temple: (1) *hieron,* which includes the temple with all its courts, and (2) *naos,* the inner sanctuary where God manifested His presence. The Corinthian body of believers is the *naos,* for God's Spirit lives in them.[45]

Because the Church (including the local assembly) is sacred, that is, dedicated to God and to His service, anyone who "destroys" (corrupts or ruins) the assembly (specifically, the local assembly) is fighting against God, and "God will destroy him" (or her), that is, punish by eternal destruction in the lake of fire (cf. 2 Peter 2:8,10,12).[46] Every member of the local church, and especially its leaders, needs to regard the entire local body as holy, for God is holy (cf. Lev. 10:3; 1 Pet. 1:14–16).

5. All Things Are Yours 3:18–23

[18]Do not deceive yourselves. If any one of you thinks he is wise by the standards of this age, he should become a "fool" so that he may become wise. [19]For the wisdom of this world is foolishness in God's sight. As it is written: "He catches the wise in their craftiness"; [20]And again, "The Lord knows that the thoughts of the wise are futile."

Paul anticipates that some will think they are so wise that they do not need the warnings he has been giving. He warns them not to deceive themselves. As he pointed out in chapter 2, the wisdom of this world (the wisdom of this age) is not as wise as what the world calls the foolishness of God. Therefore, if they are measuring their wisdom

---

[44]See also 1 Cor. 6:19, which shows the Spirit also dwells in the individual believer.

[45]Dusing, "The New Testament Church," 537.

[46]Note that in this context the word "destroy" cannot mean annihilate. No human being could annihilate God's temple (God's people). See Horton, *Our Destiny,* 239.

by the standards of this age (in contrast to the wisdom God gives [cf. James 1:5]), they need to become a "'fool,'" that is, in the eyes of the world. Only when they humble themselves in this way, dropping their conceited ideas about their own wisdom and turning away from the false wisdom of the world, can they become truly wise; only then can they build the assembly instead of tearing it down.

To emphasize this, Paul reminds them that "the wisdom of this world is foolishness in God's sight." He confirms this from Scripture by quoting from Job 5:13 and Psalm 94:11.

> **[21]So then, no more boasting about men! All things are yours, [22]whether Paul or Apollos or Cephas or the world or life or death or the present or the future—all are yours, [23]and you are of Christ, and Christ is of God.**

Since the wisdom of this world is foolishness to God, it is foolish to boast about human leaders. Instead of saying I belong to Paul or Apollos or Cephas, we need to recognize that they belong to us. What Paul and Peter wrote in their epistles and the examples of Paul, Apollos, and Peter in the Book of Acts belong to us, but we belong to Christ. The same can be said of any human leader. For example, what Martin Luther taught about justification by faith alone belongs to us; but we do not belong to Luther, we belong to Christ. What John Wesley taught about holiness and perfect love belongs to us; but we do not belong to Wesley, we belong to Christ.

Beyond that, the world (Gk. *kosmos,* the world as people or as the scene of present life) belongs to us to enjoy as God intended. We can do so because we do not belong to the world and are not guided by it, nor are we any longer enslaved by it. We belong to Christ. Then, life and death, the present and the future, all belong to us. We do not have to be afraid of any of it. We are not slaves to any of it, because we belong to Christ. Because we belong to Christ, God has already "seated us with him in the heavenly realms in Christ Jesus" (Eph. 2:6). That has meaning because Christ is God's, that is, He is God's Son and the one Mediator between God and humankind. So through Him we belong to God. Then we have the additional promise in Romans 8: 28, "We know that in all things God works for the good of those who love him, who have been called according to his purpose." So we do not have to exalt ourselves. We cannot have a higher position than we already have in Christ. So we can afford to humble ourselves and serve the Lord and one another wherever He gives opportunity.

C. Paul's Faithfulness 4:1–21

1. The Lord Will Judge 4:1–5

1So then, men ought to regard us as servants of Christ and as those entrusted with the secret things of God. 2Now it is required that those who have been given a trust must prove faithful.

In view of the fact that Paul, Apollos, and Peter belong to the believers, men (Gk. *anthrōpos,* "people," "humankind") ought to look at them and other Christian leaders as servants of Christ sent by Him to help them.

Paul, Apollos, and Peter are also entrusted with the "secret things of God" (that were unrevealed mysteries in Old Testament times but are now revealed in the gospel).

They are entrusted not to keep or protect those "secret things" but to administer them to all believers. Because they have this responsibility, they are required to be faithful; that is, they must give themselves to the task of spreading the gospel regardless of the difficulties and regardless of the consequences.

3I care very little if I am judged by you or by any human court; indeed, I do not even judge myself. 4My conscience is clear, but that does not make me innocent. It is the Lord who judges me. 5Therefore judge nothing before the appointed time; wait till the Lord comes. He will bring to light what is hidden in darkness and will expose the motives of men's hearts. At that time each will receive his praise from God.

Paul was entrusted with administering the secret things of God by the Lord. Therefore, he was responsible to God, not to any human court with its human limitations, and certainly not to the Corinthians who were judging (examining, investigating, criticizing) him. Their opinion of him, his gospel, and his administration of it didn't matter to him. Neither did his own opinion of himself matter. Some people are always questioning themselves, wondering if they have done right or done what they should, always judging themselves. Paul didn't do that either.

From what we see in the Book of Acts, Paul was sensitive to both the checks and the guidance of the Holy Spirit. He took the doors that were open. When the Spirit stopped him from going to the province of Asia, he obeyed but did not sit idly waiting. He went on until the vision of the Macedonian call gave him further guidance. He faithfully preached the gospel, taught the people, and even went from house to house (Acts 20:18–21). Thus, he could say, "My conscience is clear." (He refers here to his Corinthian ministry, not to his past life before he met Jesus on the Damascus road.) He had been faithful.

Nevertheless, he realized that this did not mean he was innocent (or that he was justified before God by this). He implies that we do not see our own heart, motives, and actions the way God sees them. He alone is our Judge, for He alone can see us as we really are. So the fact our conscience doesn't accuse us doesn't mean we have not done anything wrong. As human beings we have a way of forgetting unpleasant things we have done, and we all too often fail to look at our real motives because we want to justify ourselves.

This means we must quit judging, examining, and criticizing one another in the way the Corinthians were judging Paul.[47] We must "wait till the Lord comes." That is, we must all appear before the judgment seat of Christ. Nothing will be hid from Him. He "looks on everything we do and say as important."[48] Even though we have different backgrounds and different natural gifts, we are responsible to make right choices that will bring glory to God.

God will reveal the motives of our hearts (see 3:12–15; Rom. 14:10; 2 Cor. 5:10). This is another reason why Paul was not concerned about people's opinion of him. They could not see his heart, nor did their praise mean anything. Only the praise we shall receive from God really counts.

2. No Reason For Boasting 4:6–7

6Now, brothers, I have applied these things to myself and Apollos for your benefit, so that you may learn from us the meaning of the saying, "Do not go beyond what is written." Then you will not take pride in one man over against another. 7For who makes you different from anyone else? What do you have that you did not receive? And if you did receive it, why do you boast as though you did not?

---

[47]Paul does say other kinds of judgments can still be made. See 5:12; 6:5.

[48]Stanley M. Horton, *Our Destiny: Biblical Teachings on the Last Things* (Springfield, Mo.: Logion Press, 1996), 84.

Paul now makes an application to the Corinthian brothers and sisters,[49] and probably especially to their leaders.[50] They seem to have been taking pride in Apollos, but were exalting themselves against Paul.[51] But what he had been saying about himself and Apollos was not to depreciate Apollos but to help the Corinthians learn not to "go beyond what is written" in the (Old Testament) Scriptures.[52] As was indicated in chapters 2 and 3, they were judging by other standards, especially the standards of this age in contrast to God-given standards (3:18). By recognizing that God is the true and only impartial Judge, they will not set one person above another, as if he or she should be glorified as having power and privilege beyond others. By taking pride in leaders, they were actually exalting themselves above those who claimed to follow other leaders. This pride and self-exaltation was actually the cause of the jealousy and quarreling that was tending toward division.

It is true that we are all different, but who makes us different in the sense of being superior? God does not. He does not show favoritism (Acts 10:34). Nor can people claim superiority due to talents and abilities they possess, or even because of successful ministries. Everything we have, we have received. Therefore, there is no reason for anyone to boast or take pride in themselves as if they were superior to others. Certainly it is wrong to attack others in order to build ourselves up or even to exalt ourselves over others. To do so is also to be ungrateful to the God from whom we have received all we have and are.

3. The Apostles A Spectacle To The Universe 4:8–13

[8]Already you have all you want! Already you have become rich! You have become kings—and that without us! How I wish that you really had become kings so that we might be kings with you!

---

[49]Paul considered the church as "a family—a network of close relationships in which love is the rule." Galen Hertweck, "The Church as Community: Small Groups in the Local Church," in *Faces of Renewal,* ed. Paul Elbert (Peabody, Mass.: Hendrickson Publishers, 1988), 254.

[50]Gordon H. Clark, *First Corinthians: A Contemporary Commentary* (Nutley, N.J.: Presbyterian & Reformed Publishing Co., 1975), 70.

[51]Gordon D. Fee, *The First Epistle to the Corinthians* (Grand Rapids: Wm. B. Eerdmans, 1991), 49.

[52]The New Testament Scriptures were only being written at this time. We can include them, of course.

The Corinthian church leaders had become conceited. So Paul uses irony to show them their real condition. They were acting as if they already had all they wanted, that is, in the spiritual realm. They were spiritually rich; they were acting as if they were already kings, ruling and reigning over the Corinthian assembly.

They had lost sight of the promises of God and the hope of Christ's return. Like some who hold the so-called realized eschatology, they thought they were already living on a such a high spiritual plane that they didn't need anything or anyone else (cf. 14:37). In their pride they disregarded the apostles and gave Paul and his company (such as Timothy) no place. Almost sarcastically Paul says he wishes they really were kings so he and the other apostles might be kings and reign along with them.[53] Actually, the Corinthians and their leaders were far from being what they claimed to be.

> **[9]For it seems to me that God has put us apostles on display at the end of the procession, like men condemned to die in the arena. We have been made a spectacle to the whole universe, to angels as well as to men.**

Paul understood that when people boasted against and disregarded him and the other apostles it was not contrary to what God himself seemed to be doing. Paul compares the experience with how the Roman conquerors would return to Rome in triumphal procession: Their worst enemies would be at the end of the procession, to be taken to the arena or Roman Colosseum to be killed, perhaps by lions. They would be a spectacle. That is, the crowd would attend as if they were watching a play meant to entertain them. So Paul and the apostles were a spectacle being watched, not only by the world, by humankind, but also by angels.[54]

Paul realized, of course, that what he was doing was serious business for God, not mere entertainment. And the fact that both God and angels witness our actions is good reason for us to live according to God's Word and will.

> **[10]We are fools for Christ, but you are so wise in Christ! We are weak, but you are strong! You are honored, we are dishonored!**

---

[53]Or, this may be a rather wistful but genuine wish on Paul's part (cf. 2 Cor. 5:2–4; Phil. 1:21–24).

[54]That is, by good angels.

Paul continues his irony by contrasting himself and the other apostles with the Corinthians. He and the other apostles are "fools for Christ," that is, willing to do things for Christ that the world thinks are stupid (as the next verse illustrates). The Corinthians are "so wise in Christ" (not *for* Christ); that is, they are still in Christ but think what they are doing is sensible or prudent—but they are relying on their own wisdom. Paul and the apostles are willing to be considered weak, while the Corinthians think of themselves as strong, mighty, powerful. Again, this is irony. They are only imagining that they are strong. The Corinthians are honored—that is, they honor themselves—while Paul and the other apostles are dishonored. The next three verses show the extent of the dishonor.

> **11To this very hour we go hungry and thirsty, we are in
> rags, we are brutally treated, we are homeless. 12We
> work hard with our own hands. When we are cursed,
> we bless; when we are persecuted, we endure it;
> 13when we are slandered, we answer kindly. Up to this
> moment we have become the scum of the earth, the
> refuse of the world.**

Paul says more about this in 2 Corinthians 11:16–33. Paul and the other apostles so gave themselves to the spread of the gospel that they had little concern for their own needs. As they pressed on into new territories to establish new churches, they knew what it meant not to have enough food, water, or clothes. They were often beaten and brutally mistreated. Like Jesus (Luke 9:58), they had no place to call home. To support themselves and spread the gospel, they worked hard. Paul was a tentmaker, and worked from early morning until at least noon to support not only himself but his entire evangelistic team.

None of this adversely affected the attitudes of Paul and the other apostles or their relationship to the Lord and to people. They returned blessing for cursing (cf. Luke 6:28; 23:34), endured persecution without complaint, and answered slander (untrue accusations) with kind words. For Christ's sake and the gospel they were willing to be defamed or stigmatized and become like the offscourings of the world, just so much trash in the world's eyes.[55]

---

[55]Another possible meaning is "become scapegoats for the world." Archibald Robertson and Alfred Plummer, *A Critical and Exegetical Commentary on the First Epistle of Paul to the Corinthians,* 2d ed. In The International Critical Commentary Series (Edinburgh: T & T Clark, 1914), 87.

4. Paul Their Father Through The Gospel 4:14–17

[14]I am not writing this to shame you, but to warn you, as my dear children. [15]Even though you have ten thousand guardians in Christ, you do not have many fathers, for in Christ Jesus I became your father through the gospel. [16]Therefore I urge you to imitate me.

Paul concludes this section with a fatherly appeal (vv. 14–17) followed by a stern warning. His purpose in all he has said up to this point has not been to make them ashamed of their treatment of him or their attitude toward him, but to warn them as a father would warn, admonish, and instruct children whom he really loves. Paul has taken this responsibility because he truly was their father in the gospel: He was the first to bring them the gospel, establishing the Corinthian assembly through preaching attended by signs and wonders produced by the power of the Spirit (2:4–5). The Corinthians might have ten thousand guardians (Gk. *paidagōgous,* "custodians," "guides," "tutors"), both now and in the future, but they would never have more than one father—commissioned by Jesus to take the gospel to the Gentiles. Paul gave them the right start and wanted them to stay on the right path. That is why he urged them to follow his example of serving the Lord.

[17]For this reason I am sending to you Timothy, my son whom I love, who is faithful in the Lord. He will remind you of my way of life in Christ Jesus, which agrees with what I teach everywhere in every church.

Worldly-wise leaders had made the Corinthians forget what Paul was really like, how he lived, and what he taught. They needed to be reminded. So Paul was sending Timothy to them (or the Greek verb may mean he had already sent him). Timothy had been with Paul in Corinth so they knew him (Acts 18:5). Like the Corinthians, Timothy was also Paul's spiritual offspring, for Paul had led Timothy to the Lord and made him a companion so Paul could teach and guide him. Paul loved Timothy like a son, developing a relationship so close that Timothy would be enabled to explain Paul's way of life in Christ Jesus. Timothy would remind the Corinthians of Paul's teachings (teachings that Paul repeated in every church, so Timothy had heard them again and again). The church at Corinth could depend on what Timothy would tell them. He would help them return to a way of life that was truly in Christ Jesus.

5. Paul Will Deal With Arrogant People 4:18–21

18Some of you have become arrogant, as if I were not coming to you. 19But I will come to you very soon, if the Lord is willing, and then I will find out not only how these arrogant people are talking, but what power they have. 20For the kingdom of God is not a matter of talk but of power. 21What do you prefer? Shall I come to you with a whip, or in love and with a gentle spirit?

Paul had to give a sterner warning to some who had "become arrogant," puffed up, groundlessly inflated with pride. They were spreading rumors that Paul would never return, probably saying he was afraid to come and find that his ministry was inferior to theirs. Paul, however, was not only willing to come but was depending on the Lord's will and guidance.[56]

When he did come, he would test the claims of these conceited leaders, not by testing their words, but by testing their power. He had come with a demonstration of the Spirit's power (2:4). Signs, wonders, and transformed lives confirmed his ministry. He would find out if their ministries were just high-sounding, empty words, or backed by power. This is important, for the kingdom of God is more than mere words—it is power.

Paul was talking neither of the future kingdom age nor about the Church. By the "kingdom of God" he meant the rule and authority of God, the way God shows in the present that He is actively reigning on the throne. Paul had a similar thought in mind in Romans 14:17, where he declares that the kingdom of God, that which shows God is ruling in our lives, is not a matter of the rules we follow with respect to eating or drinking, but a matter of "righteousness, peace and joy in the Holy Spirit." Our manifesting these things shows God is truly our King.

The Spirit shows His power also as He convicts "'the world of guilt in regard to sin and righteousness and judgment'" (John 16:8). He continues the work Jesus gave Paul to "'open their eyes and turn them from darkness to light, and from the power of Satan to God, so that they may receive forgiveness of sins and a place among those who are sanctified by faith in me [Jesus]'" (Acts 26:18).

56Actually, he found it necessary in God's will to change his plans. See 2 Cor. 1:15,16,23.

Paul did not want to come to them "with a whip," that is, as a father who must discipline severely. He asked the question to try to get them to change their attitude. He would rather come to them "in love" and in the gentleness that is the fruit of the Holy Spirit.

Study questions for this section may be found in appendix B.

III. SINNING CHRISTIANS MUST BE JUDGED 5:1–6:19

A. Sexual Immorality Ignored 5:1–13

1. The Sinner Needs To Be Dealt With 5:1–5

[1]It is actually reported that there is sexual immorality among you, and of a kind that does not occur even among pagans: A man has his father's wife.

Paul now turns to other problems in the Corinthian assembly. Sin was present in their midst. This is a warning for all generations. As Dr. Bruce Marino points out, "A Church without spot or wrinkle will not be a reality until Jesus returns (Eph. 5:27; Rev. 21:27)."[1]

First, Paul deals with a problem of incest that was openly reported and that everyone in the assembly knew about. Corinth was a very immoral city, but even they did not commit the kind of incest where a man was openly living with his father's wife, that is, his stepmother. Possibly, his father was dead, but we are not told that he was. It is more likely that she brazenly left the father to cohabit with the son. This was forbidden in the law of Moses (Lev. 18:8; Deut. 22:30; 27:20). It may be that the people were misinterpreting their freedom from the Law to mean they could break some of the basic principles God established for the strength of the family. But liberty does not mean license, and certainly not licentiousness.

---

[1]Bruce R. Marino, "The Origin, Nature, and Consequences of Sin," in *Systematic Theology,* ed. Stanley M. Horton, rev. ed. (Springfield, Mo.: Logion Press, 1995), 285.

2And you are proud! Shouldn't you rather have been filled with grief and have put out of your fellowship the man who did this?

Instead of recognizing that sin must be dealt with, the people in the assembly were arrogant. They did not merely ignore it or wink at it. They must have boasted of their liberty and their tolerance. This toleration of sin was as bad as the sin itself. Paul tells them they should have been so filled with grief and sorrow because of this sin that they would put that man out of their fellowship, no longer recognizing him as a brother in Christ, and no longer having table fellowship with him either. Surely if they had paid attention to Isaiah's vision of the holiness of God (Isa. 6), they would have had a different attitude.

3Even though I am not physically present, I am with you in spirit. And I have already passed judgment on the one who did this, just as if I were present. 4When you are assembled in the name of our Lord Jesus and I am with you in spirit, and the power of our Lord Jesus is present, 5hand this man over to Satan, so that the sinful nature may be destroyed and his spirit saved on the day of the Lord.

Though Paul was not present with the Corinthian believers in body, he was present in the Spirit. That is, the Spirit was present with them, and in and by the same Spirit Paul was present with them.[2] In the name of the Lord Jesus, that is, with His authority, Paul had already decided what to do with this man.[3] The people must come together, recognizing that Paul was with them in Spirit and that the power of the Lord Jesus was with them. Then they must accept the responsibility of maintaining discipline and "hand [the] man over to Satan." This may mean the kind of permission that God gave Satan to accuse Job (Job 1:12; 2:6). Or it may mean that when they refused even table fellowship with him, they were turning him back to the realm of the world where Satan is the prince of darkness and would take control (cf. Eph. 6:12).

---

[2]See Gordon D. Fee, *The First Epistle to the Corinthians* (Grand Rapids: Wm. B. Eerdmans, 1991), 204–5. See also David L. Olford, "Romans 12:1–2: The Gospel of Renewal" in *Faces of Renewal*, ed Paul Elbert (Peabody, Mass.: Hendrickson Publishers, 1988), 46 n. 67.

[3]Clark notes that Matt. 18:15 applies only to private matters, not public sin, so it does not apply here. Gordon H. Clark, *First Corinthians: A Contemporary Commentary* (Nutley, N.J.: Presbyterian & Reformed Publishing Co., 1975), 81.

The destruction of the sinful nature (Gk. *tēs sarkos,* "of the flesh")[4] does not seem to mean that the man would die. If the man died, there would be no second chance for salvation, for after death comes judgment (Heb. 9:27). The purpose of the discipline Paul was calling for was that the man's spirit might be saved on the Day of the Lord. He implies that Satan, the adversary, would cause a physical sickness or infirmity that would become a means of bringing the man to repentance.[5]

Paul implies also that the man's sin had already made him a slave of Satan. The public handing him over to Satan would be a declaration to the world of where the man stood (cf. 1 Tim. 1:19–20, where Paul considers the same kind of handing over to Satan as a lesson that needed to be learned). It may be that sickness might cause him to repent and seek healing and forgiveness, for he would still be able to call on the elders of the assembly (James 5:14–15). It should be noted that the entire assembly was to be involved in this disciplinary action, and it was to be remedial, not judgmental.[6]

2. Get Rid Of The Old Yeast 5:6–8

**6 Your boasting is not good. Don't you know that a lit-
tle yeast works through the whole batch of dough?
7 Get rid of the old yeast that you may be a new batch
without yeast—as you really are. For Christ, our Passover lamb, has been sacrificed. 8 Therefore let us keep
the Festival, not with the old yeast, the yeast of malice
and wickedness, but with bread without yeast, the
bread of sincerity and truth.**

The Corinthians' arrogance had infected the whole assembly. Paul wants each of them to "get rid of the old yeast" with all its wrong attitudes so they can live out what they really are, a new creation in Christ, and therefore holy ("without yeast").[7] Yeast produces fermentation so the Bible often uses it as a type or symbol of spiritual or moral corruption or other types of evil that spread through the congregation. Because Christ fulfilled the typology of Passover,[8] with

---

[4]Paul usually uses the word "flesh" for the old sinful nature.

[5]Marino, "The Origin, Nature, and Consequences of Sin," 278.

[6]Fee, *First Epistle to the Corinthians,* 214.

[7]George J. Zemek, "Awesome Analogies: *Kathos* Constructs in the NT," *Journal of the Evangelical Theological Society* 38, no. 3 (September 1995): 344.

[8]The Gk. aorist indicates that this was a finished work; as Heb. 10:10 says, it was done "once for all."

which the Jews included the Feast of Unleavened Bread (yeast free), He delivers believers from spiritual death and from the slavery of sin. Through Him God makes believers a holy people (1 Pet. 2:5).

To be the holy people they are in Christ, Paul demands first that they recognize that their boasting is not good. Paul meant their boast of freedom and tolerance (which they probably considered loving tolerance) was neither morally good nor pleasing to God because it showed an attitude of pride and conceit.[9] It certainly did not contribute to the spread of the gospel. It may have even caused pagans to say they weren't interested in the gospel message because the Christians were worse than them. The Corinthian believers needed to be confronted with the seriousness of the sin they were tolerating.

Just as "a little yeast works through the whole batch of dough," so a little toleration of any sin in their midst could well encourage other members of the congregation to participate in sin, until the whole body was contaminated and sin had cut them all off from fellowship with God. Each one needed to obey; each one needed to get rid of the old yeast, especially the yeast of desire that delights in doing evil and ill will that wants to injure. Only then can they be a "new batch," new and different because the spreading yeast of sin has been removed. Only then can they "keep the Festival" with bread free from sin, the bread that includes pure, godly motives and living in line with the truths of the gospel.

The Passover was a memorial feast, remembering what God did in delivering Israel from the death angel and from Egyptian slavery. It made possible the fulfillment of God's covenant-promise to Abraham that his descendants would inherit the land (Gen. 15:18–21). Moreover, the promise to Abraham included blessing for all the families and nations of the earth (Gen. 12:3; 22:17–18). Christ as our Passover Lamb has made it possible for us to enter into a spiritual Canaan land of fellowship with God the Father and with His Son (1 John 1:3). The Lord's Supper should remind believers of these things.

3. Judge And Expel Sinning Christians 5:9–13

9I have written you in my letter not to associate with sexually immoral people—10not at all meaning the people of this world who are immoral, or the greedy

[9]Donald S. Metz, "1 Corinthians," in *The Beacon Bible Commentary,* (Kansas City, Mo.: Beacon Hill Press, 1968), 7:352.

and swindlers, or idolaters. In that case you would have to leave this world. 11But now I am writing you that you must not associate with anyone who calls himself a brother but is sexually immoral or greedy, an idolater or a slanderer, a drunkard or a swindler. With such a man do not even eat.

Paul knew how immoral the pagan Corinthians were. He knew too that when they accepted Christ, they needed to clean up their lives. So, in a previous letter (which has not been preserved) he told them not to associate with (literally, "mingle together with") people who are involved in any kind of sexual immorality, including adultery, prostitution, incest, and homosexuality. Now he clarifies this by saying that he had in mind not the pagan world in general but the self-proclaimed believer who was habitually "immoral or greedy" (greedy for gain, covetous, always wanting more), and the "swindler" (a word also used of rapacious wolves and of cheating people out of their property) or an "idolater."

Paul did not expect the believers to leave "this world." That is, he did not want them to go off by themselves and have no contact with the world at large. They would need to carry on their work, their trades, and do business with unsaved people.[10]

Paul's concern was the purity of the church. They must not associate with one who claims to be a Christian brother (or sister) and who continues in the pagan practices so common in Corinth. They are not to eat with them because eating with them implies fellowship, approval, and even honoring them.[11] The Bible wants us to see the seriousness of sin (Rom. 6:16; Gal. 3:22; James 1:15; 1 John 3:6). This needs to be reinforced today, for worldly society has lost its moral vision. "With 67% of Americans no longer believing in moral absolutes, and with American society drowning in its own individualism, values are simply what is personally desirable or important. One person's values may be entirely different from another's."[12]

12What business is it of mine to judge those outside the church? Are you not to judge those inside? 13God will judge those outside. "Expel the wicked man from among you."

---

[10]See Jesus' prayer in John 17:15–16.

[11]Metz, "1 Corinthians," 7:356.

[12]David Wells, "The Secularization of Our Moral Life," in *Okenga Connections* 3, no. 2 (summer 1998): 1.

Paul did not consider it his business to judge unbelievers, those "outside the church." His mission, like that of Jesus, was not to condemn the world, but to seek their salvation through Christ (see John 3:17). At the same time, Paul was concerned about presenting the church as a pure virgin to Christ (2 Cor. 11:2). Consequently, the Corinthian believers had a responsibility to judge anyone within the assembly who was destroying that purity. They could leave the unbelieving world outside the church to be judged by God, which He will do in due time at the Great White Throne (Rev. 20:11–15).[13] In the meantime, however, Paul demanded that the Corinthian believers expel the wicked man from their fellowship (implying he was persisting in his sin). This was mercy. Under the Law such sins were punished by death (e.g., Deut. 22:24)

Paul would probably recognize that in America driving out a member from a church might bring a lawsuit. However, the principle of not giving fellowship or sharing social times with persistent, known sinners (who may claim to be Christians or may be members of the church) is something that we too must obey. It would seem too that we do not need to participate in efforts to change sinners by other means than the gospel.

B. Let Believers Judge Believers 6:1–8

1If any of you has a dispute with another, dare he take it before the ungodly for judgment instead of before the saints? 2Do you not know that the saints will judge the world? And if you are to judge the world, are you not competent to judge trivial cases? 3Do you not know that we will judge angels? How much more the things of this life!

Paul deals next with another situation that was not helping their Christian witness. The Corinthian believers, like most of us today, could not always agree. So they were taking their disputes to the civil judgment seat in the public marketplace, before pagan judges instead of "before the saints" (holy ones, that is, the believers who are sanctified by the Spirit). Those judges would arbitrate according to pagan laws and ideas, rather than according to Christian principles.[14] Paul did not

---

13See Stanley M. Horton, *Our Destiny: Biblical Teachings on the Last Things* (Springfield, Mo.: Logion Press, 1996), 186,221–24.

14Roman law permitted Jews to settle their problems among themselves. Nothing required the Christians to go before pagan courts. Gordon H. Clark, *1 Corinthians: A Contemporary Commentary* (Grand Rapids: Wm. B. Eerdmans, 1975), 86.

mean that we may not use our civil or criminal courts for serious situations that involve unbelievers. Nor did he mean that pagan judges would never give a just verdict or settlement. But the cases between believers would be noticed by the pagan world, who would then wonder about the Christian love proclaimed by the Corinthian believers. This prospect horrified Paul.

Paul wanted the Corinthian church to look to its wise members for arbitration of their differences. Some day Christian believers will share in the rule of the world (see Matt. 19:28; 2 Tim. 2:12; Rev. 22:5).[15] In comparison to this great responsibility, the cases believers were bringing before pagan judges were "trivial." Surely the believers should already be competent to judge such cases. Paul reinforces this thought by saying that we shall also "judge angels."[16] That should make us feel even more competent to judge the things of everyday life.

> **4Therefore, if you have disputes about such matters, appoint as judges even men of little account in the church! 5I say this to shame you. Is it possible that there is nobody among you wise enough to judge a dispute between believers? 6But instead, one brother goes to law against another—and this in front of unbelievers!**

Paul is not being sarcastic here. He means what he says. Since all of us shall judge the world and judge angels, even the very least of the Christians should be able to do a better job than pagan judges. But he wants to shame them because they are acting as if there is no one wise enough among them to settle their disputes. He says this in a way that expresses shock that such should be the case—that brothers go to law against each other before unbelievers. Surely, the unbelievers were shocked by this as well![17]

> **7The very fact that you have lawsuits among you means you have been completely defeated already. Why not rather be wronged? Why not rather be cheat-**

---

[15]Stanley M. Horton, *Our Destiny: Biblical Teachings on the Last Things* (Springfield, Mo.: Logion Press, 1996), 211–12.

[16]See Jude 6, indicating fallen angels are now kept chained in darkness for judgment on the final great judgment day.

[17]Gordon Fee prefers the NEB for v. 4, "If therefore you have such business disputes, how can you entrust jurisdiction to outsiders, men who count for nothing in our community?" Gordon D. Fee, *The First Epistle to the Corinthians* (Grand Rapids: Wm. B. Eerdmans, 1991), 235–36.

ed? 8Instead, you yourselves cheat and do wrong, and you do this to your brothers.

Christians who have lawsuits against each other are already losers. Both sides are already totally defeated (in the eyes of God, as well as before the outside community). The questions Paul asks are rhetorical. It would indeed be better to be wronged or cheated than to go to court before unbelieving judges (cf. Matt. 5:39–40; Rom. 12:20).

Verse 8 indicates the reason they go to court against brothers who wrong or cheat them. They are guilty of the same things. They themselves wrong others and cheat others. They forget that they are brothers, that they are all part of the family of God.

C. The Wicked Will Not Inherit The Kingdom Of God 6:9–11

9Do you not know that the wicked will not inherit the kingdom of God? Do not be deceived: Neither the sexually immoral nor idolaters nor adulterers nor male prostitutes nor homosexual offenders 10nor thieves nor the greedy nor drunkards nor slanderers nor swindlers will inherit the kingdom of God.

"Do you not know" means they did know ("You know perfectly well"—*Jerusalem Bible*). Paul had certainly made that clear in all his teachings, for he knew they needed to be warned.[18] But those who persisted in going before pagan judges had forgotten that the wicked will not inherit the kingdom of God. As believers, we look forward to inheriting the kingdom of God, that is, we have the hope of sharing with Christ in the Kingdom to come. But God is not going to share it with those who do wrong, who do not live changed lives, holy lives.

Some suppose that because they were once saved, they are eternally secure even if they return to sinful practices or to a lifestyle that is wicked in the sight of God. They deceive themselves.

To be sure the Corinthians understand what is included in being wicked, Paul becomes very specific: It includes those who are habitually "sexually immoral" (whether through prostitution, frequenting prostitutes, or "free sex"), "idolaters" (including idolatrous practices such as witchcraft, fortune-telling, astrology, spiritism, and other occult prac-

[18]Horton, *Our Destiny,* 153.

tices), "adulterers" (who are unfaithful to their marriage partners), "male prostitutes" (soft, effeminate, the "passive" partner in the relationship, usually a youth), "homosexual offenders" (the active partner),[19] "thieves," "the greedy" (those who always want more, including those who take advantage of others to satisfy their covetousness), "drunkards," "slanderers" (including those who use abusive language as well as those who physically abuse others), and "swindlers" (a word also used of rapacious or ravenous wolves and of those who cheat others out of their property). Again Paul emphasizes that none of these will inherit the future kingdom of God or share in His rule ("their place will be in the fiery lake of burning sulfur" [Rev. 21:8]). They will be forever outside the new heavens and the new earth (Rev. 22:15). What a warning to believers! (Cf. Rom. 8:13.)

> **[11]And that is what some of you were. But you were washed, you were sanctified, you were justified in the name of the Lord Jesus Christ and by the Spirit of our God.**

The Corinthian believers knew what Paul was talking about. Some of them had been involved in those very wrongdoings. But their situation was not hopeless. Their sins had been washed away (cf. Acts 22:16).[20] Even those who were the worst sinners had been "sanctified," made holy. They had been "justified" (acquitted, pronounced not guilty, and treated as righteous) in "[Gk. *en*] the name of the Lord Jesus Christ and by [Gk. *en*] the Spirit of our God." The Greek *en* can mean "in" or "by." The point is that both the redeeming work of Jesus and the work of the Holy Spirit are involved in our justification (cf. 2 Thess. 2:13). "The form of the Greek verbs 'washed,' 'sanctified,' and 'justified' in this passage (aorist passive) gives no sense of any sort of process here. They all refer to the same instantaneous, completed experience: conversion. . . . It is not a second definite work of grace as some would have it."[21] Thank God, the same redeeming work and justification is

---

[19]These two terms can surely be applied to female homosexuality as well.

[20]Paul is not referring to water baptism here, but to the washing of the Word and the sanctifying work of the Spirit (Eph. 5:26). The Gk. middle indicates they were "actively involved in the process" Donald S. Metz, "1 Corinthians," in *The Beacon Bible Commentary* (Kansas City, Mo.: Beacon Hill Press, 1968), 7:364.

[21]Timothy P. Jenney, "The Holy Spirit and Sanctification," in *Systematic Theology,* ed. Stanley M. Horton, rev. ed. (Springfield, Mo.: Logion Press, 1995), 415–16.

still available to all. Then the Holy Spirit does continue His sanctifying work as we grow in grace.[22] Because of His help we do not need to live like those in the world.

D. Flee Sexual Immorality 6:12–19

1. The Body Is Meant For The Lord 6:12–17

**12"Everything is permissible for me"—but not every-
thing is beneficial. "Everything is permissible for me"—
but I will not be mastered by anything. 13"Food for the
stomach and the stomach for food"—but God will
destroy them both. The body is not meant for sexual
immorality, but for the Lord, and the Lord for the body.
14By his power God raised the Lord from the dead, and
he will raise us also.**

Paul next answers what some of the Corinthian believers were saying. Because they were free from the Law, they supposed they could do whatever they wished. Like some today, they may have said, "If it feels good, do it." But Paul replied that "not everything is beneficial" (useful, helpful, really good and advantageous for the body of Christ). Moreover, many things, even legitimate things, can enslave us. Paul refused to be "mastered by anything." He was subject to the authority of God and Christ. He would not let things or human desire dominate him, not even things that were not sinful in themselves.

Paul's opponents said further that "food [was] for the stomach and the stomach for food," implying that it was all right to satisfy physical desires in any way they pleased. Paul's reply meant that God would "destroy them both": the food that satisfies the desire and the stomach that one is attempting to satisfy.

That they had in mind more than physical food is shown by Paul's next statement. They were really implying that the body was made for sex and sex for the body, so sexual desires could be satisfied by any kind of immorality without any more guilt than putting food into the stomach.

It was easy for the Corinthians to take that attitude, for with their Greek background, they took a negative view of the body, considering it of little importance. Many of their philosophers considered the

---

[22]Ibid., 416.

body a prison for the soul,[23] so they thought that the things that were done in the body did not affect the soul. But God created the human body. He created Adam and Eve for each other and for himself. So the body is meant for the Lord, to be a means by which we can express ourselves in worship and service to Him. Paul's desire was "that now as always Christ will be exalted in my body, whether by life or by death" (Phil. 1:20).

The Lord is for the body not only because He created it but because He knows we need a body for the full expression of our nature as His children. He demonstrated this by raising our Lord Jesus from the dead by His power. Jesus identified himself with humankind from birth to death in order to take our place and die for us on the cross. But God did not merely raise Him up spiritually. God raised Him up with a real, tangible body. It had been changed, it was of a different order, but He could still walk, talk, and eat with His disciples (Luke 24: 37–43; Acts 1:3–4,6).[24]

God would not have given Jesus a real body in the Resurrection if He was not for the body, respecting its importance. This guarantees that He will raise us with a real body as well (cf. Rom. 8:11). Thus, since the body is so important to God and to us, we should never let sinful desires cause us to yield to immorality of any kind (cf. Rom. 8:11–17, which speaks of our obligation to put to death by the Spirit the misdeeds of the body).[25]

> **15Do you not know that your bodies are members of Christ himself? Shall I then take the members of Christ and unite them with a prostitute? Never! 16Do you not know that he who unites himself with a prostitute is one with her in body? For it is said, "The two will become one flesh." 17But he who unites himself with the Lord is one with him in spirit.**

Paul has another important objection to sexual immorality. The Bible looks at the person as a unit. It is true that the Bible speaks of

---

[23]According to Plato, Socrates said we are "entombed in this which we carry about us and call the body, in which we are imprisoned like an oyster in its shell" (Phoedrus, 250c). *Plato,* vol. 1. trans. Harold N. Fowler (Cambridge, Mass.: Harvard University Press, 1914), 485.

[24]In Acts 1:6 the Gk. indicates Jesus was sharing a meal with them. See Stanley M. Horton, *The Book of Acts* (Springfield, Mo.: Gospel Publishing House, 1981), 18.

[25]Horton, *Our Destiny,* 69–70.

body, soul, and spirit. But the Bible recognizes that in our present existence we act as a unity. We cannot say, "My body did it." We can only say, "*I* did it." When we are born from above, we are not only in fellowship with Christ, we, as individuals—and in our individual bodies—are also united with Him, part of His Body, the Church. So we cannot say, "I am united with Christ, but my body is not." If we are united with Him, our body is also united with Him. If we ask the question, "Shall I take the members of Christ (my body) and unite them with a prostitute?" the only possible answer for the person who is truly united in fellowship with Christ is an emphatic "Never!" (The Gk. can mean "Don't ever let it happen.") Sexual union with a prostitute cannot be a matter of indifference, for whenever a man and a woman are joined together sexually they become one in body, as Moses said of the first man and woman (Gen. 2:24).

Then, because religious prostitution was so common and because pagans considered it to be a way to honor gods and goddesses, Paul wanted to avoid the idea that there is anything sexually related to our union with the Lord. So he makes a strong contrast. We who are united with the Lord are "one with Him in spirit" (which probably implies in and by the Holy Spirit).

2. The Body Is The Temple Of The Holy Spirit 6:18–19

18Flee from sexual immorality. All other sins a man commits are outside his body, but he who sins sexually sins against his own body. 19Do you not know that your body is a temple of the Holy Spirit, who is in you, whom you have received from God? You are not your own; 20you were bought at a price. Therefore honor God with your body.

Because of the constant temptation of sexual immorality, Paul does more than give reasons against it. He commands us to flee from it. We can see an illustration of this response in the life of Joseph. He considered it better to suffer in prison than to yield to the temptations of Potiphar's wife and sin against God (Gen. 39:7–9).

Sexually immorality is not only abhorrent to God, it is a sin against one's own body, which Paul has just said is "for the Lord" (v. 13). Moreover, the body of the individual believer[26] is "the" temple, as indicated

---

[26]"You" in v. 19 is singular. See Michael L. Dusing, "The New Testament Church," in *Systematic Theology*, ed. Stanley M. Horton, 537.

in the KJV and other versions, (not merely "a" temple) of the indwelling Holy Spirit, who is God's gift to us, for we received the Spirit from Him.

As was noted in the commentary on chapter 3, the Greek has two words for temple, and Paul again uses *naos,* the inner sanctuary where God manifested His presence, His Shekinah (indwelling, abiding) glory.[27] For the Holy Spirit has come to dwell, to abide not merely with us but in us (John 14:16–17, KJV). Because our bodies are His temple and because Jesus paid the full price for our redemption by shedding His infinitely valuable blood on Calvary's cross, we belong to God (cf. 1 Pet. 1:18–19, "redeemed . . . with the precious blood of Christ"; Rev. 5:9). There can be only one conclusion—we should, we must, honor God with our bodies.

We can apply this further. All our bodily actions should give praise to God. We should be careful not to let films, books, magazines, or the Internet stimulate immoral thoughts or deeds. "Even legitimate pleasure must not become our reason for living."[28] We should be especially concerned that we show we belong to the Lord by yielding to His Holy Spirit, not with fleshly manifestation, but manifesting the gifts and fruit of the Spirit.

When the beginnings of the current Pentecostal revival began to get worldwide attention in 1906 at the Azusa Street Mission in Los Angeles, it was obvious that the blessing was indeed for all, as Joel and Peter emphasized, for God broke down racial barriers. In a day when racial prejudice was rampant, blacks and whites worshiped together, spoke in tongues, and prophesied.[29] Spontaneous revivals in other parts of the world broke out also. Now people of every race and almost every nation have made Christ Savior, Lord, and King and are blessed with the baptism in the Holy Spirit. May God make us holy and help us to glorify Him in and through our bodies in worship, service, and sacrifice.[30]

Study questions for this section may be found in appendix B.

---

[27]*Shekinah* is derived from the Heb. *Shakhan,* "live, dwell." It is not found in the Hebrew Bible but later rabbis used it of the glory that was continually present in the Most Holy Place of the tabernacle and temple.

[28]Stanley M. Horton, *What the Bible Says About the Holy Spirit* (Springfield, Mo.: Gospel Publishing House, 1976), 205.

[29]My mother was baptized in the Spirit at the Azusa Street Mission in 1906. She told me they were saying, "The blood line has wiped out the color line."

[30]Fee points out that the KJV "and in your spirit" (v. 20), while true, detracts from the message of the paragraph and was probably a later addition. Fee, *First Epistle to the Corinthians,* 265–66. The KJV and NKJV are the only translations that retain the phrase.

IV. QUESTIONS ANSWERED 7:1-11:2

A. Marriage 7:1-40

1. Avoid Immorality 7:1–7

[1]Now for the matters you wrote about: It is good for a man not to marry. [2]But since there is so much immorality, each man should have his own wife, and each woman her own husband.

"Now" indicates Paul is taking up a new subject (also vv. 8, 25). The letter he refers to was not from some individual but from the whole church. Apparently, the letter was not a particularly friendly one. Their questions were not asked in a spirit of humility with a desire to learn. Rather they seemed to be "over against Paul on issue after issue."[1] In what follows, Paul discusses marriage, which they were not taking seriously enough. We should keep in mind that Paul was not against marriage. He includes forbidding to marry among things taught by demons "through hypocritical liars" (1 Tim. 4:2–3), and Hebrews 13:4 says, "Marriage should be honored by all." Paul also compares the relationship of Christ and the Church to the marriage relationship, making applications to the husband and wife that show he had a high view of marriage (Eph. 5:22–33). But the Corinthians were living in difficult times, anticipating persecution. Therefore, what Paul says here should be understood in connection with verse 26, "Because of the present crisis, I think that it is good for you to remain as you are."

"Not to marry" (Gk. *gunaikos mē haptesthai*), literally, "not to touch a woman," in all extant *koine*[2] literature "is a euphemism for sexual

---

[1]Gordon D. Fee, "Tongues—Least of the Gifts?" *Pneuma* 2, no. 2 (fall 1980): 5.

[2]*Koine*, "common," is a term used of the everyday Greek of NT times. It was the language of trade, commerce, and education, and was a second language, after Latin, common over most of the Roman Empire. The NT was written in koine.

intercourse" and does not imply "take a wife," or "marry."[3] This may have been a Corinthian slogan that Paul quotes and wants to modify.[4] It is possible they were misinterpreting Luke 20:34–35, supposing that they could be like the angels now.[5]

In verse 2 Paul is arguing against the false teaching that advocates asceticism and marital celibacy. Some apparently were supposing that Christ was coming very soon and that they must be spiritual. By "spiritual" they were probably influenced by Greek ideas about the body as being something unworthy (see 6:12–20; 15:1–58). What Paul means is that each man who is already married should continue to have relations with his own wife, and each wife with her own husband. This is the norm for Christians. The immorality Paul has in mind is probably married men going to prostitutes (usually temple prostitutes encouraged by Greek religion). Verse 2 would apply to any extramarital affair today.

> **3The husband should fulfill his marital duty to his wife, and likewise the wife to her husband. 4The wife's body does not belong to her alone but also to her husband. In the same way, the husband's body does not belong to him alone but also to his wife.**

Within marriage the husband has the primary responsibility to seek to satisfy his wife sexually. The wife also should respond. Paul does not look at sexual relations as only for procreation. They are an obligation within marriage, but both husband and wife should consider each other to come to a mutual agreement about the how and when. Because in God's plan they are to be united as one flesh, each possesses the other's body. Neither is to think solely of his or her own pleasure or desires. Each should be concerned about satisfying the normal, God-given sexual desires of the other.

> **5Do not deprive each other except by mutual consent and for a time, so that you may devote yourselves to prayer. Then come together again so that Satan will not tempt you because of your lack of self-control.**

---

[3]Gordon D. Fee, "1 Corinthians 7:1 in the NIV," *Journal Of the Evangelical Theological Society* 23, no. 4 (December 1980) 307–314.

[4]J. Carl Laney, "Paul and the Permanence of Marriage in 1 Corinthians 7," *Journal of the Evangelical Theological Society* 25, no. 3 (September 1982): 283.

[5]Donald S. Metz, "1 Corinthians," in *The Beacon Bible Commentary* (Kansas City, Mo.: Beacon Hill Press,1968), 7:372.

"Do not deprive" means "stop depriving." Apparently, some in Corinth were teaching that married couples should not have sexual intercourse, or that they would be more spiritual if they did not. "Deprive" (Gk. *apostereite*) is a strong word, used also of defrauding or robbing. Sexual abstinence in marriage is not to be the norm for Christians. Nor is sex to be used for manipulating one's spouse.

The one exception is when both partners agree that for a specific period of time they will devote themselves wholly to prayer,[6] wanting nothing to detract from their communion with the Lord. But it should be for a limited time, and then they should return to mutually agreed sexual relations. Satan, the adversary, is always on the alert to tempt one to commit adultery. He should be given no opportunity to do so because of one's lack of self-control.

> **[6]I say this as a concession, not as a command. [7]I wish that all men were as I am. But each man has his own gift from God; one has this gift, another has that.**

Paul calls what he has just said "a concession." (This is the only concession.) It is just a suggestion, giving "permission to stay away from sexual relations for a time. It is not a command to do so" (v. 6, NCV). In other words, sexual abstinence is really not even necessary.

He is not saying that his instructions to those who are already married are to be taken lightly, but he goes on to wish that everyone were like him. He does not want them to think that everyone must marry. Under the difficult conditions at Corinth, marriage was not mandatory.

Many question whether Paul was ever married. However, since he did cast his vote for the martyrdom of Stephen and others (Acts 26:10), this would mean he was a member of the Sanhedrin, which required its members to be married.[7] Many believe Paul's wife died and he was now a widower.[8] He would like all men (Gk. *anthrōpous,* human beings including male and female) to be like him, unmarried. (He does not mean that he wants them to be widows or widowers, but

---

[6]This should include prayer for each other. Robert L. Brandt and Zenas J. Bicket, *The Spirit Helps us Pray* (Springfield, Mo.: Logion Press, 1993), 340.

[7]Some believe Paul was not a member of the Sanhedrin but only voted in the local synagogue law courts. See F. F. Bruce, *Commentary on the Book of Acts* (Grand Rapids: Wm. B. Eerdmans, 1954), 172–73 n. 110, 490 n. 18.

[8]I heard Dr. Merrill Tenney express this opinion in a class I attended at Gordon Divinity School in 1942.

simply unmarried). But he realized that this would take a special gift of freedom from any desire for sexual fulfillment. Paul had that gracious gift (Gk. *charisma*). But God in His sovereignty does not give everyone the same gift.

2. Advice To The Unmarried And Widows 7:8–9

8Now to the unmarried and the widows I say: It is good for them to stay unmarried, as I am. 9But if they cannot control themselves, they should marry, for it is better to marry than to burn with passion.

The "unmarried" (Gk. *agamois*) usually means a widower. By saying it is good for widows and widowers to stay unmarried like him, Paul, means it is advantageous under the circumstances of the time (probably because of the danger of severe persecution). But, as the previous verse indicates, not all have the gift, so not all are able to control themselves the way Paul did. So it is better for them to marry than "to burn," to be inflamed with sexual desire (which might lead them to prostitutes). He does not mean, however, that a person should marry for sex alone. That would be contrary to God's purpose for the family.

3. Divorce Forbidden By The Lord 7:10–11

10To the married I give this command (not I, but the Lord): A wife must not separate from her husband. 11 But if she does, she must remain unmarried or else be reconciled to her husband. And a husband must not divorce his wife.

Next Paul speaks to believers who are already married. He has sayings of Jesus to back up the command he is giving to them (see Matt. 5:31–32; 19:2–8). Some translate the command to the wife, "The wife should not allow herself to be separated from her husband." But this assumes Paul was talking to Jews: Only the husband could initiate a divorce.[9] On the other hand, Greeks and Romans did allow the wife to seek a divorce, and Jesus had a word for them (Mark 10:12).

Paul recognizes wives were divorcing their husbands, but he puts a restriction on them. They must stay unmarried or be reconciled to their husbands. Clearly, the ideal is what Jesus drew attention to. God

---

[9]Jerome Murphy-O'Conner, "The Divorced Woman in 1 Cor. 7:10–11," *Journal of Biblical Literature* 100, no. 4 (December 1981): 604.

in the beginning intended that marriage be between one man and one woman for life (Matt. 19:4–6; cf. Gen. 2:24). The same commands of Jesus forbid a husband to divorce his wife. Paul does not allow remarriage in such cases. As Christians they should find some way to be reconciled to each other.

4. Living In Peace With Unbelieving Spouses 7:12–16

**12To the rest I say this (I, not the Lord): If any brother
has a wife who is not a believer and she is willing to
live with him, he must not divorce her. 13And if a
woman has a husband who is not a believer and he is
willing to live with her, she must not divorce him. 14For
the unbelieving husband has been sanctified through
his wife, and the unbelieving wife has been sanctified
through her believing husband. Otherwise your children would be unclean, but as it is, they are holy.**

"The rest" covers people who are married and after marriage one partner becomes a Christian and the other rejects the gospel. Paul does not have a saying of Jesus to guide them. However, he is not giving them his own opinion. The word he has for them is no less inspired by the Holy Spirit.

Becoming a Christian does not change the marriage covenant. The Christian, whether husband or wife, does not have the right to initiate a divorce in such cases. The Christian partner should continue to live in loving faithfulness to the unbelieving partner as long as the unbeliever is willing.

Continuing in the marriage relationship with an unbelieving partner does not defile the believer. The believer's faith in God and Jesus has a sanctifying influence over the relationship. In that sense the unbeliever is sanctified, or set apart, from anything sinful in the relationship. If this were not so, the children born to the couple would be unclean, that is, ceremonially unclean and therefore unable to come into the presence of God. But the sanctifying influence of the Christian parent makes the children holy in the sense that they belong to the Lord and can be brought into His presence for His blessing. The Holy Spirit can make such a marriage situation into a powerful ministry.[10]

10Timothy P. Jenney, "The Holy Spirit and Sanctification," in *Systematic Theology*, ed. Stanley M. Horton, rev. ed. (Springfield, Mo.: Logion Press, 1995), 418.

15But if the unbeliever leaves, let him do so. A believing man or woman is not bound in such circumstances; God has called us to live in peace. 16How do you know, wife, whether you will save your husband? Or, how do you know, husband, whether you will save your wife?

"Leave" (Gk. *chōrizetai*) is "a well-attested technical term for divorce."[11] If the unbeliever wishes to divorce, the believer should let him or her go. From verse 13 it may be implied that the unbeliever is no longer willing to live in faithfulness to the believer. Most probably, the unbeliever is already unfaithful or involved in pagan rites with prostitutes. The divorced believer then is not bound (Gk. *dedoulōtai,* "enslaved"), that is, is set free from the marriage vows. Though Paul does not really say so, this implies freedom to remarry, but, of course, only to a believer (v. 39).

No emphasis should be put on this exception that is usually interpreted to allow for remarriage in such cases. God does not want the unbeliever to divorce. He has called us to live in peace, that is, in the well-being and blessing He provides. So as long as the unbeliever is willing to live in faithfulness to the believing partner, the believer should pursue peace in the hope that through it the unbeliever will be brought to salvation.

This does not mean that the believer badgers or condemns the unbeliever, but that the believer so shows the love and grace of Christ that the unbeliever is attracted to Him. As Peter points out to wives, once the unbelieving husband knows the Word, the wife should be submissive to the husband so that he may be won over "without words" but rather by the behavior of the wife, her "purity and reverence" (1 Pet. 3:1–2).

5. Remaining In The Situation God Calls One To 7:17–24

17Nevertheless, each one should retain the place in life that the Lord assigned to him and to which God has called him. This is the rule I lay down in all the churches. 18Was a man already circumcised when he was called? He should not become uncircumcised. Was a man uncircumcised when he was called? He should

11Murphy-O'Connor, "The Divorced Woman," 605.

not be circumcised. 19Circumcision is nothing and uncircumcision is nothing. Keeping God's commands is what counts.

Now Paul turns to another question. Does becoming a Christian demand an outward change in one's circumstances or place in life? Some may be in circumstances that God has assigned or dealt to them. Some may have a call God has given them. They are to continue to live in that place in life and not seek to change it. Paul gives the same rule to all the churches, not just to the Corinthians.

The first circumstance some Jewish believers wanted to change was their relation to the Abrahamic covenant through the sign of circumcision. They wanted to get rid of the sign that identified them as Jews.[12] On the other hand, some Gentiles were listening to Judaizers who wanted them to become Jews first, be circumcised, and then add their Christianity to their Judaism. Paul says that both are wrong, for the sign of circumcision is now meaningless, for the old covenant of the Law was abolished by Christ's sacrifice (Eph. 2:15). The only thing that counts in God's eyes is loving obedience to Him (cf. Gal. 5:6).

20Each one should remain in the situation which he
was in when God called him. 21Were you a slave when
you were called? Don't let it trouble you—although if
you can gain your freedom, do so. 22For he who was
a slave when he was called by the Lord is the Lord's freedman; similarly, he who was a free man when he was called is Christ's slave.

The second situation people wanted to change was slavery. Because the Romans made slaves of people they conquered, a high percentage of the population were slaves.[13] Though the New Testament lays down principles that should lead to the abolition of slavery, Paul did not advocate slaves starting a rebellion hoping to obtain freedom. In that society that would have meant death. Paul wanted the Christians who were slaves to accept their circumstances, not let their slavery trouble them. They should realize that the Lord had set them free: free from sin, free in spirit, free in the Holy Spirit, and free to serve God in spite of their circumstances. However, this did not mean they should refuse

[12]An operation to do so was available in those days.

[13]In the great cities of the Roman Empire as much as one-third of the population were slaves. J. D. Douglas, ed., *The New Bible Dictionary* (Grand Rapids: Wm. B. Eerdmans, 1965), 1198.

freedom if it became available. In fact, the best interpretation of the Greek means that they should make the most of opportunity.[14] But they needed also to realize that those believers who were free became Christ's slaves, taken captive by Him to serve Him and His Church (cf. Eph. 4:8,11).

23You were bought at a price; do not become slaves of men. 24Brothers, each man, as responsible to God, should remain in the situation God called him to.

All needed to remember the price paid for them—the precious blood of Jesus, who bought them back for God.[15] Therefore, they belonged to Him, not to men (Gk. *anthrōpōn,* human beings including male and female). The conclusion, then, is that Christians should not seek to change their marital or social status. Rather, they should seek to do God's will, whatever their situation.

6. Should Virgins Marry? 7:25–38

25Now about virgins: I have no command from the Lord, but I give a judgment as one who by the Lord's mercy is trustworthy. 26Because of the present crisis, I think that it is good for you to remain as you are. 27Are you married? Do not seek a divorce. Are you unmarried? Do not look for a wife. 28But if you do marry, you have not sinned; and if a virgin marries, she has not sinned. But those who marry will face many troubles in this life, and I want to spare you this.

Paul now turns to another question. Should virgins marry? "Virgins" in verse 25 is masculine plural but includes both young men and young women, most of whom were probably engaged, that is, promised by their parents according to the ancient custom. Again, Paul has no saying of Jesus for them, but he has a word they can accept because God's mercy has made Paul trustworthy. Paul is not making a judgment that would apply to everyone in every circumstance. But because of the crisis circumstances of that time, it would be better for them to remain single.

---

[14]Gordon D. Fee, *The First Epistle to the Corinthians* (Grand Rapids: Wm. B. Eerdmans, 1991), 317–18.

[15]Daniel B. Pecota, "The Saving Work of Christ," in *Systematic Theology,* ed. Horton, 350.

Paul then reminds the married that the present crisis does not mean they should seek to change their status by a divorce, nor should the unmarried (widowers) seek a wife. However, if an unmarried man does marry, he has not sinned, and if a woman who is a virgin marries, she has not sinned.

Paul is not against marriage. It is a holy estate. But he knows that under the present circumstances marriage would bring "many troubles" (pressures, difficult circumstances, probably caused by persecution). He wants them to accept his advice so they will be spared a great deal of trouble. It would be easier for them to endure whatever circumstances that might come if they did not have to care for a husband or wife at the same time.

> **29What I mean, brothers, is that the time is short. From now on those who have wives should live as if they had none; 30those who mourn, as if they did not; those who are happy, as if they were not; those who buy something, as if it were not theirs to keep; 31those who use the things of the world, as if not engrossed in them. For this world in its present form is passing away.**

Because of the present crisis the time has been shortened or restricted. "Time" (Gk. *kairos*) in this sense means a point in time or short period or season. It can also mean a time of crisis or a time of opportunity. Paul's point is that because of the present situation individuals should not focus on their current circumstances. Their marriage, their sorrows, their happiness, their buying, and their possessions should not be the center of their attention. Instead of being engrossed in or absorbed by these things, they should recognize that God has something better ahead.

The "present form," or outward appearance, of this world with its earthly joys, cares, possessions, and sufferings is "passing away." This can also mean that the things in this world are going by so that we cannot hold on to them anyway. (Some suppose Paul had the nearness of Christ's second coming in mind, but this does not fit the context of the "present crisis" he speaks of.)We can apply this to ourselves. We should not make things, property, or our present circumstances the center of our attention. Then, as we approach the end of the age, we can see an even greater need of focusing our attention on Jesus (cf. Heb. 11:13–16; 12:2–3).

We must recognize also that the world is headed for judgment

(Dan. 2:44–45); but we seek first the kingdom of God and His righteousness so that we will be prepared to share in God's "eternal purpose which he accomplished in Christ Jesus our Lord" (Eph. 3:11).[16]

> **32I would like you to be free from concern. An unmarried man is concerned about the Lord's affairs—how he can please the Lord. 33But a married man is concerned about the affairs of this world—how he can please his wife—34and his interests are divided. An unmarried woman or virgin is concerned about the Lord's affairs: Her aim is to be devoted to the Lord in both body and spirit. But a married woman is concerned about the affairs of this world—how she can please her husband. 35I am saying this for your own good, not to restrict you, but that you may live in a right way in undivided devotion to the Lord.**

Paul wanted them to be free from any concern that would keep them either in body or in spirit from giving to the Lord's affairs. He recognized that being a Christian does not relieve spouses from the responsibility of caring for and pleasing each other; they have to give attention to the affairs of this world. This is not wrong—it is a fact of life—but it means their interests are divided. And Paul wants them to do both, care for each other and serve the Lord, without worry or anxiety.

So even though remaining unmarried was considered a disgrace by most Jews, Paul did not consider it inferior to the married state. He preferred under the circumstances that men, widows, and virgins remain unmarried—for their own good as well as to enable them to live with full devotion to the Lord. Paul simply considered the unmarried state an advantage.

> **36If anyone thinks he is acting improperly toward the virgin he is engaged to, and if she is getting along in years and he feels he ought to marry, he should do as he wants. He is not sinning. They should get married. 37But the man who has settled the matter in his own mind, who is under no compulsion but has control over his own will, and who has made up his mind not to marry the virgin—this man also does the right thing.**

16Stanley M. Horton, *Our Destiny: Biblical Teachings on the Last Things* (Springfield, Mo.: Logion Press, 1996), 19.

38So then, he who marries the virgin does right, but he who does not marry her does even better.

With young people in mind, Paul qualifies the previous statements further. "Virgin" here clearly means a young woman engaged to be married. Thus the NIV takes this passage to mean a man who is engaged to be married (to a virgin) does not sin if he goes ahead and marries. But, again under the present circumstances, if he is fully decided and has the will to refrain from marriage, he does even better.

On the other hand, many commentators see parental authority presupposed in this passage[17] and interpret it of a father who sees his daughter's unhappiness and does not sin if he arranges the wedding, but the one who does not give her in marriage does better.[18] However, the phrase in verse 36, "They should get married," is against that view.[19]

7. A Widow Is Free To Remarry 7:39–40

39A woman is bound to her husband as long as he lives. But if her husband dies, she is free to marry anyone she wishes, but he must belong to the Lord. 40In my judgment, she is happier if she stays as she is— and I think that I too have the Spirit of God.

Marriage is for life, as Jesus emphasized in contrast to the easy divorce practiced by the Jews of that day. But it is also true that the marriage contract is only for *this* life. Jesus indicated this when He told the Sadducees, "'When the dead rise, they will neither marry nor be given in marriage; they will be like the angels in heaven'" (Mark 12:25). So Paul says a widow is free to remarry "anyone she wishes," only it must be someone who is "in the Lord"(v. 39, KJV), that is, living a Christian life in full communion with the Lord and the local assembly (which is the Lord's body). It is foolish and should be unthinkable for a Christian woman to marry an unbeliever in the hope of converting him. Too many have found it so to their sorrow.

But Paul is not contradicting what he has already said about marriage. His judgment is the same. She will be happier (under the present circumstances where persecution is imminent) if she stays single.

17Metz, "1 Corinthians," 7:385.

18Fred Fisher, *Commentary on 1 and 2 Corinthians* (Waco, Tex.: Word Books, 1975), 122–124.

19The Gk. *gamizōn* in v. 38 is probably used for variety, and does not mean "give in marriage" here, but simply "marry."

Paul's judgment is not merely personal opinion. He thinks (rather, "considers," "believes") that he also has this from the Spirit. That is, he is inspired by the Spirit of the Lord.[20]

B. Food Sacrificed To Idols 8:1–13

1. Love Builds Up 8:1–3

[1]Now about food sacrificed to idols: We know that we all possess knowledge. Knowledge puffs up, but love builds up. [2]The man who thinks he knows something does not yet know as he ought to know. [3]But the man who loves God is known by God.

"Now" indicates Paul is changing the subject and taking up another question: food sacrificed to idols. Before he begins to discuss it, he must have noticed something about the way the question came to him. There must have been a sense that people were condemning one another because of what they claimed to know about the subject. Knowledge, however, would never settle the question, for where there is argument, knowledge only "puffs up," making each one more sure he or she is right. Without love, even our knowledge of spiritual truths breeds pride, arrogance, and conceit. Our clever answer only humiliates others as it puffs us up. But love builds up, so the question must be decided on the basis of what love calls for.

This is all the more true because, in this life, no matter who we are or what we think we know, our knowledge is incomplete. None of us knows what we ought to know to really settle questions by our own reasoning powers.

On the other hand, the person who loves God is "known by God," having a personal relationship of love, and having His approval.[21] Then, love helps us honor both God and fellow believers so that we promote the good of all. Such love is truly the fruit of the Holy Spirit. It often involves the fruit of self-discipline and even self-denial as well. It depends also on "the wisdom that comes from heaven," which "is first

---

[20]Others take this as irony, meaning he could say he had the Spirit as much or more than any who opposed his teaching. See Norman Hillyer, "1 and 2 Corinthians," in *The New Bible Commentary,* ed. D. Guthrie and J.A. Motyer, 3d ed. (Grand Rapids: Wm. B. Eerdmans, 1970), 1062.

[21]Paul probably had in mind the Heb. word for "know," *yadah,* which means "to know personally" or "to know by experience."

of all pure; then peace-loving, considerate, submissive, full of mercy and good fruit, impartial and sincere." It makes us "peacemakers who sow in peace [and] raise a harvest of righteousness" (James 3:17–18).

2. Idols Are Nothing 8:4–6

[4]So then, about eating food sacrificed to idols: We know that an idol is nothing at all in the world and that there is no God but one. [5]For even if there are so-called gods, whether in heaven or on earth (as indeed there are many "gods" and many "lords"), [6]yet for us there is but one God, the Father, from whom all things came and for whom we live; and there is but one Lord, Jesus Christ, through whom all things came and through whom we live.

The question basically implies that some were going to idol temples and participating in the pagan ceremonies in order to eat the food offered to idols.[22] Paul starts by emphasizing that an idol is a nothing. That is, it has no reality and no power in this world. The many so-called gods and lords worshiped by pagans are all nothings. The Old Testament prophets said the same thing. The idols were nothing but pieces of wood, stone, or metal, made by men's hands. There was nothing supernatural about them, and they had no power to speak or act. Paul knew the passages in Isaiah that show with tremendous irony the foolishness of idolatry (Isa. 2:8; 40:18–20; 41:7; 44:9–20; 46:1–2). Paul realized that there were many "so-called gods" and "lords" worshiped by the pagans.[23] The city of Corinth was full of their temples and shrines. But believers know there is only one God (cf. Deut. 6:4; 32:39; 1 Sam. 2:2; Isa. 44:8). "Within spiritual reality, there is only one true Divine Being: '. . . no *theos* but one' . . . (1 Cor. 8:4). God makes exclusive claim to this term as a further revelation of himself."[24] He is the Creator of everything, the source of "every good and perfect

[22]Many commentators suppose the meat was bought in the market and eaten in their homes.

[23]The Gk. *theos* can be translated "god" or "God" "depending on the literary context. . . . However, the use of this Greek word in no way makes concession to the existence of other gods, since literary context is not the same as spiritual context." Russell E. Joyner, "The One True God" in *Systematic Theology,* ed. Stanley M. Horton, rev. ed. (Springfield, Mo.: Logion Press, 1995), 140.

[24]Ibid.

gift" (James 1:17). We were created for Him, and as believers we live for Him. We know too that there is only "one Lord, Jesus Christ." He is the one through whom God created "all things" (John 1:3). Through Him also we receive both physical and spiritual life.[25]

3. Do Not Become A Stumbling Block To The Weak 8:7–13

7But not everyone knows this. Some people are still so accustomed to idols that when they eat such food they think of it as having been sacrificed to an idol, and since their conscience is weak, it is defiled. 8But food does not bring us near to God; we are no worse if we do not eat, and no better if we do.

Now Paul is applying the principle of love. He recognizes that even though all Christians subscribe to the truth that there is one true God, not everyone knows or understands this by personal experience. Many of the Corinthians' lives before conversion were so taken up with worship of idols that they couldn't forget that this food was sacrificed to them.

"Their conscience [was] weak." Our consciences depend on what we are taught and have come to believe is true. A weak conscience has not been built up by the truth to the point that it is no longer bothered by false ideas. Thus, the weak conscience of these former idol worshipers was oversensitive, being bothered and defiled. In a word, it made them feel guilty. Worse, they *were* guilty, for in going against their conscience they had become rebels, saying to themselves, "I still believe it is wrong, but I'll do it anyway." Rebellion is a dangerous sin and can lead to hardness of heart and a forfeiture of salvation.[26]

There is no real reason for guilt. The whole matter of eating food that has been offered to an idol is one of indifference as far as God is concerned, for the idols are nothings. The food we eat does not affect our relationship to Him, nor are we better or worse in His eyes because of what we eat (cf. Rom. 14:5–6).

9Be careful, however, that the exercise of your freedom does not become a stumbling block to the weak.

---

[25]Timothy Munyon, "The Creation of the Universe and Humankind," in *Systematic Theology*, ed. Horton, 219–220.

[26]Bruce R. Marino, "The Origin, Nature, and Consequences of Sin," in *Systematic Theology*, ed. Horton, 281.

[10]For if anyone with a weak conscience sees you who have this knowledge eating in an idol's temple, won't he be emboldened to eat what has been sacrificed to idols? [11]So this weak brother, for whom Christ died, is destroyed by your knowledge. [12]When you sin against your brothers in this way and wound their weak conscience, you sin against Christ. [13]Therefore, if what I eat causes my brother to fall into sin, I will never eat meat again, so that I will not cause him to fall.

Paul has in mind the same principle of love emphasized in Romans 14:13–23. Though we may know something is not wrong or sinful, we should remember the weaker brother or sister whose conscience still tells them it is wrong or sinful. In this case, seeing a more mature Christian in a pagan temple eating food sacrificed to idols may cause them to dare to do the same. Then, their conscience makes them feel so guilty and sinful that they are destroyed spiritually. That is, they may say, "What's the use in trying to serve God," and go back into the world. We must remember that the weaker brother (or sister) is part of the body of Christ, a person for whom He died. So when we indulge in self-centered desires (that may not be wrong for us) and hurt another's weak conscience we not only sin against that person, we sin against Christ.

Paul is so concerned about the weaker brother (and this implies the weaker sisters as well) that even though he knows there is nothing wrong or sinful about eating meat offered to idols, he will avoid eating it for the rest of his life rather than cause the weak one to fall into sin. Love gave him insight into the needs of others and caused him to freely give up his rights in such matters.

C. Paul's Apostleship 9:1–27

1. Paul's Claim To Apostleship 9:1–2

[1]Am I not free? Am I not an apostle? Have I not seen Jesus our Lord? Are you not the result of my work in the Lord? [2]Even though I may not be an apostle to others, surely I am to you! For you are the seal of my apostleship in the Lord.

Paul has just warned those who were eating meat offered to idols: They must not let their freedom (based on their knowledge that God is One and idols are nothing) become a stumbling block to the weak. But that did not make them less free. Paul himself refused to become a stumbling block—yet he was still free. In fact, he had the freedom Christ had given him as an apostle.

It seems that some in Corinth, like some in Galatia (Gal. 1:15 to 2:10), did not want to accept Paul as a genuine apostle. But he was not only a genuine apostle, he had truly seen the Lord on the Damascus Road (Acts 9:1–9; 22:6–16; 26:12–18). Moreover, the Corinthian believers themselves were the result of Paul's ministry in (and by) the Lord. Those who had not experienced Paul's ministry might not recognize him as an apostle, but the Corinthian believers surely should. Just as a seal attested that a document was genuine, so they were the seal, that is, "the real proof,"[27] that attested to the genuineness of Paul's apostleship (and apostolic ministry, with its manifestation of the gifts and power of the Holy Spirit), given by and exercised in the Lord.

2. The Rights Of Preachers 9:3–14

3This is my defense to those who sit in judgment on
me. 4Don't we have the right to food and drink? 5Don't
we have the right to take a believing wife along with
us, as do the other apostles and the Lord's brothers
and Cephas? 6Or is it only I and Barnabas who must
work for a living?

Paul said he would not exercise his right to eat food offered to idols. But others were still sitting in judgment on him because he did not act like the other apostles (which may include the 72 as well as the 12; note how parallel Luke 9:1–5 and 10:1,7,11,19 are).

The questions of verses 4–5 call for a positive answer. Like the other apostles, he did have the right to ask local assemblies for food and drink. He had the right to get married and take a believing wife along with him in his missionary journeys. The other apostles and the brothers of Jesus and Peter did, and the assemblies supported them. But Paul willingly gave up those apostolic rights.

Paul and Barnabas, however, seemed to be the only ones who had to work for a living (and to support their ministry). Paul spent his morning at his trade of tentmaking to support himself and his evan-

---

[27] David G. Clark, "Ephesians 4:7–16: The Pauline Perspective of Pentecost," in *Faces of Renewal*, ed. Paul Elbert (Peabody, Mass.: Hendrickson Publishers, 1988), 134.

gelistic party (Acts 18:3; 1 Cor. 4:12; 1 Thess. 2:9; 2 Thess. 3:7–9). Probably, Apollos and others accepted support from the Corinthian believers. The Corinthians may then have thought Paul and Barnabas were doing something wrong by working at a secular occupation instead of giving full time to the work of the gospel.

7Who serves as a soldier at his own expense? Who plants a vineyard and does not eat of its grapes? Who tends a flock and does not drink of the milk? 8Do I say this merely from a human point of view? Doesn't the Law say the same thing? 9For it is written in the Law of Moses: "Do not muzzle an ox while it is treading out the grain." Is it about oxen that God is concerned?
10Surely he says this for us, doesn't he? Yes, this was written for us, because when the plowman plows and the thresher threshes, they ought to do so in the hope of sharing in the harvest. 11If we have sown spiritual seed among you, is it too much if we reap a material harvest from you?

To bring out the fact that he (as well as other apostles and ministers) had the right to expect local assemblies to support him so he would not have to do "secular" work for a living, Paul asks a series of questions that call for a positive answer. No one served as a soldier at his own expense. No one planted a vineyard and did not eat the grapes. No one tended a flock and did not drink the milk.

This was common sense, but Paul was not just depending on the point of view of human wisdom. He appealed to the Scriptures. The Law said the same thing when it forbade muzzling an ox that was treading out grain (on a threshing floor; Deut. 25:4). Some might have answered that that verse applied only to oxen. But Paul recognized a principle that God applied to oxen because it applies to us as well. The principle applies to the plowman who made possible the planting of the grain and to the thresher who actually makes the grain available for human food. It is right for both to expect a share in the harvest.

But Jesus sent His apostles out into a greater harvest, a spiritual harvest (John 4:35–36). The next question calls for the same logical answer. Paul sowed spiritual seed among the Corinthian believers. A material harvest (supplying needs for food, clothing, and other expenses) should not be too much to expect from them.

[12]If others have this right of support from you, shouldn't we have it all the more? But we did not use this right. On the contrary, we put up with anything rather than hinder the gospel of Christ. [13]Don't you know that those who work in the temple get their food from the temple, and those who serve at the altar share in what is offered on the altar? [14]In the same way, the Lord has commanded that those who preach the gospel should receive their living from the gospel.

The Corinthian believers acknowledged that others had the right to such support from them. Surely Paul and his company of missionaries deserved it as well or even more. Yet Paul did not use this right. He recognized that for him to ask for it might hinder the spread of the gospel. He and his companions in ministry were willing to put up with anything rather than do that.

Yet Paul's not claiming material support did not change the fact that it is right for local assemblies to support their ministers. When Paul said, "Don't you know . . . " he means they did know ("Surely you know . . ." –NCV). Even pagan priests were supported by what was brought to the temples of their idols. Moreover, the Old Testament shows that Levitical priests ate from the temple of the Lord and from His offerings such as the fellowship offering (Lev. 7:28–36; Num. 18:8–20). The same principle applies to preachers of the gospel, not only because of the Old Testament examples, but also because the Lord commanded it; that is, His apostles weren't to have to take time from spreading the gospel by doing other work (cf. Acts 6:1–4). This would include the discipling (Matt. 28:19–20) and maturing of believers; the Lord took apostles, prophets, evangelists, and pastor-teachers captive for that very thing (Eph. 4:11–16).

We should keep in mind, however, that Paul was not encouraging a professionalism that treats the ministry as just another way of making money, rather than subordinating everything to the promotion of the gospel.

3. Paul Did Not Make Use Of His Rights 9:15–18

[15]But I have not used any of these rights. And I am not writing this in the hope that you will do such things for me. I would rather die than have anyone deprive me of this boast. [16]Yet when I preach the gospel, I cannot boast, for I am compelled to preach. Woe to me if I do

not preach the gospel! [17]If I preach voluntarily, I have a reward; if not voluntarily, I am simply discharging the trust committed to me. [18]What then is my reward? Just this: that in preaching the gospel I may offer it free of charge, and so not make use of my rights in preaching it.

Because of the situation in Corinth, Paul reemphasizes that he did not use any of these rights. He wants the Corinthian believers to understand that he is stating these principles for the benefit of the local assemblies and their ministers in general. He is not asking them to send him any material support.

He is so concerned about his "boast," of seeking no material support in order not to hinder spreading of the gospel, that he would "rather die" than be deprived of that boast. He means he would rather die than hinder the spread of the gospel.

Yet when it comes to preaching the gospel, he cannot boast, for he is "compelled to preach." He feels an inner compulsion (that surely came from the commission Jesus gave him on the Damascus Road, a commission confirmed by Ananias as well as the Holy Spirit; Acts 9:6,15–16). He must have felt like Amos, who said, "'The lion has roared—who will not fear? the Sovereign Lord has spoken—who can but prophesy?'" (Amos 3:8), or Jeremiah, who said, "His word is in my heart like a fire, a fire shut up in my bones. I am weary of holding it in; indeed, I cannot" (Jer. 20:9). Paul did not intend to preach the gospel when he set out on the Damascus Road. If he had decided on his own to preach the gospel willingly, he would have had a reward. But he was not doing so because of his own will. He was discharging a trust that Jesus had committed to him (when he called him to be an apostle to the Gentiles).

That is not to say Paul had no reward. It was rewarding to him to be able to preach the gospel, offering it "free of charge," not claiming his rights to material support from his preaching.

4. Paul's Servant Leadership 9:19–22

[19]Though I am free and belong to no man, I make myself a slave to everyone, to win as many as possible. [20]To the Jews I became like a Jew, to win the Jews. To those under the law I became like one under the law (though I myself am not under the law), so as to win those under the law. [21]To those not having the

law I became like one not having the law (though I am not free from God's law but am under Christ's law), so as to win those not having the law. [22]To the weak I became weak, to win the weak. I have become all things to all men so that by all possible means I might save some.

Paul now tells of another aspect to his freedom that should be an example to us. Though he was a free man who belonged to no human being, he was free to make himself "a slave to everyone." A slave had no rights. A slave must serve his master. So Paul took the place of a servant and claimed no rights in order that he might win "as many as possible" to the Lord.

This included giving up the right to follow his own customs and his own freedoms. His missionary strategy was to follow the customs of those around him as much as possible, that is, wherever doing so would not be against the Word of God or the principles of the gospel. So when he was with Jews, he lived like a Jew (which would involve eating kosher food, not eating pork, etc.). He did not do things to shock or antagonize them because he wanted to win them to Christ.

He explains this further: Though he was not "under the law" (of Moses), he was not lawless. He was careful to follow what the Law called for so that he might win the Jews who considered themselves still under the Law.

Then to those Gentiles who had no knowledge of the law of Moses, he did not make an issue of things that the Judaizers might have insisted on. He followed their ways of doing things, for example, eating their food (though still not lawless, but keeping himself under the law of God that Christ reveals, the law that Paul calls "Christ's law"). In other words, he did not take part in idolatrous pagan customs but kept God's law—not as a means of earning salvation, but as an expression of Christian love by a person who lives in the Spirit.

Then, to "the weak" (i.e., a weak conscience full of scruples, see 8:9–12; cf. Rom. 15:1–2), he "became weak," not showing his spiritual strength that would allow him to do things they could not do, for he wanted to win them. In all these cases, Paul wanted to win them to Christ, not to religious forms and ceremonies.

Paul summarizes this by saying he became (and continued to become) "all things" to everybody in hopes that he might "save some" (which included discipling them, encouraging a Christian lifestyle, focusing their hope on Jesus). This kind of servanthood "is one of the most important themes in the Bible."[28] What an example of servant leadership Paul was!

5. Paul's Self-Discipline 9:23–27

23I do all this for the sake of the gospel, that I may share in its blessings. 24Do you not know that in a race all the runners run, but only one gets the prize? Run in such a way as to get the prize. 25Everyone who competes in the games goes into strict training. They do it to get a crown that will not last; but we do it to get a crown that will last forever. 26Therefore I do not run like a man running aimlessly; I do not fight like a man beating the air. 27No, I beat my body and make it my slave so that after I have preached to others, I myself will not be disqualified for the prize.

Though Paul did not ask the Corinthian assembly to support him and was not concerned about receiving material benefits, this does not mean he had no hope for future rewards. He lived the life of a servant, a slave, for the sake of the progress of the gospel, expecting to share in its blessings.[29] The gospel is good news, full of promises of both present and future blessings. Of those blessings Paul was especially concerned about the promises of future glory (see 2 Cor. 4:17).

Paul worked hard at cultivating, developing, and carrying out his Christian life and service to the Lord. He compares it to running a race and to athletes in training.[30] Some runners may not care about winning. But no one in something like the Olympic games runs a race casually. They all run with the intent of winning a prize. We should live for Christ with the same intensity. Not only so, we should be in strict training under the direction of the Holy Spirit. We have no time to waste in frivolous, harmful, or sinful pursuits if we wish to win the prize, the "Well done!" from our Lord and the crown of glory He has for us (Matt. 25:21,23; 2 Tim. 4:8).

This means cooperating with the Spirit in sanctification, developing the fruit of the Spirit, especially self-control, and eradicating bad

---

[28]A. C. George, *Dimensions of Spirituality* (Thiruvanmiyur, Chennai, India: Bethesda Communications, 1997), 59.

[29]Gordon D. Fee, *The First Epistle to the Corinthians* (Grand Rapids: Wm. B. Eerdmans, 1991), 432.

[30]Corinthians were familiar with these things, since the Isthmian games were held every two years near Corinth.

habits and sins. "This text has a lot to say to Protestants today who do not work very hard at cultivating the Christian life. It speaks especially to some Charismatics who lack the last fruit of the Spirit, self-control."[31]

To Paul this meant he did not "run . . . aimlessly." He kept God-given goals before him. He did not fight the battle against sin, evil, and unbelief by random human effort. He aimed where the Spirit directed him to.

Above all, he did not let the fleshly desires of the physical body dominate him. This was a danger for those who ate in the temples of idols, for their rituals encouraged immorality. The Greek *hupōpiazō* was a term used by boxers for giving a black eye. Paul means he treated his body with severe discipline and made it his slave, so that it would obey his desires to serve Christ and win victories for Him. He knew that if he failed in this area all his preaching to others would count for nothing: He would be disqualified for the prize and rejected (Gk. *adokimos*).

Paul is referring to more than losing rewards. The word *adokimos* is used elsewhere of the depraved minds of sinners (Rom. 1:28) and of false teachers who are going to hell and dragging others with them (Titus 1:15–16). The Septuagint uses the term of people who have become dross, good for nothing but to be cast out in the slag heap or waste dump (Isa. 1:22). Paul could lose out altogether (John 15:6; Rom. 11:17–21; Gal. 5:4; 1 Tim. 1:19; 4:1; 2 Tim. 2:12; Heb. 3:12).[32] He was well aware of the exceeding sinfulness of sin and of its drastic results. The warning here is real and we should not let Calvinistic presuppositions cause us to ignore or soften it (cf. the warnings Jesus gave in Luke 21:34,36).

The verbs "run . . . fight . . . beat" are in the Greek present tense which indicates continuous action. Paul kept himself in training. "The fruit of the Spirit which is self-control is not some luxury to be enjoyed by an elite among Christians; it is a reality in the life of everyone who has been claimed by Christ. Hence to be a Christian is to be self-controlled all the time."[33] On the other hand, we must be careful

---

[31]Richard Lovelace, "Baptism in the Holy Spirit and the Evangelical Tradition," in *Faces of Renewal*, ed. Elbert, 212.

[32]Daniel B. Pecota, "The Saving Work of Christ," in *Systematic Theology*, ed. Stanley M. Horton, rev. ed. (Springfield, Mo.: Logion Press, 1995), 371.

[33]John W. Sanderson, *The Fruit of the Spirit* (Phillipsburg, N.J.: Presbyterian and Reformed Publishing Company, 1985), 140.

not to depend on good works or human willpower instead of depending on Christ and the Holy Spirit. Neither should we fall into a monastic style of life that withdraws from everyday affairs. Paul set the example when he said, "One thing I do: Forgetting what is behind and straining toward what is ahead, I press on toward the goal to win the prize for which God has called me heavenward in Christ Jesus" (Phil. 3:13–14).

D. Examples From Israel's History 10:1–13

1. God's Displeasure With Most Who Crossed The Red Sea 10:1–5

**1For I do not want you to be ignorant of the fact, broth-
ers, that our forefathers were all under the cloud and
that they all passed through the sea. 2They were all
baptized into Moses in the cloud and in the sea. 3They
all ate the same spiritual food 4and drank the same
spiritual drink; for they drank from the spiritual rock
that accompanied them, and that rock was Christ.
5Nevertheless, God was not pleased with most of
them; their bodies were scattered over the desert.**

As an illustration to emphasize the fact that God's redeemed, Spirit-filled people can lose out, fail to win the prize, and be rejected (in the Corinthian believers' case, if they persist in eating in the temples of idols), Paul turns to the Old Testament Scriptures. He reminds them that their ancestors (who are now spiritual "ancestors" of all who by faith become children of Abraham, Gal. 3:7–9) who came through the Red Sea were brought into a relationship with God by Moses (Exod. 19:4). They were led by God and they had the hope of entering the Promised Land.

Paul calls their deliverance a baptism in the sense the glory cloud was over them and the waters of the Red Sea were on each side of them.[34] It marked their identification as the people of God delivered from Egypt, just as baptism testifies to our identification with Jesus who by His death and resurrection has delivered us from the Egypt of sin. Moreover, God's provision for them of the manna and water from

---

[34]Paul emphasizes that "all" were baptized. Cf. v. 5, "most of them." See Fred Fisher, *Commentary on 1 and 2 Corinthians* (Waco, Tex.: Word Books, 1975), 153.

the rock was supernatural, and in that sense was spiritual and parallel to the Lord's Supper.

The rock was not on wheels. Water came from one rock at Horeb (Exod. 17:6) and another at Kadesh (Num. 20:11).[35] But the source of the miracle was Christ. Calling Him a rock is in line with the many times God is called Israel's "Rock" (1 Sam. 2:2; 2 Sam. 22:2,32,47; Ps. 18:2; 19:14; 28:1; 31:3; 62:2; 71:3; 78:35; 94:22; etc.). He was with them at Horeb. He was with them at Kadesh. He was with them all along the way.

God, however, did not approve the great majority of the children of Israel. Because of their fear of giants and walled cities—as reported by ten of the twelve spies who scouted out the Promised Land—they had said they wouldn't go. So, except for Joshua and Caleb, those who were twenty years old and older when the spies brought back their report never reached the Promised Land. Their bones bleached on the desert floor (see Num. 14:29–30).

2. Reasons For God's Displeasure 10:6–10

**6Now these things occurred as examples to keep us
from setting our hearts on evil things as they did. 7Do
not be idolaters, as some of them were; as it is written:
"The people sat down to eat and drink and got up to
indulge in pagan revelry." 8We should not commit sexual immorality, as some of them did—and in one day
twenty-three thousand of them died. 9We should not
test the Lord, as some of them did—and were killed by
snakes. 10And do not grumble, as some of them did—
and were killed by the destroying angel.**

The history in the Old Testament is not there simply to satisfy our curiosity about ancient times. The Holy Spirit inspired such a record because there would be lessons in it for future generations, including both the Corinthians and us. God was faithful both to bless and to judge the people of Israel. So they became examples to warn us and keep us from committing the sins they did. God knew we would need the warning.

Those wicked, evil things they did included idolatry, where the people carried on pagan-type revelry (which included sexual orgies, along

---

[35]Jewish tradition did say the stream from the rock at Horeb followed them. See Gordon D. Fee, *The First Epistle to the Corinthians* (Grand Rapids: Wm. B. Eerdmans, 1991), 447–48.

with their singing and dancing) in front of the golden calf Aaron made (Exod. 32:6,18–19). Moses commanded the Levites to execute the leaders with the sword, and three thousand were slain. Then God sent a plague (Exod. 32:25) that brought the total to twenty-three thousand.[36]

Those who were "killed by snakes" were people who had spoken against God and against Moses (Num. 21:5); this was sinning by putting God to the test (cf. Exod. 17:2). The Book of Numbers has eight instances of murmuring, or grumbling. Paul probably had in mind Numbers 14:1–38 and Numbers 16:41, where the grumbling brought divine judgment, which Paul understood was accomplished by the same destroying angel who brought the plague on Egypt's firstborn. God's promise was that if they would obey, He would not put the diseases, or plague, on them that He had put on the Egyptians (Exod. 15:26). But when they didn't do what was right, God was free to send that destroying angel again.

Too many are worshiping false gods today. The idolatry that substitutes something for the one true God leads to corruption, immorality, and heathen pleasures today just as it did in Bible times. New Age doctrines also tear down biblical values, even though they may use some biblical terminology. Though God is patient and long-suffering, He will not tolerate idolatry, sin, and false teaching now any more than He did then.

3. Warnings For Us 10:11–13

[11]These things happened to them as examples and were written down as warnings for us, on whom the fulfillment of the ages has come. [12]So, if you think you are standing firm, be careful that you don't fall!

Paul emphasizes what he has said in verse 6 about the Old Testament being "examples." He adds that they are "warnings"—"warnings for us, on whom the fulfillment of the ages has come." With that, he includes not only the Corinthian believers but all believers in the Church Age. All the ages that preceded it led up to the first

---

[36]Some confuse this with the plague at Shittim (Num. 25:9) where twenty-four thousand died. However, Paul is referring to the sin of the golden calf here and gives the total that died at that time. See Gleason L. Archer, *Encyclopedia of Bible Difficulties* (Grand Rapids: Zondervan Publishing House, 1982), 141,401.

coming of Christ and to His death and resurrection, which inaugurated the Church Age. Thus the Church Age is the fulfillment of it all, the last age preceding the promised millennial kingdom where we shall rule and reign with Christ. And these warnings given to the Corinthians nearly two thousand years ago "are even more applicable today. His coming is indeed nearer than when we first believed!"[37]

When we consider the past ages, especially the history of Israel's failures, this should warn us not to be overconfident. Even if we think we are standing firm, if we don't pay attention to the examples and warnings found in the Bible, we can still fall. Let us remind each other of these things and discipline ourselves. We must be careful that we do not imagine that we can never fall. Jesus gave many similar warnings (e.g., Matt. 24:45–51; 25:30). Young Christians may yield to temptation and let discouragement and depression cause them to continue in defeat and spiritual poverty. Older Christians may resist temptation but become complacent or even proud. But we have help. The Holy Spirit is a Spirit of power, of love, and of self-discipline (2 Tim. 1:7). We also have the assurance of 1 John 1:9—"If we confess our sins [including pride and complacency], he [Jesus] is faithful and just and will forgive us our sins and purify us from all unrighteousness." The believer, young or old, is alive in Christ and does not need to become a slave of sin (Col. 2:13–15).

> **[13]No temptation has seized you except what is common to man. And God is faithful; he will not let you be tempted beyond what you can bear. But when you are tempted, he will also provide a way out so that you can stand up under it.**

Paul not only warns us, he encourages us. We are not doomed to fall. We will have temptations, tests, and trials. That is part of the human condition since Adam and Eve fell. But we do not need to fall. We have a God who is faithful.[38] He will not abandon us, nor will He let us be tried beyond our endurance, beyond what we are able to bear.

With every trial our faithful God will provide a way out,[39] that is, a

---

[37]Stanley M. Horton, *Our Destiny: Biblical Teachings on the Last Things* (Springfield, Mo.: Logion Press, 1996), 159.

[38]5See Russell E. Joyner, "The One True God," in *Systematic Theology,* ed. Stanley M. Horton, rev. ed. (Springfield, Mo.: Logion Press, 1995), 126.

[39]The Gk. *ekbasin* was sometimes used of finding a pass when trapped in the mountains.

successful outcome, so we can bear up under it. That is, because we are sure the Lord is with us and will see us through, we can bear it instead of giving up. We must remember also that "Temptation must never be confused with sin. . . . If temptation were sin, God would not provide help to endure it."[40]

We have the further assurance that Jesus knows how we feel. In Gethsemane, His burden was almost unbearable, but God sent an angel who strengthened Him (Luke 22:41–43). "What encouragement this is for us when we confront life's impossibilities. Surely we can count on God to send His angels 'to serve those who will inherit salvation' (Heb. 1:14)."[41]

E. Flee Idolatry 10:14–22

**14Therefore, my dear friends, flee from idolatry. 15I
speak to sensible people; judge for yourselves what I
say. 16Is not the cup of thanksgiving for which we give
thanks a participation in the blood of Christ? And is not
the bread that we break a participation in the body of
Christ? 17Because there is one loaf, we, who are many,
are one body, for we all partake of the one loaf.**

Perhaps the greatest temptation facing the Corinthians was idolatry, especially the temptation to enjoy the food at feasts in pagan temples. Corinthian believers were surrounded by temples of idols and by idolatrous practices in the homes of all their pagan neighbors and relatives. So Paul says, "Flee!" For us, this would include refusing to let anything come between us and the one true God. The command is still to love the Lord our God with all our heart and with all our soul and with all our mind and with all our strength (Mark 12:30).

Paul wants the Corinthians as "sensible people" to think this through for themselves. His questions call for a positive answer. In the celebration of the Lord's Supper, the cup of thanksgiving (Gk *eulogias,* "blessing, praise") includes thanks for the life we have in Christ because He died. By partaking of the cup we declare that by faith we participate in the blood of Christ, that is, in its benefits: the salvation and forgiveness and cleansing He provides. Partaking of the bread also

---

40Bruce R. Marino, "The Origin, Nature, and Consequences of Sin," in *Systematic Theology,* ed. Horton, 279.

41Robert L. Brandt and Zenas J. Bicket, *The Spirit Helps Us Pray* (Springfield, Mo.: Logion Press, 1993), 362.

symbolizes "participation in the body of Christ," both our relationship to Him and our fellowship with one another, a fellowship that overcomes "all barriers (social, economic, cultural, etc.)."[42] Just as one loaf was broken by Jesus during the Last Supper, so there is but "one loaf," one body of Christ. The many believers of all races, nationalities, colors, and backgrounds are all part of the one Body and partake of the one loaf, that is, of the benefits of His body that was nailed to the cross for us, freely given for our redemption.[43]

> **18Consider the people of Israel: Do not those who eat**
> **the sacrifices participate in the altar? 19Do I mean then**
> **that a sacrifice offered to an idol is anything, or that an**
> **idol is anything? 20No, but the sacrifices of pagans are**
> **offered to demons, not to God, and I do not want you**
> **to be participants with demons. 21You cannot drink the**
> **cup of the Lord and the cup of demons too; you can-**
> **not have a part in both the Lord's table and the table**
> **of demons. 22Are we trying to arouse the Lord's jeal-**
> **ousy? Are we stronger than he?**

To emphasize further that they must "flee from idolatry," Paul points out that those Israelites who partook of the sacrifices, such as the fellowship offering, participated in all that the altar means (cf. Deut. 12:7). Paul still has in mind the temptation to join in the feasting at pagan temples. Even though sacrifices to idols and the idols themselves are nothing, it is still dangerous to partake.

Behind the idol worship, and encouraging it, are demons. So the sacrifices offered to idols are really offered to demons, even if the offerers do not know it. There is a whole hierarchy of demons that we must take a stand against (Eph. 6:10–18). Paul did not want the Corinthians to be participants with demons, nor should we. In fact, it is an impossibility to drink properly the cup of the Lord and at the same time drink the cup of demons. To put it plainly, no one can partake of the Lord's Supper in a way that truly remembers and honors Him and also partake of pagan feasts in pagan temples, for in doing so, they are identifying themselves with the demons who promote the idolatry.

Paul sensed that some were saying they were not afraid to partake

---

[42]Michael L. Dusing, "The New Testament Church," in *Systematic Theology,* ed. Horton, 563.

[43]There are no grounds for "closed communion" such as is practiced by the Roman Catholic Church and some Protestants. The table is "the Lord's table," rather than any denomination's table.

of the pagan feasts. They believed they were spiritually strong enough to do it and not let it affect their relationship with the Lord. Paul, in effect, asks them what they think they are doing and who do they think they are? The Old Testament reminds Israel again and again that God is a jealous God. That is, He wants all their love, all their devotion, all their worship, because He alone is God and He alone can bless and help them. By going to idolatrous feasts, the Corinthians were acting as if they wanted to stir up God's jealousy. If they think they are strong, they will find out they are not as strong as God. Judgment is implied.

Paul's lesson here surely has an application to Christians who think they can participate in modern idolatry—astrology, the occult, the drug culture, and the sinful practices these things encourage—without it affecting their relationship with God. His judgment will come on them sooner or later. All those things, including any miracles or supernatural events that they produce, speak with the voice "of Satan and his demons."[44]

F. Seek The Good Of Others 10:23–11:2

23"Everything is permissible"—but not everything is beneficial. "Everything is permissible"—but not everything is constructive. 24Nobody should seek his own good, but the good of others.

"Everything is permissible" seems to be a quotation of what some of the Corinthian leaders were saying. Because they were free from the law of Moses, they taught that they were free to do whatever they wished. Paul modifies what they were saying in three ways. Everything is not "beneficial" (useful or helpful). Everything is not "constructive." Everything does not edify or build up spiritually.

Those who were saying that everything is permissible were thinking only of themselves, what they wanted to do, what they felt was good for them or would do something for them. Paul shows this is wrong. As followers of Christ, we should not seek our own good, but the good of others (cf. Gal. 6:10; Heb. 13:16).

25Eat anything sold in the meat market without raising questions of conscience, 26for, "The earth is the Lord's, and everything in it."

---

[44]John R. Higgins, "God's Inspired Word," in *Systematic Theology*, ed. Horton, 68.

Paul anticipates a further question. What about those who do not join in the feasts in pagan temples but eat the meat offered to idols when it is sold in the meat markets? His answer is to buy it and eat it without asking any questions that would cause a person to have a guilty conscience. After all, the meat did not belong to the idols. The earth and everything in it really belongs to the Lord. It is His by right of creation and because of who He is (Pss. 24:1; 50:12; 89:11–12). Furthermore, we have His permission to eat meat (Gen. 9:3). The world's misuse of God's gifts should not keep us from their proper use.

> **27If some unbeliever invites you to a meal and you**
> **want to go, eat whatever is put before you without**
> **raising questions of conscience. 28But if anyone says to**
> **you, "This has been offered in sacrifice," then do not**
> **eat it, both for the sake of the man who told you and**
> **for conscience' sake— 29the other man's conscience, I**
> **mean, not yours. For why should my freedom be**
> **judged by another's conscience? 30If I take part in the**
> **meal with thankfulness, why am I denounced because**
> **of something I thank God for?**

Another question Paul anticipates is "What should we do if an unbeliever asks us to share a meal in his home?" Paul wants believers to avoid sin, not sinners. Jesus ate with tax collectors and sinners as well as Pharisees. There can be excellent opportunities for witness during and after a good meal. So believers should eat whatever is put before them and ask no questions.

There would be one exception: "If anyone says to you, 'This has been offered in sacrifice.'" Many interpret the speaker to be a believer with a weak, oversensitive conscience as saying this. Then, for the sake of the weak believer and his conscience, stop eating the food in question. However, Paul has already indicated that the fact the meat has been offered to idols is of no concern to the Christian (v. 25). Fee suggests that a pagan who knew about Jewish concerns might think he is helping the Christian out by mentioning that the food was offered to idols, so as a consideration of the pagan's moral consciousness about what a Christian should do, the Christian should stop eating the meat.[45]

Even so, this should not affect believers who have strong faith and a strong conscience. Nor should they let anyone put judgment on them if they choose to eat. Whatever Paul eats, he thanks God for, so why should

---

[45]Fee, *First Epistle to the Corinthians*, 483–87.

anyone denounce him for that? Paul refuses to let himself be affected by the denunciations of others who might regard him like the Pharisees did Christ.

> **[31]So whether you eat or drink or whatever you do, do it all for the glory of God. [32]Do not cause anyone to stumble, whether Jews, Greeks or the church of God— [33]even as I try to please everybody in every way. For I am not seeking my own good but the good of many, so that they may be saved.**

Paul concludes this discussion by reemphasizing two things. First, whatever you eat, drink, or do, "do it all for the glory of God." Our worship of God, our glorifying Him, should not be limited to what we do in church services. Everything should be done in a spirit of worship to our wonderful Lord, desiring to exalt Him.[46] We should do nothing that would detract from His glory, or keep others from glorifying God as Lord, Savior, Redeemer, and Friend. Second, do not do anything that would "cause anyone to stumble" (or go astray). This includes Jews, Greeks (non-Christians, pagans), as well as the church (assembly) of God.

As in 9:19–23, Paul wants to please,[47] not offend, the people he is trying to reach for Christ and establish as mature believers. He wants them all to be saved—not merely converted, but saved with the final salvation that includes our new bodies and our ruling and reigning with Christ, a salvation that will be ours in its fullness when Jesus comes again.

> **[1]Follow my example, as I follow the example of Christ. [2]I praise you for remembering me in everything and for holding to the teachings, just as I passed them on to you.**

The first verse belongs to the summation at the end of chapter 10. Paul wants the believers to exercise their will to become imitators of him to the extent that he is an imitator of Christ.[48] He does not mean

---

[46]Dusing, "The New Testament Church," 544.

[47]This does not mean Paul was trying to curry favor for himself, nor did it mean he was trying to please them by condoning their sin. He did not try to win the approval of men, or please people in a way that would not be pleasing to God (Gal. 1:10). He wanted to show them he was concerned about their good, about their eternal welfare.

[48]It is possible that Paul has a limited example of Christ in mind, limited to his discussion of eating meat offered to idols: For example, Christ did eat with sinners without sinning, He kept in mind the weak in faith (Matt. 12:20), and He did things for the sake of others rather than for the sake of himself (John 11:42).

that he is the perfect example; Christ is. His sinlessness; His love and compassion; His humility, gentleness, patience, and mercy; His concern for women and children, for the sick and the poor; His obedience to the Father's will in sacrificing himself for our salvation—all make Him the perfect example. More than that, He is "the radiance of God's glory and the exact representation of his being" (Heb. 1:3). He is more than our example, of course, for He is Savior and Lord. We must remember that we cannot follow Him or even imitate Paul's imitating of Jesus until we do make Him our personal Lord and Savior.

As an introduction to the next section of this letter Paul commends the Corinthian believers. He praises them especially for holding to his teachings just as he passed them on (from the Lord) to them (cf. 11:23). He means he is praising them for obeying them. He says this because he is very concerned that they accept and obey the teaching he is about to give.

Study questions for this section may be found in appendix B.

V. DIRECTIONS FOR WORSHIP 11:3–33

A. Propriety In Prayer And Prophecy 11:3–16

3Now I want you to realize that the head of every man is Christ, and the head of the woman is man, and the head of Christ is God.

Traditionally, this passage is interpreted by taking "head" to mean authority, or ruler. Others interpret it "to refer primarily to the concept of honor, in that one's physical head is the seat of his honor (cf. vv. 4–5). Thus as Christ honored God, man is to honor Christ and woman is to honor her husband."[1] It is more likely that "head" means "source of life."[2] Paul begins by drawing attention to a sequence where God the Father is the head of Christ, Christ is the head of every indi-

[1]W. Harold Mare, "1 Corinthians," in *The NIV Study Bible*, ed. Kenneth Barker (Grand Rapids: Zondervan Bible Publishers, 1985), 1748.

[2]Gordon D. Fee, *The First Epistle to the Corinthians* (Grand Rapids: Wm. B. Eerdmans, 1991), 503.

vidual man, and the man is the head of the woman. This is explained further in verse 8, which directs our attention to creation.

God the Father and Christ are both fully divine. They are "coeternal, coequal, and coexistent,"[3] but Jesus receives from the Father (John 14:24) and comes from the Father (John 16:28). Thus, there is a voluntary "economic subordination," or functional subordination, of the Son to the Father where the Son works in unity with the Father.[4] Since Paul draws a distinction between Christ as "the head of every man," but the man being "the head of the woman," it cannot mean that every man is the head of all women: The reference is again to the order of creation, the man, Adam, being created first. However, Adam said Eve was both "'bone of my bones and flesh of my flesh'" (Gen. 2:23), sharing the same essence.[5] Since "man" and "woman" can mean husband and wife, there is an application to the situation in Corinth as well.

Those who take it that headship means authority say disobedience is insubordination.[6] However, Christ is not inferior to the Father who is His Head. Neither is the wife inferior to the husband. "The word 'helper' (Gen. 2:18) is often used of God (Exod. 18:4) and does not indicate a lower status. Moreover, when the New Testament places wives in a role of functional subordination to their husbands (Eph. 5:24; Col. 3:18; Titus 2:5; 1 Pet. 3:1), it does not necessarily follow that females are inferior to males, or even that females should be functionally subordinate to males generally (the NT pattern is that wives are subordinate to their own husbands)."[7]

The relationship of the husband and wife is not comparable to that of master and servant or army officer and soldier, for reference to it follows a command for mutual submission out of reverence for Christ. Ephesians 5:21–33 compares it to the relationship of Christ and the Church. The husband's part is to love his wife: give himself up for her in order to encourage her to be holy (dedicated to the worship and

---

[3]Kerry D. McRoberts, "The Holy Trinity," in *Systematic Theology,* ed. Stanley M. Horton, rev. ed. (Springfield, Mo.: Logion Press, 1995), 153.

[4]Ibid., 165.

[5]Timothy Munyon, "The Creation of the Universe and Humankind" in *Systematic Theology,* ed. Horton, 238.

[6]James G. Sigountos and Myron Shank, "Public Roles for Women in the Pauline Church: A Reappraisal of the Evidence," *Journal of the Evangelical Theological Society* 26, no. 3 (September 1983): 284.

[7]Munyon, "Creation," 248–49.

service of the Lord), feed and care for her, recognize her worth, love her as his own body (as he loves himself), and be united to her. The wife's part is in love to submit voluntarily to his love and encouragement and to respect him. Thus, the wife works in unity with the husband. His leadership must be servant leadership (Matt. 20:25–28). When there is fundamental submission to Christ servant leadership will follow easily.

4Every man who prays or prophesies with his head covered dishonors his head. 5And every woman who prays or prophesies with her head uncovered dishonors her head—it is just as though her head were shaved. 6If a woman does not cover her head, she should have her hair cut off; and if it is a disgrace for a woman to have her hair cut or shaved off, she should cover her head.

Though both men and women are equally free to pray and prophesy publicly in the congregation, they do need to consider the customs of the time in order not to disgrace themselves, implying that it would also disgrace the cause of Christ. In the society of Corinth a man who prayed or prophesied in the assembly with his head covered (with a cloth covering) disgraced his own head.[8] A woman who prayed or prophesied in the assembly with her head uncovered[9] disgraced her own head[10] to the point that if it were shaved it would be no greater disgrace. Obviously Paul is talking about her own physical head here, not her husband.

The principle behind covering the head is still important today. As Don Stamps wrote, "When dressing modestly and properly for the glory of God, a woman enhances her own God-given place of dignity and worth."[11]

7A man ought not to cover his head, since he is the image and glory of God; but the woman is the glory of man. 8For man did not come from woman, but woman from man; 9neither was man created for woman, but

---

8This custom later changed. Orthodox Jewish men now must wear a yarmulke (skullcap) or hat when in prayer.

9 "Uncovered" may mean with loosed hair, something women did not do in public in those days.

10Or, this may mean she disgraced her own husband.

11Donald C. Stamps, ed., *The Full Life Study Bible* (Grand Rapids: Zondervan Publishing House, 1992), 1767.

woman for man. [10]For this reason, and because of the angels, the woman ought to have a sign of authority on her head.

Something more than human custom is involved in the relationship of the husband and wife. Paul goes back to God's creation of the first man and woman to give scriptural grounds.

The man is the image and glory of God;[12] that is, God created Adam to be holy as He is holy (cf. Eph. 4:24) and to bring praise, honor, and glory to Him. Then the woman was created as Adam's glory, because it was not good for him to be alone. He needed her as his counterpart and partner. This is explained by saying that the woman came out of the man: He was her "head"—her source. "She is not therefore subordinate to him, but necessary for him . . . so that he might be complete."[13]

Because the wife is the husband's glory, she ought to have authority (Gk. *exousia*) over her head. Some take this to mean that she ought to wear a veil as a sign that she is under authority; however, the Greek grammar indicates it means she has authority over her own head to do what she wishes or chooses to do.[14] But what she does should also be "because of the angels." What this means is not explained. It may refer back to 6:3: Since women will also take part in judging angels, they should be able to judge what to do in the matter of praying and prophesying with their heads covered. Or it may mean they were thinking of themselves as being spiritually like angels, so they didn't need to pay attention to the distinction between sexes. Another possibility is that it may mean that because angels are concerned with honoring God they are "shocked at conduct not according to God's will."[15]

[11]In the Lord, however, woman is not independent of man, nor is man independent of woman. [12]For as woman came from man, so also man is born of woman. But everything comes from God.

"In the Lord," that is, among believers who are in right relation to the Lord, neither the husband nor the wife is to operate independently of each other. That is, neither is self-sufficient, neither has any right to

---

[12]For a good discussion of the image of God in human beings see Munyon, "Creation," 250–53.

[13]Fee, *First Epistle to the Corinthians,* 517.

[14]Ibid., 520.

[15]Stamps, *Full Life Study Bible,* 1786.

look down on the other. God did take the first woman from the first man. But ever since then, every man is born of a woman. So the woman is not inferior to the man. As husband and wife, they need each other. But God is the Creator, the source of all human life, male and female. Both were created in His image. We are all dependent on Him. He is the true source of both physical and spiritual life for us all.

> **13Judge for yourselves: Is it proper for a woman to pray**
> **to God with her head uncovered? 14Does not the very**
> **nature of things teach you that if a man has long hair,**
> **it is a disgrace to him, 15but that if a woman has long**
> **hair, it is her glory? For long hair is given to her as a**
> **covering. 16If anyone wants to be contentious about**
> **this, we have no other practice—nor do the churches**
> **of God.**

Now Paul clarifies the basis of his argument. They surely have the good sense to realize that it is not "proper" (fitting, pleasing, right) for a woman to pray to God in public with her head uncovered. If they looked around they would see in the natural order of things[16] in their society that long hair was considered a disgrace for men[17] while long hair was considered a glory for women. This points also to her need in their society to have her head covered by a shawl or cloth covering.

To conclude this argument Paul suggests that those who were "contentious about this" and not covering their heads needed to pay attention to the customs in the local assemblies of God in every other place. So we need to be careful that our dress and actions are not contrary to what our assemblies today consider appropriate, lest we bring shame on our Head, Christ.[18]

---

[16]Paul is not referring to what is often called "Mother Nature," but to the customs natural to their day or customs inherited from their ancestors. Walter Bauer, *A Greek-English Lexicon of the New Testament and Other Early Christian Literature*, trans. F. Wilbur Gingrich and Frederick W. Danker, 2d ed. (Chicago: University of Chicago Press, 1979), 869.

[17]Artists who picture Jesus as having long hair are wrong. Jesus was not a Nazirite. Paul would not have said this if Jesus had had long hair. Both Jewish and Gentile men wore their hair short in NT times. Ancient records confirm this.

[18]Robert L. Brandt and Zenas J. Bicket, *The Spirit Helps Us Pray* (Springfield, Mo.: Logion Press, 1993), 274.

B. Propriety In The Lord's Supper 11:17–34

1. Divisions Expressed 11:17–22

[17]In the following directives I have no praise for you, for your meetings do more harm than good. [18]In the first place, I hear that when you come together as a church, there are divisions among you, and to some extent I believe it. [19]No doubt there have to be differences among you to show which of you have God's approval.

Paul started out this chapter with praise (v. 2), for he knew the majority were already following the directions about head coverings. But he has no praise for the way the Corinthians were coming together "as a church," an assembly of believers, because of the reported divisions among them. Note the irony of verse 19. Instead of praising them he sarcastically said they needed the divisions so they could show which groups among them had "God's approval."

The Book of Acts keeps emphasizing that the believers came together "in one accord" (2:1, KJV). They were one in genuine fellowship, one in purpose, one in their praises to God, one in their devotion to the apostles' teaching (which is now recorded in the New Testament), united in prayer, and filled with the Holy Spirit (Acts 2:42; 4:24, 31; 5:12; cf. Phil. 2:2). Without this kind of fellowship it is not a New Testament church; it is not the kind of assembly of believers the New Testament calls an *ekklēsia.* Without this kind of fellowship it is no different than the crowd assembled in a theater or at a ball game. Without this real fellowship their observance of the Lord's Supper was a mere performance.[19] Without this fellowship their meetings were doing "more harm than good": They were harming each other. They were harming the world outside who saw their divisions and were repelled by the lack of love.

[20]When you come together, it is not the Lord's Supper you eat, [21]for as you eat, each of you goes ahead without waiting for anybody else. One remains hungry, another gets drunk. [22]Don't you have homes to eat and drink in? Or do you despise the church of God and humiliate those who have nothing? What shall I say to you? Shall I praise you for this? Certainly not!

---

[19]Eduard Schweizer, "The Service of Worship" *Interpretation* 13, no. 4 (October 1959), 401.

What they were observing was really "not the Lord's Supper." He contrasts this with their suppers in their own homes where they would not show a lack of hospitality or consideration for others.

Because Jesus instituted the Lord's Supper in connection with the Passover meal, the Corinthian believers continued to observe it in connection with a meal, which Jude 12 and some later writers refer to as a "love feast." Each one brought his or her own meal. The rich went ahead eating with their rich friends, without waiting for latecomers, people (especially slaves) who could not get away from their work early enough to join the others. Thus, the rich gorged themselves with food and wine in their own private supper[20] while others did not have enough to satisfy their hunger.

It is possible, too, that the differences in their human loyalties spilled over into this time, a follower of Apollos, for example, not sharing with a follower of Cephas. The division here, however, seems to be between the rich and the poor. The rich had their own homes where they could eat their suppers. They did not need to despise God's assembled believers and destroy the unity of the assembly (cf. Gal. 3:28; 5:21; Eph. 5:18; Col. 3:11). Their conduct shows that the supper they are observing cannot be identified as the *Lord's* Supper.

2. The Lord's Directions 11:23–26

23For I received from the Lord what I also passed on to you: The Lord Jesus, on the night he was betrayed, took bread, 24and when he had given thanks, he broke it and said, "This is my body, which is for you; do this in remembrance of me."

Paul reminds them of what Jesus personally told him, possibly during his three years in Arabia (Gal. 1:11–12,15–17). Mentioning "the night He was betrayed" reminds us Judas was present. Paul wants the Corinthian believers to remember that one of Jesus' own disciples betrayed Him, something we too must remember. But the presence of Judas did not detract from the love that filled the heart of Jesus (see John 13:1).

The giving of thanks also showed His love for God the Father and

---

[20]"Gets drunk" (Gk. *methuei*) does not necessarily mean they were intoxicated. It can also mean "to eat and drink to complete satisfaction." Donald S. Metz, "1 Corinthians," in *The Beacon Bible Commentary* (Kansas City, Mo.: Beacon Hill Press, 1968), 7:418.

for the disciples as well. Then He broke the thin loaf of unleavened bread and, using metaphorical language, said, "'This is my body, which is for you.'"[21] Since Jesus was bodily present, He meant, "This represents my body." "'Do this'" is a continuous present tense: "Keep on doing this" (until Jesus comes again; cf. Luke 22:19). Doing it "'in remembrance'" of Christ also addresses the Corinthians' apparent failure to remember anything but their appetites when coming together supposedly for the Lord's Supper.

Those who have interpreted this to mean that the Lord's Supper involves a fresh sacrifice of Christ each time it is observed need to pay strict attention to Hebrews 9:26–28, which makes it clear that Christ was sacrificed "once for all," in contrast to the repeated sacrifices necessary under the Law. So we keep celebrating the Lord's Supper in remembrance of His "once for all" sacrifice on the cross, a sacrifice which was both for us and in our place as well.

> The term translated "remembrance" (Gk. *anamnesis*) may not mean quite what you think. Whereas today to remember something is to think back to some past occasion, the New Testament understanding of *anamnesis* is just the opposite. Such a remembrance was meant to "transport an action which is buried in the past in such a way that its original potency and vitality are not lost, but carried over into the present."[65] Such a concept is even reflected in the Old Testament (cf. Deut. 16:3; 1 Kings 17:18).
>
> ---
>
> [65]Ralph P. Martin, Worship in the Early Church (Grand Rapids: Wm. B. Eerdmans, 1964),126.[22]

Therefore, every time we celebrate The Lord's Supper, we should "remember" by claiming anew the benefits of His death and resurrection.

> **[25]In the same way, after supper he took the cup, saying, "This cup is the new covenant in my blood; do this, whenever you drink it, in remembrance of me."**
> **[26]For whenever you eat this bread and drink this cup, you proclaim the Lord's death until he comes.**

---

[21]The word "'broken'" (KJV) is not in the best ancient manuscripts. See John 19:31–36. His body was not broken; cf. Ps. 34:20.

[22]Michael L. Dusing, "The New Testament Church," in *Systematic Theology*, ed. Horton, 562.

The Passover meal came in between the distribution of the bread and the taking of the cup. "'This cup'" refers to the contents of the cup which represented the new, fresh covenant put into effect by the shedding of Jesus' blood (see Heb. 9:11–12,14–15,24–25), thus making the old covenant obsolete. Doing this would be a means of calling to remembrance the shedding of His blood, the new covenant, and all the blessings it includes. In other words, the Lord's Supper not only looks back at Calvary, it looks ahead to the consummation when at the wedding supper of the Lamb people from every nation, tribe, people, and language will participate (Matt. 8:11; 22:10; Rev. 7:9; 19:7–9).

Jesus did not say how often to do this. The Law called for the Passover celebration only once a year. However, some suppose that the Lord's Supper should be observed every time believers come together. Others suppose it should be observed once a week or once a month. Jesus made no requirements about the frequency, except that it should be "until He comes," that is, until the time when He comes to snatch away the Church in the Rapture. The only requirement is that we focus our attention on Him and "proclaim" His death: Our very act of partaking announces to the world that we have identified with Christ in His death, received the benefits of His shed blood, and are a new people in Him.

3. Partaking In An Unworthy Manner 11:27–34

27Therefore, whoever eats the bread or drinks the cup of the Lord in an unworthy manner will be guilty of sinning against the body and blood of the Lord. 28A man ought to examine himself before he eats of the bread and drinks of the cup. 29For anyone who eats and drinks without recognizing the body of the Lord eats and drinks judgment on himself. 30That is why many among you are weak and sick, and a number of you have fallen asleep.

The failure to wait for others and the failure to have genuine fellowship meant they were partaking of the Lord's Supper "in an unworthy manner." This meant they were "guilty of sinning against the body and blood of the Lord"; that is, they were just as bad as the Jewish leaders and the Romans who crucified Christ. They were not recognizing what the Cross meant, nor were they showing the love that God showed in giving His Son (John 3:16).

Paul does not say that any believer should refrain from partaking of the Lord's Supper. That would be telling the world that you do not believe in the power and effectiveness of Christ's sacrifice and His shed blood.[23] But believers must examine themselves to see whether they are recognizing the body of the Lord. By the "body of the Lord," Paul means the body of believers, the local assembly gathered together (see 1 Cor. 10:16–17).[24]

In view of what is said before and after this passage, it is clear Paul is concerned about the unity of the body of Christ, by which he means the unity of the body of believers with Christ as their head. Those who were allowing divisions among the body were not recognizing other believers as part of the body of Christ. Therefore they were "sinning against the body" and were eating and drinking judgment on themselves, that is, calling down judgment (Gk. *krima,* "condemnation, punishment") on themselves for their wrong attitudes and unloving behavior.

These attitudes and this lack of love were already bringing judgment on many of the Corinthian believers in the form of physical weakness, sickness, and even death. "It is not likely that any effort at gaining healing would have been fruitful until the cause was remedied."[25]

> **31But if we judged ourselves, we would not come under judgment. 32When we are judged by the Lord, we are being disciplined so that we will not be condemned with the world.**

If we examine and judge ourselves, including correcting our unloving attitudes and behavior, as well as our motives, we would not "come under judgment." If we do not do this, the Lord will judge; nevertheless, His purpose is not to destroy us or send us to hell, but to discipline us as

---

[23]I remember noticing a man who refused to partake of the Lord's Supper. He told me he was afraid he might have done something wrong and would bring judgment on himself. I asked him if he was holding a grudge against anyone in the assembly or if he knew of any sin he had not confessed. He said, "No." Then I asked him how long he thought it would take the Blood to cover him. He then partook, began to grow in the Lord, and one of his sons later became a deacon in that church.

[24]For a discussion of the Roman Catholic, Lutheran, Zwinglian, and Calvinistic views of the body of Christ see Dusing, "The New Testament Church," 563–65.

[25]Brandt and Bicket, *The Spirit Helps us Pray,* 278.

a loving father does his children (Heb. 12:7–11; cf. 1 Cor. 5:5; 1 Tim. 1:20). He wants us to repent, to live holy lives, to grow in grace and show His love.[26]

He wants us to respond as obedient children and not reject His discipline. As Hebrews 12:4–6 says, "In your struggle against sin, you have not yet resisted to the point of shedding your blood. And you have forgotten that word of encouragement that addresses you as sons: 'My son, do not make light of the Lord's discipline, and do not lose heart when he rebukes you, because the Lord disciplines those he loves, and he punishes everyone he accepts as a son.'" (Cf. 1 Pet. 4:12–19.) It would be a terrible thing to reject the Lord's discipline and be judged as a rebel and be condemned to the lake of fire along with the rest of the world.

> **33So then, my brothers, when you come together to eat, wait for each other. 34If anyone is hungry, he should eat at home, so that when you meet together it may not result in judgment. And when I come I will give further directions.**

Paul concludes this exhortation by referring to the love feast which included the celebration of the Lord's Supper. They must "wait for each other," until they can eat together in true Christian love and unity of the body. "Wait for" includes the idea of receiving and welcoming with open anticipation. Then, to avoid the temptation to gorge oneself and disregard others in a way that will bring God's judgment, Paul suggests that anyone who is hungry eat something first at home. This implies also that it is not wrong to eat a meal before partaking of the Lord's Supper; Paul does not call for fasting in preparation for it.

From this it is easy to see that Jesus commanded the partaking of the elements of the bread and the wine (rather, grape juice, since He speaks of "'the *fruit* of the vine,'" Matt. 26:29; Luke 22:18),[27] but He did not command the repetition of the Passover Feast, nor did He intend to institute a love feast. Thus, it is not necessary to partake of the elements of the Lord's Supper in connection with a meal. However, the same receiving and welcoming each other, the same waiting for each other to come into a unity of the Spirit in the love of Jesus so that we can focus on His death and the benefits of His shed blood, is still very important.

26See comments on 5:5.

27See Stamps, *Full Life Study Bible*, 1538, 1578.

Paul was aware of other questions and problems in Corinth; he promised to give further directions concerning them when he came. For the present he wanted to attend to something else that needed correction—the overuse of tongues and an imbalance in the gifts of the Spirit—so the church might be built up.

Study questions for this section may be found in appendix B.

VI. SPIRITUAL GIFTS 12:1–14:40

A. A Variety Of Gifts Given And Needed 12:1–31

1. Do Not Be Ignorant Of Spiritual Gifts 12:1–3

[1]Now about spiritual gifts,[1] brothers, I do not want you to be ignorant. [2]You know that when you were pagans, somehow or other you were influenced and led astray to mute idols. [3]Therefore I tell you that no one who is speaking by the Spirit of God says, "Jesus be cursed," and no one can say, "Jesus is Lord," except by the Holy Spirit.

"Now" indicates Paul is taking up another new topic, that of *pneumatikōn,* "spiritual things," by which he means spiritual gifts. Yet it is not entirely new. He is still concerned about the fruit of the Spirit, and he has already said that the Corinthian believers did not lack any spiritual gift, so he does not mean they are totally ignorant of them. But there are certain aspects of the gifts and their use the Corinthians need a better understanding of.

What he proceeds to say leads to the problem of the misuse of tongues. By listing tongues last, he does not mean it is unimportant—he means "it is the problem."[2]

---

[1]"Spiritual gifts" is one word in the Gk., *pneumatikōn,* a word "used for the totality of the gifts of the Spirit." See also 14:1. See Anthony Palma, "Spiritual Gifts—Basic Considerations," *Pneuma* 1, no. 2 (fall 1979): 6. The word emphasizes that they are supernatural and that the Holy Spirit is their immediate source.

[2]Gordon D. Fee, *The First Epistle to the Corinthians* (Grand Rapids: Wm. B. Eerdmans, 1991), 572.

He does not question the gifts themselves. They are from God, supernaturally distributed by the Holy Spirit. But they needed to be exercised with love. They also needed to be exercised in a way that would honor Jesus and recognize Him as Lord. The Holy Spirit always wants to honor Jesus. He is the living Word who came to make the Father known to us (John 1:18). Now that Jesus has ascended to the right hand of the Father's throne, the Holy Spirit makes Jesus known to us.

How different this is from the former state of the Gentile Corinthian believers, who had been "influenced and led astray to mute idols," small idols ("the little bronze statues in pagan homes"[3]) that could not speak and had no word for them. "Somehow or other" apparently sensible people are still led astray by pagan worship, even devil worship, and it is happening even in America.

Because the Spirit always honors Jesus, no one speaking by the Spirit will ever say, "Jesus be cursed!" A demon spirit might say that. False teachers with the spirit of Antichrist might say it, trying to make a difference between the man Jesus and the spiritual Christ (cf. 1 John 4:2–3). Even some who misunderstood Paul's teaching of Christ "becoming a curse for us" (Gal. 3:13) might say it.[4] Or, backslidden Christians might say it.[5] Whatever the case, we must understand that spirits other than the Holy Spirit can "inspire" someone's utterance (1 John 4:1).

On the other hand, only the Holy Spirit can enable anyone to say "Jesus is Lord," that is, divine Lord, the exalted King of kings and Lord of lords (Rom. 14:9; Phil. 2:9–11). Many may say the words only to hear Jesus say, "'I never knew you. Away from me, you evildoers!'" (Matt. 7:22–23). Calling Jesus "Lord" is meaningless unless the Holy Spirit makes Jesus Lord personally in our lives so that we are fully committed to Him as divine Lord and we truly love, follow, and obey Him. But we do not need to be afraid.

When we seek the Holy Spirit and His gifts, and yield to Him, He will always honor Jesus and help us keep Jesus central in our lives. Then we will "do His will instead of following our own plans and

---

[3]Arnold Bittlinger, *Gifts and Graces*, trans. Kerber Klassen (Grand Rapids: Wm. B. Eerdmans, 1976), 14.

[4]Norman Hillyer, "1 and 2 Corinthians," in *The New Bible Commentary* ed. D. Guthrie and J.A. Motyer, 3d ed. (Grand Rapids: Wm. B. Eerdmans, 1970) 1067.

[5]Bittlinger, *Gifts and Graces*, 16–17.

desires. . . . as the Holy Spirit begins to transform us into the image of God."[6]

2. THE WORK OF THE TRINITY 12:4–6

[4]There are different kinds of gifts, but the same Spirit. [5]There are different kinds of service, but the same Lord. [6]There are different kinds of working, but the same God works all of them in all men.

Next, Paul emphasizes that a variety of gifts are needed. But this variety must have the underlying unity of the Trinity, as the Father, Son, and Holy Spirit cooperate to bring a harmonious expression that edifies the assembly.

The Holy Spirit wants to honor Jesus, not only by calling Him Lord but by distributing "different kinds"[7] of spiritual gifts (Gk. *charismata,* freely given, gracious gifts; cf. *charis,* "grace"). The one Holy Spirit is the source of them all. Similarly, the variety of kinds of service, or ministry, (Gk. *diakoniōn*) has its source in the one Lord Jesus, and the different kinds of working, or activities, (Gk. *energēmatōn*) come from the one God who works effectively in all of them and in everyone (see Eph. 3:20; Col. 1:29).

The terms "gifts, service[s], working[s]" express similar aspects of the gifts and ministries needed for the edification and maturing of believers. Though each of these terms "is associated with a member of the Holy Trinity," all "are operations of the Holy Spirit (see verse 11)."[8] Thus, all are manifestations of the Holy Spirit (v. 11) and all are gifts of the Spirit (v. 4). As "services" the gifts serve the Lord Jesus and His Body, especially the local assembly gathered together. As "workings, or activities," they express the power of God. As R. L Brandt points out, "our concern is more with seeing God in the gifts than with seeing the gifts in *people.*"[9]

That God works in everyone, that is, in every believer, (cf. Phil. 2:13) shows God wants all, both Jew and Gentile, to be channels for

---

[6]Mark D. McLean, "The Holy Spirit" in *Systematic Theology,* ed. Stanley M. Horton, rev. ed. (Springfield, Mo.: Logion Press, 1995), 388.

[7]"Different kinds," Gk. *diaireseis*, does indicate a variety of gifts, but the word primarily means dividing and distributing (see 12:11).

[8]Palma, "Spiritual Gifts," 8.

[9]R. L. Brandt, *Gifts for the Marketplace* (Tulsa: Christian Publishing Services, Inc. 1989), 74.

charismatic gifts. Ultimately it is His purpose to become the "all in all" (Gk. *ta panta en pasin*) when the resurrection and Rapture bring the end of alienation and death for all believers (1 Cor. 15:25–28).

3. Distributed By The Spirit For The Common Good 12:7–11

[7]Now to each one the manifestation[10] of the Spirit is given for the common good.

Paul gives three lists of gifts in this chapter (12:8–10,28,29–30). Each gift he mentions seems to be something that can be manifest in a variety of ways as the Holy Spirit wills. Some suppose the first list is complete and comprehensive. "But Paul does not say 'These *are* the gifts of the Spirit.' He simply goes down the list saying, here is a gift given by the Spirit, then another by the same Spirit."[11] He is emphasizing that all the gifts come from the one Holy Spirit. He is an infinite Person and we can be sure He has an infinite supply to meet every need.[12]

The Holy Spirit gives manifestations (disclosures, means by which the Holy Spirit makes himself known openly)[13] to each believer, but not for the individual's own benefit or for some blessing one can claim for oneself. Nor does Paul mean each believer *has* some gift or is "gifted."[14] The point is that whatever gifts the Holy Spirit gives are given through individuals "for the common good," for the good of the local body as a whole. The gifts will help build up the local assembly, both spiritually and in numbers, just as the Holy Spirit's gifts did in the Book of Acts.

Dr. Palma classifies these gifts as "(1) utterance of wisdom and utterance of knowledge; (2) faith, gifts of healing and working of miracles; (3) prophecy, ability to distinguish between spirits, tongues, and interpretation of tongues."[15] Dr. Lim sees a "functional division" based on "Paul's use of the Greek word *heteros* ('another of a different kind')[:] twice in 1 Corinthians 12:5–8, we can see the gifts divided

---

[10]Gk. *phanerōsis,* the Spirit manifests himself in each gift. The manifestations the Spirit wants to give are the gift.

[11]Stanley M. Horton, *What the Bible Says About the Holy Spirit* (Springfield, Mo.: Gospel Publishing House, 1976), 209.

[12]Taking these lists along with those in Rom. 12:6–8 and Eph. 4:11 will give 18–20 gifts, some of which overlap; cf. 1 Cor. 14:3 and Rom. 12:8.

[13]Paul uses this word to focus attention on the Holy Spirit and His activity.

[14]Fee, *First Epistle to the Corinthians,* 589.

[15]Palma, "Spiritual Gifts," 15.

into three categories of two, five, and two gifts respectively."[16] He calls the first two "Teaching (and Preaching) Gifts"; the next five "Ministry Gifts (to the church and world)"; and the last two, "Worship Gifts."[17] However, it does not seem that Paul was emphasizing any sort of classification. Each gift can be a manifestation of the Holy Spirit in a variety of ways to meet a variety of needs; thus each may be taken as a class of gifts to be exercised one at a time as the Spirit directs.

Paul does not explain the nature and use of these gifts here. He is more concerned that the people see the availability of, and the need for, a variety of these extraordinary, supernatural manifestations. All the gifts let them know that the Spirit is working in their midst. He wants them to see also that in all the variety there is a single purpose, the good of the whole body of believers. "Paul is interested in practical results, which will set the body of Christ free for discipling, evangelism, unity, and Christlikeness."[18]

8aTo one there is given through the Spirit the message of wisdom,

The first gift Paul mentions is the "message [proclamation, declaration] of wisdom." "Through this gift supernatural insight into both the need and . . . God's Word bring the practical application of that Word to the need or problem at hand."[19] The Spirit does not make a person wise by this gift, nor does it mean the person cannot later make mistakes (cf. the example of King Solomon who, in his later life, not only made mistakes but sinned). It is just a message to meet the need. It may be guidance for the assembly (Acts 6:2–4; 15:13–21) or wisdom for how to resist adversaries (Luke 21:15; cf. Acts 4:8–14,19–21; 6:9–10). It clearly goes beyond common sense and the best of human wisdom "and human preparation."[20] Paul has already made this clear in 2:4–16. See also Proverbs 2:6, "For the Lord gives wisdom, and from his mouth come knowledge and understanding."

8bto another the message of knowledge by means of the same Spirit,

The "message [proclamation, declaration] of knowledge" is supernatural insight into what the Bible says about God, Christ, and God's

---

16David Lim, "Spiritual Gifts" in *Systematic Theology,* ed. Horton, 464.
17Ibid.
18Ibid., 469.
19Horton, *What the Bible Says About the Holy Spirit,* 271.
20Lim, "Spiritual Gifts," 465.

will. Paul said, "My purpose is that they [believers in Colosse and Laodicea who had not met Paul] may be encouraged in heart and united in love, so that they may have the full riches of complete understanding, in order that they may know the mystery of God, namely, Christ, in whom are hidden all the treasures of wisdom and knowledge" (Col. 2:2–3).

God is the one who accomplishes this. His purpose is to "give us the light of the knowledge of the glory of God in the face of Christ" (2 Cor. 4:6) so that we can spread everywhere the fragrance of the knowledge of Christ (2 Cor. 2:14). Through the Spirit we come to know Him better (Eph. 1:17). Paul asked God to fill the Colossians "with the knowledge of his will through all spiritual wisdom and understanding" (Col. 1:9; see also Rom. 10:2; 1 Cor. 2:12–13; 1 Tim. 2:4; Heb. 10:26; James 3:13; 1 Pet. 3:7; 2 Pet. 1:5,8). The Holy Spirit is the Spirit of Truth who will teach us all things (John 14:26), testify about Jesus (John 15:26), and guide us into all truth (John 16:13).

At the house of Cornelius, for example, Peter gave a message of knowledge that the baptism in the Spirit with the evidence of speaking in tongues was God's approval on the Gentiles (Acts 10:47–48; see also Acts 15:7–11). Clearly, the message of knowledge has to do with Bible truth or the application of it. It has nothing to do with where to find lost articles or what sin or disease a person may be suffering from—though God can give help for these things.

9a to another faith by the same Spirit,

"Another" (Gk. *heteros*), here, means "another of a different kind." Elsewhere in this passage, "another" (Gk. *allos*) means "another of the same kind," for example, another believer (another member of the local assembly gathered together). Paul may be using *heteros* here to mark a difference in the gifts before and after, rather than meaning a different kind of believer. Possibly the messages of wisdom and knowledge might be considered as communicating light and the five following gifts as communicating power—not to the intelligence but to the will.[21] Or he may simply be reminding the Corinthians that not everyone will be used in every gift. Or he may have set the message of wisdom and the message of knowledge apart because the Corinthians were too taken up with natural wisdom and knowledge and needed these gifts in a special way.

---

[21]Pièrre Bonnard, *Commentaire sur la Permière Épitre aux Corinthiens* vol. 2 (Neuchatel: éditions de l'imprimerie nouvelle, L.A. Monner, 1965), 206.

The gift of faith (1 Cor. 13:2) is not saving faith, but must be taken as a gift that will help or benefit the whole local body. It might be taken as a special gift of faith for a particular need. Some define it as "mountain moving faith," bringing unusual or extraordinary manifestations of God's power.[22] But just as the message of wisdom is a specific impartation of a word to meet the need for wisdom, the gift of faith may be a specific impartation of faith to meet the need of the body as a whole (cf. what Paul did in the midst of a storm [Acts 27:25]). I have seen the Holy Spirit use a song, a prayer, a testimony, or something dropped into the mind of the preacher to raise the level of faith in the local body (see 2 Cor. 3:6; Gal. 3:2,5).

[9b]to another gifts of healing by that one Spirit,

"Gifts" and "healings" are both plural in the Greek. This may indicate that there are various gifts to heal various kinds of sicknesses and diseases. Or it may mean the Holy Spirit wants to use a variety of people to minister these gifts. Or it may mean that the Spirit's gifts will heal not just one item of sickness or disease but everything that is wrong. He wants to heal the whole person.

It also lets us know that no one can say "I have the gift of healing," as if it could be owned and ministered at one's pleasure. Each healing takes a special gift that is given not to the person who ministers the gift, but through that person to the sick individual, so that God receives all the glory. He is the one who heals (Acts 4:30).

When Peter said to the crippled man at the Beautiful Gate, "'What I have I give you'" (Acts 3:6), "'what I have'" is singular and means the Spirit gave Peter a specific gift for the crippled man. Peter did not have a reservoir of gifts of healing. He had to receive from the Spirit a new, fresh gift for each person he ministered to. The same is true today. Though James 5:14–15 tells us to call the elders of the church, if that is not possible, the Holy Spirit can use any member of the body to minister gifts of healings to the sick.

[10a]to another miraculous powers,

"Miraculous powers" (Gk. *energēmata dunameōn,* "activities of miraculous powers," or "workings of miracles"—again two plurals) suggests many varieties of miracles or deeds of mighty, supernatural

[22]G. Raymond Carlson, *Spiritual Dynamics* (Springfield, Mo.: Gospel Publishing House, 1976), 103–4; Anthony D. Palma, *The Spirit—God in Action* (Springfield, Mo.: Gospel Publishing House, 1974), 83.

power. Energēmata most often is used of divine activity (Matt. 14:2; Mark 6:14; Gal. 3:5; Phil. 3:21) or of Satan's activity (Eph. 2:2; 2 Thess. 2:7,9). We need these mighty miracles to defeat Satan, for example, as in the judgment of blindness on Elymas (Acts 13:9–11).[23] "The Greek word for 'miracle' (Gk. *sēmeion*) in John emphasizes its sign value to encourage people to believe and keep on believing. The Book of Acts emphasizes the continuation of that work in the Church, showing that Jesus is Victor."[24]

[10b]to another prophecy,

The Hebrew word for prophet, *navi,* comes from an old word meaning a speaker. It became a technical term for a speaker for God, one who was inspired by the Spirit to give God's message to the people (2 Pet. 1:21).

The gift of prophecy is available to all believers, not just to prophets (see Acts 2:17–18). The Spirit uses it in a variety of ways to bring God's message to the body of believers. Peter's "sermon" on the Day of Pentecost was not a sermon in the ordinary sense of the word. Rather, it was a manifestation of the gift of prophecy. Peter stood up and "spoke out" (Gk. *apephthengxatoi* [Acts 2:14]) spontaneously by the inspiration of the Holy Spirit. (In Acts 2:4 a form of the same Greek word is used of speaking in tongues as the Spirit, literally, "gave them to speak out" [Gk. *apophthengesthai*].)

The gift of prophecy will be a word from the Lord that "touches sensitive spots, reveals what was secret, and brings conviction and worship, as well as encouragement and stimulation to action."[25] Acts 15:32 is a good example: "Judas and Silas, who themselves were prophets, said much to encourage and strengthen the brothers [and sisters]." See the comments on chapter 14 for more about this gift.

[10c]to another distinguishing between spirits,

"Distinguishing" (or "discernings") is plural in the Greek, again indicating this gift may be manifest in various ways. It may be involved in "weighing carefully" what prophets say (1 Cor. 14:29).[26] First John 4:1 says, "Dear friends, do not believe every spirit, but test the spirits to

---

[23]Anthony D. Palma, "The Working of Miracles," *Advance,* (October 1974), 36.

[24]Lim, "Spiritual Gifts," 466.

[25]Horton, *What the Bible Says About the Holy Spirit,* 276.

[26]Fee, *First Epistle to the Corinthians,* 597.

see whether they are from God, because many false prophets have gone out into the world." John does give one test: "Every Spirit that acknowledges that Jesus Christ has come in the flesh is from God, but every spirit that does not acknowledge Jesus is not from God" (4:2–3a). But sometimes the Bible speaks of the human spirit as well as the spirit of the devil and demon spirits. This gift will distinguish between them (see Acts 5:3; 8:20–23; 13:10; 16:16–18). "It allows us to use all the gifts and the Word of God to work against Satan in order to then make a full, free proclamation of the gospel."[27]

10d to another speaking in different kinds of tongues,

Again there is variety in this gift. It will be expressed in different kinds, or families, of languages. It is not gibberish or nonsense syllables, for it involves communication. By it we speak to God. By it we "utter mysteries" (14:2), that is, spiritual truths that have been revealed in the New Testament.[28] More will be said about this gift in the comments on chapter 14.

10e and to still another the interpretation of tongues.

"Interpretation" can mean translation, paraphrase, or even commentary. See Nehemiah 8:8 where Ezra read in Hebrew and the Levites gave the meaning in Aramaic, "so that the people could understand what was being read." In that case, the Levites understood and spoke both languages. However, the gift of interpretation is a supernatural gift given through a person who does not understand the language spoken by the speaker in tongues. It "comes as one gives attention to the Lord, rather than to the tongues that are being given. . . . A step of faith may be required also in that the Spirit very often gives only a few words of the interpretation at first. Then, when these are given in faith, the rest comes as the Spirit gives utterance."[29]

11 All these are the work of one and the same Spirit, and he gives them to each one, just as he determines.

Paul does not say these nine gifts are the only ones, nor does he give them in any order of importance. They are just examples of the statement in verse 4. They are all manifestations of the one Holy Spirit. Paul's concern is that every believer have a part in the ministry of the

---

[27]Lim, "Spiritual Gifts," 467.

[28]See comments on 2:7.

[29]Horton, *What the Bible Says About the Holy Spirit*, 279.

Spirit, as the chapter goes on to show. They are not given as a deposit in the body of believers. They are given to individuals. Yet they are not for the individual's benefit but for the body's benefit, to build it up spiritually and in numbers. They are sovereignly given by the Holy Spirit as He wills[30] (pleases, or determines), not as any believer wills or desires; He alone knows what is truly needed and He uses whomever He wishes (cf. John 3:8).

The question might be asked, Does the Holy Spirit give gifts to believers who are not yet baptized in the Spirit with the evidence of speaking in other tongues? The answer is that it is as He wills or determines. Old Testament prophets prophesied and performed miracles. The disciples ministered healing before the Day of Pentecost (Matt. 10:8). "Yet it can safely be said that the baptism in the Spirit results in a higher incidence of spiritual manifestations among those so baptized."[31]

4. One Body With Many Parts 12:12–20

12The body is a unit, though it is made up of many parts; and though all its parts are many, they form one body. So it is with Christ. 13For we were all baptized by one Spirit into one body—whether Jews or Greeks, slave or free—and we were all given the one Spirit to drink.

By comparing the local assembly to the human body Paul stresses that unity does not mean uniformity but interrelatedness and interdependence.[32] "The unity that the Spirit brings is the unity of a living organism. It retains its variety. It is able to adjust to new situations and meet new opportunities and challenges."[33] The statement "So it is with Christ" then draws attention to the fact that our union is with Christ, so that we belong to Him—and only then to His Church.

The unity of the Body is emphasized further by the fact that there is only one Spirit and only one Body. All believers (cf. Eph. 4:16), whatever their background, race, or social status, have a part in it

---

[30]The Greek word is present tense, implying the Holy Spirit's personality and continuing work.

[31]Palma, "Spiritual Gifts," 11.

[32]Galen Hertweck, "The Church as Community: Small Groups in the Local Church," in *Faces of Renewal*, ed. Paul Elbert (Peabody, Mass.: Hendrickson Publishers, 1988), 251.

[33]Horton, *What the Bible Says About the Holy Spirit*, 213.

because the Spirit baptizes every one of them into that one Body. Some would translate verse 13, "For *in* one Spirit also we were baptized so as to form one body," saying the Greek *en* must mean "in." However, *en* often means "by" (see Luke 2:27, "moved by the Spirit"; Luke 4:1, "led by the Spirit"; Rom. 2:29, "circumcision…by the Spirit"; 1 Cor. 12:3 and 14:2, "speaking by the Spirit"; Eph. 3:5, "revealed by the Spirit"). Thus, "by one Spirit" is the correct translation here and is in fact found in most English versions, including the King James Version, the New International Version, the New American Standard Version, Today's English Version, and the versions by Moffatt, Phillips, Williams, and Beck. "Clearly, it is not just Pentecostal hermeneutical bias that makes a distinction between the baptism by the Spirit, which incorporates believers into the body of Christ, and the baptism in the Holy Spirit, in which Christ is the Baptizer"[34]

The preceding passage of the biblical text draws attention to the unity of the Body, with gifts given by the one Holy Spirit. Consequently the baptism in 12:13 is by the Spirit into the Body "and is therefore distinct from the baptism by Christ into the Holy Spirit on the Day of Pentecost."[35]

However, that is not all. Those baptized into the one Body are then "given the one Spirit to drink," or "made to drink with the same Spirit" (author's translation). This is a new fact[36] and can mean we are watered, imbued, or saturated with the one Spirit, and can thus refer to an experience of the outpouring of the Spirit like that on the Day of Pentecost (cf. Isa. 29:10, where the Septuagint translates the Hebrew *nasakh,* "pour out," with *pepotiken,* "made to drink"; see also Isa. 32:15; 44:3). This implies not only the initial baptism in the Spirit but a continuing experience with the Spirit, "which nourishes the eschatological community."[37] As Ephesians 5:18 commands us, we need to "ever be filled with the Spirit" (Williams translation).

14Now the body is not made up of one part but of
many. 15If the foot should say, "Because I am not a
hand, I do not belong to the body," it would not for

[34]Stanley M. Horton, "The Pentecostal Perspective," in Melvin E. Dieter et al., *Five Views on Sanctification* (Grand Rapids: Zondervan Publishing House, 1987), 129–30.

[35]Ibid., 216.

[36]Bonnard, *Commentaire,* 219.

[37]Jean-Jacques Suurmond, "The Meaning and Purpose of Spirit-Baptism and the Charisms," *EPTA Bulletin* 9, no. 4 (1990): 116–17.

**that reason cease to be part of the body. 16And if the
ear should say, "Because I am not an eye, I do not
belong to the body," it would not for that reason cease
to be part of the body. 17If the whole body were an
eye, where would the sense of hearing be? If the
whole body were an ear, where would the sense of
smell be? 18But in fact God has arranged the parts in
the body, every one of them, just as he wanted them
to be. 19If they were all one part, where would the
body be? 20As it is, there are many parts, but one
body.**

After drawing attention to the one Holy Spirit and the unity of the Body, Paul draws attention again to the variety needed and to the importance of every member. This diversity is the real emphasis of the passage, for it was what the believers in Corinth needed.[38]

The foot cannot say it is not a part of the body because it is not the hand, nor can the ear say it is not a part of the body because it is not an eye. "If every part of the body had the same function, if it were all a big eye or a big ear, it would not be a body and would not be able to function. Thus a church where everyone had the same gift or ministry would be a monstrosity, not a functioning body of Christ."[39] God has arranged for variety in the local assembly so that it will function in ways to please and glorify Him. We need to appreciate and value differences in ministries and gifts.

5. Every Part Needed 12:21–26

**21The eye cannot say to the hand, "I don't need you!"
And the head cannot say to the feet, "I don't need
you!" 22On the contrary, those parts of the body that
seem to be weaker are indispensable, 23and the parts
that we think are less honorable we treat with special
honor. And the parts that are unpresentable are treated with special modesty, 24while our presentable parts
need no special treatment. But God has combined the
members of the body and has given greater honor to
the parts that lacked it, 25so that there should be no
division in the body, but that its parts should have
equal concern for each other. 26If one part suffers,**

[38]Fee, *First Epistle to the Corinthians,* 601.

[39]Horton, *What the Bible Says About the Holy Spirit,* 217.

every part suffers with it; if one part is honored, every part rejoices with it.

Still comparing the local assembly with the human body, Paul next illustrates the interdependence of the parts. Each part needs every other part. The eye needs the hand, and the head needs the feet. God has formed the human body in such a way that all the members work in perfect harmony. Every part is necessary, including those that "seem to be weaker," that is, less prominent or less important. When any part of the body hurts, we all hurt. When any part of the body is honored, we all rejoice. The world often does the reverse, for "human nature prefers to be judgmental."[40] The local assembly needs to apply this to itself and its members, especially when some are undergoing and enduring suffering (cf. Gal. 6:2). "The body needs all its functions working, each for the good of the whole, each recognizing the value and importance of the others."[41] It is arrogance not to do so.

6. A Variety Appointed In The Church 12:27–31

27Now you are the body of Christ, and each one of you
is a part of it. 28And in the church God has appointed
first of all apostles, second prophets, third teachers, then workers of miracles, also those having gifts of healing, those able to help others, those with gifts of administration, and those speaking in different kinds of tongues.

Paul does apply this to the Church, mentioning the body of Christ to indicate that the gifts are given within the body and have the primary purpose of building up the body. He draws attention to "unity first, then diversity of individual members."[42] Each one has an important part in the body of Christ.

To make his application clear, Paul mentions that God has specifically appointed in the Church[43] first apostles (sent by Jesus personally while He was on earth, with the exception of Paul who was

---

40Lim, "Spiritual Gifts," 472.

41John Ruthven, "On The Cessation of the Charismata," *Pneuma* 12, no. 1 (spring 1990): 29.

42Palma, "Spiritual Gifts," 10.

43Not just the local church, but the Church as a whole, so those with these ministries moved from place to place. New churches needed these itinerate ministries. See also next paragraph.

appointed later), second prophets (Spirit-directed speakers for God), third teachers, then workers of miracles, those having gifts of healing, those able to help others, those with gifts of administration, and those speaking in different kinds of tongues. Fee points out that the first three are ministries "that find expression in various persons." The rest are "gracious endowments of the Spirit, given to various persons in the church for its mutual upbuilding."[44]

The enumeration here may be chronological with respect to the history of the Early Church.[45] Apostles were the primary witnesses to the life, death, resurrection, and teachings of Jesus. They included not only the Twelve but Paul, Barnabas, James, Andronicus and Junias,[46] and the seventy-two others Jesus sent out (Luke 10:1–20). Prophets and teachers were also given by the resurrected and ascended Jesus to establish and mature the believers: so that every one of them could do works of service, or ministry, and build up the body of Christ "until we all reach unity in the faith and in the knowledge of the Son of God and become mature, attaining to the whole measure of the fullness of Christ. Then we will no longer be infants. . . . Instead, speaking the truth in love, we will in all things grow up into him who is the Head, that is, Christ. From him the whole body, joined and held together by every supporting ligament, grows and builds itself up in love, as each part does its work" (Eph. 4:13–16).

The rest of the gifts are also necessary for this, not only the obviously supernatural gifts of miracles, healings, and speaking in tongues, but also the gifts of "helps" (KJV; i.e., doing helpful deeds) and administrations (governments).

The plural of *antilēmpseis,* "helps," indicates that all sorts of helpful deeds may be inspired by the Holy Spirit in this gift. The corresponding verb is used of helping the weak (Acts 20:35) and of masters being helped by good service (1 Tim. 6:2). The word was also used as a technical term for a chief accountant and would fit the work of the seven chosen in Acts 6:2–3, where "'tables'" means "money tables," and refers to the same cash fund that Paul later brought offerings to. These seven were "'full of the Spirit and wisdom'" (Acts 6:3) and surely ministered through the gifts of the Spirit.

---

[44]Fee, *First Epistle to the Corinthians,* 619.

[45]Lim, "Spiritual Gifts," 470.

[46]Junias (Rom. 16:7) is a feminine name. Those sent out in pairs may have included brother and sister or husband and wife.

Kubernēseis ("administrations," "governments," "guidance") is also plural and provides for a variety of expressions of the gift for those who are in a position of leadership. Acts 27:11 uses *kubernētē,* a closely related noun, to mean a steersman or pilot of a ship. Thus, it implies guidance and counseling, or even the managing of business affairs as well as giving spiritual leadership and guidance to the local assembly.

> **29Are all apostles? Are all prophets? Are all teachers? Do all work miracles? 30Do all have gifts of healing? Do all speak in tongues? Do all interpret? 31aBut eagerly desire the greater gifts.**

Paul next asks a series of questions which call for the answer no. He is dealing with ministries and gifts exercised or manifest when the assembly of believers comes together. He implies that no one will be used in the public meeting by the Spirit in all the gifts. This verse is not dealing with gifts such as tongues exercised in private prayer, nor tongues as the initial outward evidence of the baptism in the Holy Spirit. "Do all speak in tongues" is in the continuous present tense in the Greek and may mean, "Do all continue to speak in tongues?" implying that not everyone will have a continuing ministry in the local assembly of speaking in tongues.

He goes on to tell them to "eagerly desire the greater gifts." This may mean "keep desiring eagerly," that is, with a zeal that never lets up. They were exercising the gifts but needed to give more attention to those that are greater.

Fee lists four possible interpretations of the "greater gifts." (1) "Desire" is imperative, and means to seek the greater gifts rather than speaking in tongues (2). On the basis of 14:12 Paul is quoting the Corinthians who were eager to seek the greater gifts. (3) "But" (Gk. *de*) is adversative and "eagerly desire" (Gk. *zēloute*) is indicative, rather than imperative. Paul wants them to seek after love rather than gifts. However, *zēloute* continues the thought in 14:1 and is clearly imperative. (4). *Zēloute* is imperative, but does not refer back to the gifts in chapter 12: "Rather, he is looking ahead to his next point, the need for intelligibility in the community . . . but before he can get that point made, he interrupts himself to give the proper framework in which the 'greater gifts' are to function, namely, love."[47] The greater gifts would

---

[47]Gordon D. Fee, "Tongues—Least of the Gifts?" *Pneuma* 2, no. 2 (fall 1980): 13.

thus be all the intelligible gifts as greater than the gift of tongues.[48]

31bAnd now I will show you the most excellent way.

Paul has been taking the Corinthians who did not "lack any spiritual gift" (1:7) and showing them the need to appreciate both the variety of the gifts and the unity of the body. Now He wants to point out "the most excellent way" to exercise the gifts, the way of love.[49] He does not suggest that the gifts are inferior to the fruit of the Spirit (which are all included in love). Nor does he mean that spiritual gifts and manifestations are not needed if they have love. Though God's love and the love of Christ are the source of our salvation and all God has for us, love is not called a spiritual gift (one of the *charismata*).[50] All that has been said in chapter 12 shows that the gifts are necessary for Christian life and ministry. But in Corinth they needed correction. The gifts were genuine, but the motives of the believers were not all they should be.[51] Let us not forget that God has modeled this love for us "in His person and work."[52]

B. Gifts Must Be Exercised With Love 13:1–13

1. The Necessity Of Love 13:1–3

The contrast in this chapter is between spiritual gifts without love and spiritual gifts with love. Paul has already shown that love is seen in action, especially in God's gift of Jesus and His death on the cross. But Paul does not degrade the gifts, nor does he say love is better than the gifts. "The whole point is simply that without love the highest gifts

---

[48]Another possibility is that "greater gifts" is being used ironically, as Eugene H. Peterson paraphrases v. 31 in *The Message* (Colorado Springs: NavPress Publishing Group, 1993): "And yet some of you keep competing for so-called 'important' parts"—when in reality all the gifts are of equal value. Only in the Corinthian mind was there a ranking of the gifts.

[49]"Most excellent" (Gk. *kath' huperbolēn*, "according to excellence") is not a comparative. Paul is not comparing love and the gifts.

[50]Love is a fruit, not a gift. The NT never calls love a *charisma*. Nor is it an alternative to the gifts. Bittlinger, *Gifts and Graces*, 74–75.

[51]Bonnard, *Commentaire*, 219.

[52]Russell E. Joyner, "The One True God," in *Systematic Theology*, ed. Horton, 128.

lose their proper effectiveness, value, and reward."[53] Paul brings this out with seven examples of spiritual ministry valued by the Corinthians.

> **1If I speak in the tongues of men and of angels, but**
> **have not love, I am only a resounding gong or a**
> **clanging cymbal. 2If I have the gift of prophecy and**
> **can fathom all mysteries and all knowledge, and if I**
> **have a faith that can move mountains, but have not**
> **love, I am nothing. 3If I give all I possess to the poor**
> **and surrender my body to the flames, but have not**
> **love, I gain nothing.**

Tongues were highly valued, so much so that some may have thought they were speaking in "tongues of . . . angels"[54] (or this may be a figure of speech Paul uses to indicate the Corinthians' high regard for tongues). But whether human or angelic, without love such languages had no more effect than "a resounding gong or a clanging cymbal." They get attention but that is all. So tongues without love may get attention, but do not contribute to genuine worship.

In Corinth, tongues were not bringing edification even to the individuals who spoke them, because the Corinthians' lack of love let them "tolerate, or endorse, illicit sexuality, greed, and idolatry (5:9–10; illustrated in 5:1–5; 6:1–11; 6:12–20; 8:1–10:22)."[55]

Prophecy is a genuine gift. Understanding with supernatural insight all the mysteries that were not revealed in Old Testament times but are revealed in what is now the New Testament, receiving all kinds of supernatural knowledge, and having a gift of faith that can move mountain after mountain—all are genuine gifts of the Spirit. Yet, without love, without acting in love, the person who ministers such gifts is nothing, of no value to the Lord or the local assembly of believers, even if people acclaim the gifts. In Corinth their knowledge only made them proud (8:1–2), and it sometimes brought destruction to a weak brother "for whom Christ died" (8:11).

Others may think they are deserving reward because of giving everything to the poor or surrendering their bodies to the flames

---

[53]Stanley M. Horton, *What the Bible Says About the Holy Spirit* (Springfield, Mo.: Gospel Publishing House, 1976), 220.

[54]Some Jews did believe angels had their own heavenly languages. See Gordon D. Fee, *The First Epistle to the Corinthians* (Grand Rapids: Wm. B. Eerdmans, 1987), 630.

[55]Fee, *First Epistle to the Corinthians*, 627.

(probably as martyrs),[56] for the Bible says, "Jesus Christ laid down his life for us. And we ought to lay down our lives for our brothers. If anyone has material possessions and sees his brother in need but has no pity on him, how can the love of God be in him?" (1 John 3:16–17).[57] But if we do these things without love, we will gain nothing even though many may be blessed, helped, and challenged; that is, we will have no reward, for our works will be treated as wood, hay, or straw to be burned (1 Cor. 3:12).[58]

2. The Nature Of Love 13:4–7

4Love is patient, love is kind. It does not envy, it does not boast, it is not proud. 5It is not rude, it is not self-seeking, it is not easily angered, it keeps no record of wrongs. 6Love does not delight in evil but rejoices with the truth. 7It always protects, always trusts, always hopes, always perseveres.

Since the word "love" is used in so many different contexts, Paul identifies twelve characteristics that describe the kind of love needed in the seeking and manifesting of spiritual gifts.[59]

Love is patient and people who provoke or injure us. It does not allow resentment to arise, even when wrongs go unrighted. It goes the second mile, turns the other cheek, endures insult, bears with those who disagree or mock or gibe (Matt. 5:39,41). It reflects the patience of God with sinners: It cannot be short-tempered with those for whom Christ died.

---

[56]Some early manuscripts have "give my body that I may boast," which draws attention to themselves (and to their wrong attitude). Fee prefers this reading because the burnings of Nero had not yet taken place. He also suggests that the boasting may be legitimate, like that of Rom. 5:2–3; 2 Cor. 1:14. See Fee, *First Epistle to the Corinthians,* 634–35.

[57]See also Matt. 25:31–46; Luke 10:25–37; Heb. 13:16. Love will not let social service be a neglected area.

[58]See Stanley M. Horton, *Our Destiny: Biblical Teachings on the Last Things* (Springfield, Mo.: Logion Press, 1996), 94.

[59]In King James's time "charity" was a synonym for love, so the KJV translates the Gk. word used here (*agapē*) as "love" eighty-two times and as "charity" twenty-six times. Part of this was due to the fact that different groups translated different sections of the Bible and did not compare with each other. The Gk. *agapê* is used often of love of God and His love, but is often used interchangeably with *phileō,* friendly love, love of things, etc.; vv. 4–8 give the definition of what Paul means here.

Love does not stop with a mere patience that puts up with those who heap abuse. It is actively kind, returns good for evil (cf. Luke 6:27; Rom. 12:21), seeks out what it can do for others, puts itself in the service of others, encourages others to speak and minister (cf. 14:30–31).

Love is not envious, never jealous, never expresses ill will, malice, or peevishness. Its heart is too big to engage in littleness or jealous rivalry or competition. It sees the good in others and desires to promote the good of the body of believers. It honors the Holy Spirit for the gifts He gives to others as He determines (12:11).

Love is not boastful, never a braggart, but is truly humble. It never shows off, never parades its own virtues, never shows pride in being used in gifts, never calls attention to itself. After love does its work of kindness it steals back into the shadows so that Christ may receive all the glory.

Love is not proud, puffed up, or self-important, nor is it anxious for honor. Nor is it like some people who make a show of being humble but inwardly feel how important they are. It does not "lord it over" those less fortunate, nor does it treat others as inferiors. It is never self-satisfied, arrogant, or overbearing. It never demands its rights nor feels recognition for faithful service is its due (see Matt. 20:26–28; Luke 17:7–10). It is also willing to receive correction (cf. 14:29–30).

Love is never rude or unbecoming, never behaves disgracefully or shamefully. Jesus was a perfect gentleman. His love is always considerate, polite, and gentle; never coarse or vulgar. Love never needlessly embarrasses, injures, or humiliates another but is always courteous. Positively, it seeks the well-being of the whole body of Christ.

Love is not self-seeking, never selfish, grasping, or greedy. God so loved that He gave (John 3:16). The same divine love will make us more concerned about giving than getting. It seeks the good of others. It does not demand its own way but accepts God-given leadership (cf. 14:37).

Love is not "easily angered." The word "easily" is not in the Greek ("is not provoked" –NASB). Love is not angered or irritated no matter what the circumstances. Any irritability that arises comes from a different source. But love keeps the victory even when everything seems to go wrong.

Love keeps no record of wrongs. It is not mindful of evil done to it, but instead takes no notice of it. It is forgiving and never holds a grudge. It never reminds others of hurtful words or injuries said or done in the past. There is no limit to its forgiveness. Love takes the one who has wronged it into its heart, forgetting the past.

Love does not delight in evil, nor in the downfall or misfortunes of others. Love never says "I told you so" or "It serves your right." Nor does it dig up the sins of the past or desire to expose or gossip about the faults of others. Love wants to see sins forgiven and rejoices when the truth of the gospel is advanced.

Love always protects, trusts, hopes, and perseveres. It never gives up, it bears up. It is obedient, faithful, trustful, and buoyant. It keeps pressing on with faith and confident hope. It sees where help is needed and gets under the load without being asked or begged. It provides sincere encouragement for others.

If these things seem difficult to attain, let us remember that we can look to God to pour His love into our hearts by the Holy Spirit (Rom. 5:5). We may need to repent for our lack of love. Then His love will bring us to the goal.

3. The Priority Of Love 13:8–13

**[8]Love never fails. But where there are prophecies, they
will cease; where there are tongues, they will be
stilled; where there is knowledge, it will pass away.
[9]For we know in part and we prophesy in part, [10]but
when perfection comes, the imperfect disappears.**

Love like this will never fail (Gk. *piptai,* "fall"), come to an end, or become invalid. Prophecies "will cease" (Gk. *katargēthēsontai,* "be done away with," a different word from love "failing"). Tongues "will be stilled," or stop (Gk. *pausontai,* a still different word). The spiritual gift of the word of knowledge will also cease.

When? Not today when all the gifts are so needed to edify the believers, but when "perfection," or completeness, comes. "When perfection comes" refers to the perfection that Jesus will bring when He comes again and we receive our new bodies that are immortal and incorruptible (15:53–54) and enter into millennial blessings. Until then we are subject to our present limitations (Rom. 8:18–25). Now "we eagerly await a Savior from there [from heaven], the Lord Jesus Christ, who by the power that enables him to bring everything under his control, will transform our lowly bodies so that they will be like his glorious body" (Phil. 3:20–21). We do strive to please God, "For the grace of God that brings salvation has appeared to all men. It teaches us to say 'No' to ungodliness and worldly passions, and to live self-controlled, upright and godly lives in this present age, while we wait for the blessed hope—the glorious appearing of our great God and Savior, Jesus Christ, who gave himself for us to redeem us from all wickedness and to purify for himself a people that are his very own, eager to do what is good" (Titus 2:11–14). Thus, we are all still looking ahead to the time when perfection, or completion, will come.

No other position is exegetically possible.[60] "Only in the eschaton will there be a perfect mutual indwelling with ultimate reality, God, who will be 'all in all' (I Cor. 15:26) and we 'shall know fully, even as (we are) fully known' so that the charisms will no longer be necessary (I Cor. 13:8–12)."[61] Until then they are useful.[62]

During the entire Church Age our understanding and knowledge have been and still are partial. This did not change when the New Testament was completed, nor at the end of the first century. Many older commentaries agree, including those by Alford, Barnes, Ellicott, and Lange. F. F. Bruce, a recent British scholar, concurs: "It is true that, according to I Cor. 13:8–10, prophecies, tongues, and knowledge are to be done away, but only 'when that which is perfect is come.' That which is perfect is not come yet . . . the literature of the period following the apostolic age makes it plain that the gifts did not come to a full stop with the closing of the New Testament canon." [63]

11When I was a child, I talked like a child, I thought like a child, I reasoned like a child. When I became a man, I put childish ways behind me. 12Now we see but a poor reflection as in a mirror; then we shall see face to face. Now I know in part; then I shall know fully, even as I am fully known.

Paul illustrates his meaning further by contrasting a child's ways with a man's ways, that is, full maturity. In the present Church Age we

---

[60]For a good discussion of the availability of the baptism in the Holy Spirit today see John W. Wycoff, "The Baptism in the Holy Spirit," in *Systematic Theology,* ed. Stanley M. Horton, rev. ed. (Springfield, Mo.: Logion Press, 1995), 444–47.

[61]Jean-Jacques Suurmond, "The Meaning and Purpose of Spirit Baptism and the Charisms," *EPTA Bulletin* 9, no. 4 (1990): 114.

[62]Archibald Robertson and Alfred Plummer, *A Critical and Exegetical Commentary on the First Epistle of St. Paul to the Corinthians,* 2d ed. In The International Critical Commentary Series (Edinburgh: T. & T. Clark, 1914), 297.

[63]F.F. Bruce, "Answers to Questions," *The Harvester,* August 1964.

need spiritual gifts of speech and knowledge for edification and spiritual growth. After the Rapture, in our changed bodies, we shall have greater powers and knowledge and will not need these gifts any longer.

As a further illustration, Paul compares our present understanding and knowledge to the indirect image in a mirror (mirrors in those days were of polished bronze).[64] But when Jesus comes, the perfect state will be unveiled: We shall see no longer indirectly, but face to face. Now there are many things that perplex us. We are able to claim only part of what God has for us. But the day is coming when "we shall see him as he is" (1 John 3:2). Then we shall no longer need what is now "in part." We do know God now, but spiritual gifts reveal only bits and pieces. When Jesus comes, and as Jon Ruthven points out, in heaven we shall "know God (*kathōs*) exactly as, and to the same degree" that, God knows us now.[65]

> **13And now these three remain: faith, hope and love.**
> **But the greatest of these is love.**

In contrast to temporary blessings of charismatic gifts given for this age, three things we have now are permanent: faith, hope, and love. Even when faith becomes sight, faith in the sense of trustful obedience will always be the right attitude toward God. Even when the promised hope is realized, hope in the sense of expectation of future good will remain, for God is the God of hope (Rom. 15:13). But love, though mentioned last, is the greatest. We shall never forget John 3:16 and the glory of the Cross. Love was and is God's primary motive and must become ours, for God is love (1 John 4:8).[66]

C. The Gifts Of Prophecy And Tongues 14:1–40

The whole of chapter 12 leads to the recommendation to "eagerly desire the greater gifts" (12:31). In chapter 13 these gifts are placed under the direction of a high, holy outflowing love. Now, with this love in mind, chapter 14 begins to give practical directions for the exercise, or operation, of these spiritual gifts. Again and again in this chapter

---

[64]Fee, *First Epistle to the Corinthians,* 648.

[65]Jon Ruthven, "On the Cessation of the Charismata: The Protestant Polemic of Benjamin B. Warfield" *Pneuma* 12, no. 1 (spring 1990): 23.

[66]The final judgment will separate the wicked from the light of God. "The faith, hope, love that remain for us...will be forever lacking in that environment." Horton, *Our Destiny,* 231.

we see how love is the guiding principle of these practical directions.

Though chapter 12 shows that all the manifestations of the Spirit are necessary and beneficial, the Corinthian believers needed special direction and guidance concerning the operation of two: tongues and prophecy. Chapter 14 gives most of its attention to them, though many of the basic principles could be applied to other gifts as well.

1. Prophecy Edifies The Church 14:1–5

1Follow the way of love and eagerly desire spiritual gifts, especially the gift of prophecy.

Here Paul echoes 12:31 about spiritual gifts. All believers are to pursue the way of love, strive to act in love. But this does not mean we can then afford to despise or neglect spiritual gifts. Both love and the gifts are from the same Spirit. So all believers, not just apostles[67] or leaders, must have a deep concern for the gifts (Gk., *pneumatika,* "spiritual things"): a zeal for them that makes us strive for them, desiring eagerly and earnestly that each member function freely in this body ministry. But it is most important to seek and strive for the gift of prophecy.[68]

This word of instruction was apparently much needed in Corinth. Since speaking in tongues is the initial outward evidence of the baptism in the Holy Spirit, it is easy then to respond in faith to the Spirit as He gives the gift of tongues. It also becomes easy to pray in tongues. Thus, there is the pitfall that we may give so much time to tongues that we fail to be open to the other gifts the Holy Spirit has for us.

**2For anyone who speaks in a tongue does not speak
to men but to God. Indeed, no one understands him;
he utters mysteries with his spirit. 3But everyone who
prophesies speaks to men for their strengthening,
encouragement and comfort. 4He who speaks in a
tongue edifies himself, but he who prophesies edifies
the church. 5I would like every one of you to speak in
tongues, but I would rather have you prophesy. He
who prophesies is greater than one who speaks in**

67Some suppose the gifts were primarily given for accreditation, and thus not needed after the apostles passed off the scene, but the Book of Acts shows many ordinary believers being used in the gifts.

68Prophecy is not preaching, as some have supposed. It is spontaneous speaking given by the Spirit.

tongues, unless he interprets, so that the church may be edified.

The problem Paul needed to deal with was the overuse of tongues without interpretation. He knew that what the Spirit wants to do is use the manifestation of the gifts to build up the local assembly both spiritually and in numbers. So he contrasts uninterpreted tongues with prophecy.

When tongues are not interpreted, only God understands. In that sense, then, the tongues speaker "does not speak to men but to God." (Consequently, no one in the congregation understands what is said or learns anything from it.) Though the human spirit is responding to God's Spirit and the tongues speaker is edified, all that is said remains as "mysteries" (secret truths, truths of the gospel; cf. 2:7–10; Rom. 16:25).

On the other hand, prophecy is in the language the people understand and brings a spontaneous, Spirit-given message that strengthens them (builds them up spiritually, develops and confirms their faith), encourages them (awakening them and helping them to move forward in faithfulness and love),[69] and comforts them (cheers, revives, and stirs hope and expectation).[70]

Paul doesn't say that tongues are less supernatural than prophecy or inferior to prophecy. But on the principle of love, prophecy is to be preferred because it edifies the local assembly, while tongues edifies only the individual. Now, it is not wrong for the individual to be edified. We all need that. Paul still wants all believers to keep on speaking in tongues (which, as has been noted, the Gk. tense indicates). However, they do not need to take up the time of the rest of the assembly while they are edifying themselves. This clearly indicates that tongues are important in our individual worship and prayer. Many charismatics today refer to tongues as a "prayer language."

As we have seen in chapter 12, the Holy Spirit's concern is to use the individual to bless and build the whole body. It is His purpose that everyone shall "in all things grow up into him who is the Head, that is, Christ. From him the whole body, joined and held together by [the spiritual activity of] every supporting ligament, grows and builds itself up in love, as each part does its work" (Eph. 4:15–16). Love will lead

---

[69]Encouragement is treated as a separate gift from prophecy in Rom. 12:6–8.

[70]Stanley M. Horton, *What the Bible Says About the Holy Spirit* (Springfield, Mo.: Gospel Publishing House, 1976), 277.

us therefore to strive for prophecy above other spiritual gifts because it does more to build up the assembly both spiritually and numerically. In this way the person who prophesies is "greater than the one who speaks in tongues."

However, tongues with interpretation will also edify the assembly. It is uninterpreted, tongues that do not "speak to men" (v. 2). But when interpreted, the one who speaks in tongues is doing something just as praiseworthy as the one who prophesies. This may well mean that tongues with interpretation can fulfill the same function as prophecy.[71] At least, tongues with interpretation benefits the congregation as much as prophecy does.

2. Tongues Need Interpretation 14:6–19

6Now, brothers, if I come to you and speak in tongues, what good will I be to you, unless I bring you some revelation or knowledge or prophecy or word of instruction? 7Even in the case of lifeless things that make sounds, such as the flute or harp, how will anyone know what tune is being played unless there is a distinction in the notes? 8Again, if the trumpet does not sound a clear call, who will get ready for battle? 9So it is with you. Unless you speak intelligible words with your tongue, how will anyone know what you are saying? You will just be speaking into the air.

Verse 6 gives a strong argument for the need of interpretation. If we come speaking in tongues without interpretation, we do not do any good for the local assembly. But tongues when interpreted may bring insight into spiritual truths (a "revelation"); "knowledge," including spiritual understanding; a message to strengthen, encourage, and comfort ("prophecy"); or a "word of instruction" (not in the sense of establishing new doctrine but clarifying spiritual truth and helping the hearers to apply it).

On the other hand, tongues without interpretation may be compared to a flute or a harp played without clear notes or a definite

---

71Most Pentecostals take this to mean that tongues with interpretation "are equivalent to prophecy." Frank M. Boyd, *The Spirit Works Today* (Springfield, Mo.: Gospel Publishing House, 1970), 115. Others (including W. I. Evans, Anthony Palma, Raymond Levang, Gordon Fee, and R. L. Brandt) take it that tongues are always prayer and praise addressed to God. R. L. Brandt, *Gifts for the Marketplace* (Tulsa: Christian Publishing Services, 1989), 199.

melody, and therefore no communication of anything to the listener. Similarly, a trumpet communicates no message to the army if its notes are indistinct and its call unrecognizable. How then can the assembly be satisfied with tongues that are not interpreted! The assembly and the one speaking in tongues would miss the message the Spirit wants to communicate. Just as a trumpet giving a "clear call" communicates to the soldier, so tongues when interpreted can communicate with the congregation.

> **10Undoubtedly there are all sorts of languages in the world, yet none of them is without meaning. 11If then I do not grasp the meaning of what someone is saying, I am a foreigner to the speaker, and he is a foreigner to me. 12So it is with you. Since you are eager to have spiritual gifts, try to excel in gifts that build up the church. 13For this reason anyone who speaks in a tongue should pray that he may interpret what he says.**

As a further argument for the need for interpretation Paul points out that the Holy Spirit has many languages to draw from when He gives a person the gift of tongues, and those languages all convey meaning.[72] But if the language is foreign to the hearer, he does not understand the meaning. Thus, a person who speaks in tongues without interpretation treats the hearer as a foreigner,[73] and the speaker might as well be a foreigner as far as any benefit the hearer derives.

Having said this, Paul again commends the Corinthian believers for their zeal and desire for spiritual gifts. His teaching was in no sense a rebuke. They were right in responding to the Spirit. Love, however, would encourage them to accept his teaching and to direct their seeking toward those gifts which do the most to build up the assembly.

Again, the idea is not to neglect any spiritual gift, but to seek to excel, abound, and overflow for the local assembly. This is why Paul urged that the person who speaks in tongues should pray for the interpretation. This takes a step of faith and obedience. But the Lord will

---

[72]C. F. Voegelin estimates 20,000 languages and dialects over the course of history (15,500 of which have died out). *Classification and Index of the World's Languages* (New York: Elsevier, 1977).

[73]Gk. *barbaros*, "barbarian." In NT times those who could not speak Greek were called barbarians. The spread of Greek language over the eastern half of the Roman Empire made it easier to spread the gospel.

not disappoint the person who takes courage and responds to the Holy Spirit in this way. The Spirit wants to give the needed interpretation.

14For if I pray in a tongue, my spirit prays, but my mind is unfruitful. 15So what shall I do? I will pray with my spirit, but I will also pray with my mind; I will sing with my spirit, but I will also sing with my mind. 16If you are praising God with your spirit, how can one who finds himself among those who do not understand say "Amen" to your thanksgiving, since he does not know what you are saying? 17You may be giving thanks well enough, but the other man is not edified.

Tongues need interpretation. Even when Paul prays in tongues, his spirit joining with the Holy Spirit and going out to God, his mind, or understanding, cannot enter in and remains "unfruitful," unproductive. So Paul asks himself what to do. He will continue the practice of praying with his spirit, using the supernatural, spiritual gift of speaking in tongues (cf. Jude 20). This is "a most effective way of praying and an effective means of avoiding the tendency for prayer to deteriorate into mere ritual."[74] He will also pray with his mind and understanding, still spontaneously moved by the Spirit.

When musical instruments are playing he will break out spontaneously singing in tongues. (The Gk. word means to sing with musical accompaniment.) He will also sing with his mind, his understanding, also anointed by the Spirit.

His speaking in tongues is in this case praise, "giving thanks" (or worship). But if it is not interpreted, the one who does not understand it cannot join in, cannot put an "amen" (Heb. for "surely") to it. Saying "amen" accepts something as being true and valid.[75] "Some observers of the Early Church in worship compared the loud chorus of 'amens' to the echo of distant thunder. The concurring 'amen' of the congregation was regarded as no less important than the prayer itself. (See Rev. 5:13–14; 22:2)."[76]

74Robert L. Brandt and Zenas J. Bicket, *The Spirit Helps Us Pray* (Springfield, Mo.: Logion Press, 1993), 393. Thus Jude 20 has led many to speak of glossalalia as a prayer language, some saying that tongues are most often a prayer. Jean Héring, *La Première Épitre de Saint Paul aux Corinthiens,* 2d ed. (Neuchatel: Éditions delachaux & Nestlé, 1959), p. 126.

75William L. Holladay, *A Concise Hebrew and Aramaic Lexicon of the Old Testament* (Grand Rapids: Wm. B. Eerdmans, 1971), 20.

76Brandt and Bicket, *The Spirit Helps Us Pray*, 276.

Verse 16, in fact, can mean that the one who in public worships in tongues by himself or herself puts the rest of the assembly in the place of those who are "without understanding" (NCV): unlearned, untrained, inexperienced. This implies that worship in the local assembly should be in one accord, with everyone joining in, with everyone united in heart, mind, and soul. But this does not imply that worship in tongues even without interpretation has no value. The person who does so worships, or gives thanks, "well" (rightly, commendably); nevertheless, love would want others edified.

18I thank God that I speak in tongues more than all of you. 19But in the church I would rather speak five intelligible words to instruct others than ten thousand words in a tongue.

The manifestation of spiritual gifts is such a spontaneous thing that taking time for teaching sometimes seems to "quench the Spirit." It may have seemed to the Corinthian believers also that such teaching might discourage speaking in tongues and perhaps cause the gift to be suppressed. (It was actually a growing worldliness, not Biblical teaching, that caused the gift to die out over the next several centuries.)

At every point, Paul stops to make it clear that what he is teaching is not meant in any way to hinder or stop the exercise of any spiritual gift. The Holy Spirit had already given Paul this teaching, but it did not stop him from speaking in tongues. In fact, he thanks God that he spoke in tongues more than any of them (implying he spoke in tongues now more than ever before; also implying that he spoke in tongues when he was baptized in the Holy Spirit[77]).

However, when he was with others in the assembly he would rather speak five words that could be understood and give teaching "than ten thousand words in a tongue." He came with the heart of a shepherd, wanting to feed the flock (the Heb. word for shepherd, *ro'eh,* literally means "feeder"). Teaching takes divine truth from God's Word (1 Pet. 2:2) and puts it in a form which may be received and assimilated with profit and blessing. For Paul to take up all the time of the assembly with a gift which brought edification primarily to himself would hardly show a shepherd's heart, nor would it show the love that chapter 13 describes.

---

[77]John W. Wyckoff, "The Baptism in the Holy Spirit," in *Systematic Theology,* ed. Stanley M. Horton, rev. ed. (Springfield, Mo.: Logion Press, 1995), 441.

Paul must have exercised the gift of tongues when he was alone in his private devotions. There he could open his heart toward God and let the Spirit-given words roll out in prayer, praise, and thanksgiving. In some inner room, some secret place, he could give free course to the operation of this gift and let it bless and strengthen him. It may be that the Corinthian believers were missing a great blessing by failing to exercise the gift of tongues in their personal prayer life.

3. The Effects Of Tongues And Prophecy 14:20–25

20Brothers, stop thinking like children. In regard to evil be infants, but in your thinking be adults.

The Corinthians needed to accept what Paul was teaching. He knew how they loved the free expression of the Spirit. He anticipated that some would already be closing their minds to what he was writing. Some might be finding fault, becoming angry, or feeling ill will. The person who is mature is willing to give up the lesser for the greater, to turn from that which seems good in order to have something better.

Children do not develop deep-seated malice or habitual faultfinding, however. So as far as "evil," or malice, is concerned we should remain like infants. But in our thinking and understanding we need to be mature adults. It takes mature thinking to receive teaching on spiritual gifts, especially with regard to ministering them in love. But Paul expected it of the Corinthian church—and God expects it of us all.

21In the Law it is written: "Through men of strange tongues and through the lips of foreigners I will speak to this people, but even then they will not listen to me," says the Lord. 22Tongues, then, are a sign, not for believers but for unbelievers; prophecy, however, is for believers, not for unbelievers.

Lest the Corinthians jump to the conclusion that there was no place for speaking in tongues in the public worship, Paul quickly draws their attention to Isaiah 28:11–12. In the context of Isaiah's prophecy, proud Israelites were saying that Isaiah was treating them like spiritual babies and they resented it. Isaiah then made it clear that because of their unbelief, the message meant for blessing would bring judgment. God would send foreign conquerors whose language they would not understand, but whose actions would make it clear that these Israelites were separated from God, cut off from His blessing and under His judgment. Paul applies this to speaking in tongues (languages) they did not understand. So speaking in tongues is necessary as a judgment sign to unbelievers, making them realize that they are separated from God and cannot understand His message.[78]

Tongues can also be a sign to unbelievers in that it draws their attention and lets them know something supernatural is present. This was apparently the case on the Day of Pentecost when the sound of tongues brought a crowd together (Acts 2:6).

Prophecy, however, is not a sign (something obviously miraculous) to unbelievers, for it is in the language they understand, and they do not recognize it as supernatural. On the other hand, believers who are in tune with the Holy Spirit recognize the gift of prophecy as supernatural, full of the Spirit's power.

> **23So if the whole church comes together and everyone**
> **speaks in tongues, and some who do not understand**
> **or some unbelievers come in, will they not say that you**
> **are out of your mind? 24But if an unbeliever or some-**
> **one who does not understand comes in while every-**
> **body is prophesying, he will be convinced by all that**
> **he is a sinner and will be judged by all, 25and the**
> **secrets of his heart will be laid bare. So he will fall**
> **down and worship God, exclaiming, "God is really**
> **among you!"**

On the other hand, if the whole church keeps on speaking in tongues, all at the same time, the initial effect of it will pass and unbelievers or those who are not instructed in spiritual things will say all the people speaking in tongues are out of their mind. These outsiders are the important people, the people the church must reach.

This was exactly the case on the Day of Pentecost. The crowd initially was amazed because they heard the 120 speaking in languages of the countries they came from. Eventually, however, as the 120 kept speaking in tongues, the crowd said they had had too much wine, which was just another way of saying they were out of their minds (Acts 2:13). Clearly the tongues did not lead the hearers to accept Jesus as Lord and Savior. Then the 120 stopped and Peter stood up to speak.

---

[78]Archibald Robertson and Alfred Plummer, *A Critical and Exegetical Commentary on the First Epistle of St. Paul to the Corinthians,* 2d ed. In The International Critical Commentary Series (Edinburgh: T & T. Clark, 1914), 317.

Prophecy, in contrast to tongues, speaks to the mind and heart of those who are unbelievers or spiritually ignorant. It brings them conviction, and by it the Holy Spirit is able to do His work of convicting and convincing the world of sin, righteousness, and judgment (John 16:8). He makes sinners realize they are sinners and that sin is sin. He also calls them to account as the gift of prophecy brings a message that spotlights the secrets of their inner hearts and reveals their guilt. They see themselves in a true light and recognize that the message comes from God. This makes them fall down to worship and honor God. Instead of saying that the tongues speakers are out of their mind, these unbelievers will recognize that God is speaking. "To fall down and worship" means they are converted. This also is a sign to the believers that God is truly among them.

This too was exactly the situation on the Day of Pentecost. When Peter stood up to speak in the language they all understood, he did not give his own reasoning. The phrase in Acts 2:14 "addressed the crowd" is, literally, "spoke forth to them." Peter spoke as the Spirit gave utterance, but this time in prophecy instead of in tongues. This word spoke to their hearts (Acts 2:37,41) and brought the truth about Jesus Christ "into the very situation of the hearers."[79] This was followed by the gift of exhortation, of Peter's warning and pleading with the people (Acts 2:40). The result was such that three thousand were saved.

The gift of prophecy will always apply the truth to the situation where the people are, where they actually live. Note, too, that Paul expects that all can speak in tongues and that all can prophesy. They all had been baptized in the Holy Spirit and He distributes the gifts as He wills. He does not limit them to people who have an office.

4. Worship In An Orderly Way 14:26–40

a) Contribution To Worship By All 14:26

26What then shall we say, brothers? When you come together, everyone has a hymn, or a word of instruction, a revelation, a tongue or an interpretation. All of these must be done for the strengthening of the church.

"What then shall we say" shows that Paul expected the Corinthian believers to draw the right conclusions from the principles of love and

[79]Eduard Schweizer, "The Service of Worship," *Interpretation* 13, no. 4 (October 1959): 406.

edification of the local assembly.

The first rule for the expression of spiritual gifts is that no gift is unimportant and no gift should be set aside. People baptized in the Spirit will have the fullness of the gifts available for the health of the church. "Everyone has" means that everyone should have a part and contribute something to the building up of the whole assembly. Over too much of church history, the body of Christ has been paralyzed, with clergy dominating the laity and smothering their gifts.[80] We are not to be like a theater audience, where one or several paid actors act on the stage while everybody else merely looks on.

"Each one takes part with his special gift."[81] This may include a "hymn" (Gk. *psalmon,* a song or hymn with musical accompaniment) which might be old or new, learned or freshly given, but anointed by the Holy Spirit and made a spiritual ministry. (The Book of Psalms was the hymnbook of the Early Church and should still be a part of our worship.) Another may bring a "word of instruction," Spirit-illuminated from God's Word. Another may bring a "revelation," that is, one of the gifts of revelation such as a message of wisdom or a message of knowledge. Another may bring a tongue, another an interpretation.

While these gifts are ministered we can be sure the whole congregation should be actively listening and silently interceding in faith. The important thing is that all contribute to the variety with the purpose of strengthening the assembly (cf. 12:7, "for the common good"). "Liberty in the Spirit must be governed by responsibility to the body."[82]

b) Directions For Tongues Speakers 14:27–28

27If anyone speaks in a tongue, two—or at the most three—should speak, one at a time, and someone must interpret. 28If there is no interpreter, the speaker should keep quiet in the church and speak to himself and God.

Paul has already made it clear that tongues need interpretation to edify and to become part of the "greater gifts" (12:31). To reemphasize

[80]Richard Lovelace, "Baptism in the Holy Spirit and the Evangelical Tradition," in *Faces of Renewal,* ed. Paul Elbert (Peabody, Mass.: Hendrickson Publishers, 1988), 230.

[81]Schweizer, "The Service of Worship," 401.

[82]Anthony Palma, "Spiritual Gifts—Basic Considerations," *Pneuma* 1, no. 2 (fall 1979): 20.

this, he picks tongues out of the variety of expression mentioned in verse 25 to show that if we are to have variety there must be some limitation, and since the Corinthians were overusing tongues, he gives four rules which will bring proper limitation on their expression.

First, they should be limited to "two—or at the most three." Some interpret this to mean two or three in succession, then allowing two or three more later in the meeting. Others say it means two or three by the same person, thus allowing two or three more by the next person. But this is not in line with the purpose to allow a greater variety of spiritual gifts to be manifested. Furthermore, the word "by" (v. 27, KJV, NASB) is the Greek *kata,* which is used distributively, that is, two or at most three in each meeting or each time the believers gather. Again, Paul's purpose is not to quench the Spirit but to encourage believers to seek and exercise other spiritual gifts.

Second, they should speak "one at a time." Love does not allow two to speak at once, as if in competition.

Third, "someone must interpret." Opportunity should be given for interpretation after a message in tongues. Some take this to mean that one person in the assembly should do all the interpreting. But this idea does not fit well with the exhortation that follows.

Fourth, if no interpreter is present (no person who has been used in the manifestation of that gift), then no tongues should be given aloud, for to do so would not edify the assembly. The person can still express the gift in a right way, however, by quietly speaking directly to God. This will still fulfill one purpose of the gift: to edify the person speaking (14:4). The balancing exhortation should be kept in mind also: The tongues speakers should pray for the gift of interpretation (14:13).

Do these verses (22–27) rule out speaking in tongues in corporate worship? David Lim points out, on the basis of Acts 2:4; 10:44–46; and 19:6, that "Everyone worshiping in tongues at the same time cannot be denied from a biased interpretation of 1 Corinthians 14:2,22–25. Paul and Luke do not contradict each other."[83]

c) Directions For Prophets 14:29–33

29Two or three prophets should speak, and the others should weigh carefully what is said. 30And if a revelation comes to someone who is sitting down, the first speaker should stop. 31For you can all prophesy in turn

---

[83]David Lim, "Spiritual Gifts," in *Systematic Theology,* ed. Horton, 476.

so that everyone may be instructed and encouraged. [32]The spirits of prophets are subject to the control of prophets. [33a]For God is not a God of disorder but of peace.

The gift of prophecy also needs direction and instruction, though not the same kind of limitation as tongues. In verse 29 the Greek word *kata* is not used. The sense here seems to be that "two or three" prophets may speak in succession. Then before others prophesy, other believers in the assembly should weigh carefully, "and publicly,"[84] with deliberate consideration and evaluation, what the Spirit is saying. This would include how it lines up with the written Word of God,[85] how it meets the need, what is God's purpose, and what the believers should do about it to build up the body.

Paul may be recognizing also that people may add to the Spirit's expression out of their own feelings (perhaps unintentionally). This seems to be what happened when those in Tyre "through the Spirit" urged Paul not to go to Jerusalem (Acts 21:4). The word "through" in the Greek means here "in consequence of," or "on account of." The same thing happened in Acts 21:11,12. Other passages indicate it was indeed God's will for Paul to go to Jerusalem (cf. Acts 9:16 and Acts 27:23,24). But the people added their own fears and feelings to what the Spirit said. Paul does not teach us to accept without question every message given in a meeting.

Then, if a person is giving a message in prophecy and another person stands, indicating he or she has been given a revelation by God, then the first person should give the second person opportunity. Thus, love will not let a person jump up and interrupt another, neither will it let any one individual monopolize the time. Rather, love will give all (not just those with a special ministry as prophets) an opportunity to exercise the gift of prophecy to bring instruction and encouragement to everyone in the assembly.

This kind of love, courtesy, and consideration is possible because "the spirits of prophets are subject to the control of prophets." The Holy Spirit manifests His gifts as our spirits respond to Him, so that the Holy Spirit ministers through our spirits (cf. vv. 14–15). But He expects us to remember that "God is not a God of disorder but of

---

[84]Ibid., 467.

[85]John R. Higgins, "God's Inspired Word," in *Systematic Theology,* ed. Horton, 112.

peace" (including harmony). "Peace is foundational to moving ahead in unity, to receiving the ministries of others, and to learning even through failure."[86]

Those who exercise spiritual gifts are not hypnotized, somnambulistic. The operation of the gifts involves no loss of self-consciousness. Heathen prophets, mediums, and other demonic manifestations are very often not able to control when or what they do or say.[87] In contrast, the Holy Spirit does not function this way. God makes us fellow workers under His direction (3:9).

This means that we can wait for an appropriate time to minister the gift the Holy Spirit is impressing upon us. We need not interrupt everything the moment we feel Him moving us. We lose nothing if we wait until the Spirit provides an opportunity to manifest the gift without causing confusion and disorder. Holding steady will, in fact, only deepen the Spirit's impression and keep the gift from being ineffective.[88]

d) Directions For Women 14:34–35

33bAs in all the congregations of the saints, 34women should remain silent in the churches. They are not allowed to speak, but must be in submission, as the Law says. 35If they want to inquire about something, they should ask their own husbands at home; for it is disgraceful for a woman to speak in the church.

Other types of disorder should also be avoided, such as women interrupting and asking questions in an improper manner, thus contributing to confusion. (Most women were uneducated in that day.)[89] Such instruction could be applied to both men and women in matters that local custom considers unbecoming.[90] Paul did expect women to

---

86Lim, "Spiritual Gifts," 480.

87Erich Nestler, "Was Montanism a Heresy?" *Pneuma* 6, no. 1 (spring 1984): 69.

88I learned this early in my teaching ministry at Central Bible College. On one occasion the Spirit impressed a few words on my mind while I was seated in the chapel. I waited until a lull in the service and asked permission to speak. When I stepped to the pulpit it was like stepping into an electric field. I gave the words the Spirit had impressed on me and more words flowed out. Students rushed to the altar and a number were filled with the Holy Spirit.

89Many apply "remain silent" solely to questions asked. Pièrre Bonnard, *Commentaire sur la Première Épitre aux Corinthiens,* vol. 2 (Neuchatel: éditions de l'imprimerie nouvelle L.A. Monner, 1965), 314.

90See 9:19–23 for Paul's view of how to relate to the culture of the time.

pray and prophesy in public if the Spirit gave them a ministry (11:5). The Bible makes no differentiation between men and women with regard to spiritual manifestations. God used women as prophets in both Old and New Testament times (e.g. Miriam, Exod. 15:20; Deborah, Judg. 4:4; Huldah, 2 Kings 22:14; four daughters of Philip the evangelist, Acts 21:9).

On the other hand, there may have been a situation in Corinth like the one Paul describes in 2 Timothy 3:6–7, where false teachers who oppose the truth "worm their way into homes and gain control over weak-willed women, who are loaded down with sins and are swayed by all kinds of evil desires, always learning but never able to acknowledge the truth." The presence of such women in the Corinthian congregation would be reason enough to tell them to "remain silent." But this does not mean we should restrict women from genuine gifts and ministries given by the Spirit.[91]

e) The Lord's Command 14:36–40

**36Did the word of God originate with you? Or are you
the only people it has reached? 37If anybody thinks he
is a prophet or spiritually gifted, let him acknowledge
that what I am writing to you is the Lord's command.
38If he ignores this, he himself will be ignored.**

Paul now speaks to the entire assembly (Gk. *monous,* "only" is masculine plural). Probably because of the opposition expressed in their letter to him, he asks in irony if the Word of God originated with them or if they were the only ones "it has reached." That is, did they think they were superior to the Word of God brought them by Paul? Or did they have a right to interpret it differently from all the other assemblies, as if the others had not received the Word?

They apparently thought they were more spiritual than Paul. But if they were really prophets and spiritually gifted they would recognize that what Paul wrote to them is God's command. But if they ignore it, they "will be ignored"; implying that only the spiritually ignorant will disregard Paul's God-given, Spirit-inspired instructions.

---

[91]Gordon Fee argues that vv. 34–35 were not written by Paul but were added by a later copyist. He notes that all the Western text manuscripts place them after v. 40. Gordon Fee, *The First Epistle to the Corinthians* (Grand Rapids: Wm. B. Eerdmans, 1987), 699–708.

39Therefore, my brothers, be eager to prophesy, and do not forbid speaking in tongues. 40But everything should be done in a fitting and orderly way.

Paul concludes by affectionately addressing the Corinthians as brothers (and sisters) as he reinforces the main theme of this chapter: Prophecy is the gift they should eagerly seek. But he plainly says, "Do not forbid speaking in tongues." Also he may be implying that sensitivity to the Spirit's prompting of His manifestations can be lost by a careless attitude or by forbidding one of them, such as tongues. "Fear of extremes often causes churches to shrink from a complete gift ministry. . . . Sometimes we judge mercilessly and legalistically those who make mistakes. Then we dampen the will of others to begin ministry in gifts."[92] We should indeed encourage everything to be done "in a fitting and orderly way," but if we do so in an unloving way, this can also lead to a loss of the Spirit's gifts (perhaps by substituting either emotional expressions by some or form and ceremony by others).

Study questions for this section may be found in appendix B.

VII. CHRIST'S RESURRECTION AND OURS 15:1–58

The idea of resurrection was not fully developed in the Old Testament. Job did see it (Job 19:25–26). Isaiah 25:8; 26:19 and Daniel 12:2 anticipated it. The Pharisees believed in it, but the Sadducees, because of the influence of Greek philosophy, rejected it. They came to Jesus with a question intended to make the idea of resurrection look ridiculous. Jesus told them they were in error because they did not know the Scriptures or the power of God. Then, because the Sadducees also rejected the authority of the prophets, Jesus took a passage they accepted to show that they were mistaken: "'Now about the dead rising—have you not read in the book of Moses, in the account of the bush, how God said to him "I am the God of Abraham, the God of Isaac, and the God of Jacob"? He is not the God of the dead, but of the living. You are badly mistaken!'" (Mark 12:18–27; cf. Exod. 3:6).

92Lim, "Spiritual Gifts," 478.

The Early Church also proclaimed the resurrection of Jesus and of believers (Acts 2:25–32; 4:2; 13:35–37).[1] "The gift of the Spirit is also a guarantee of what is to come."[2] But at Athens some sneered at the idea of the resurrection (Acts 17:32), and Greek philosophy undoubtedly affected some of the Christians at Corinth. They probably thought that "life in the Spirit meant a final ridding oneself of the body, not because it was evil but because it was inferior and beneath them."[3] Thus, Paul found it necessary to emphasize that the truth of Christ's resurrection and that of believers is essential to the gospel.

A. The Gospel Paul Preached 15:1–11

[1]Now, brothers, I want to remind you of the gospel I preached to you, which you received and on which you have taken your stand. [2]By this gospel you are saved, if you hold firmly to the word I preached to you. Otherwise, you have believed in vain.

Though Paul had a great concern over the gifts of the Spirit and their manifestation, he now returns to his major concern, the gospel, the good news of our salvation through Christ's death and resurrection. Paul announced it to the Corinthians. They received it and took a stand for it, and stood in it. But apparently some who considered themselves more "spiritual" than others needed to be reminded of the truths Paul had taught them.

By the gospel Paul preached they not only were, but still are being, saved (the Gk. *sōzesthe* is a continuous present passive, indicating they were continually receiving of salvation). But they will only continue being saved if they hold fast to the word Paul preached to them, that is, to the gospel. Otherwise even their initial belief is "in vain," useless, to no purpose. Paul can say this because there is no other gospel than the one he preached, and anyone who preaches another gospel will be eternally condemned (Gal. 1:6–9).

[3]For what I received I passed on to you as of first importance: that Christ died for our sins according to the Scriptures, [4]that he was buried, that he was raised

---

[1]Stanley M. Horton, *Our Destiny: Biblical Teachings on the Last Things* (Springfield, Mo.: Logion Press, 1996), 67–68.

[2]Ibid., 70.

[3]Gordon D. Fee, *The First Epistle to the Corinthians* (Grand Rapids: Wm. B. Eerdmans, 1987), 715.

on the third day according to the Scriptures, [5]and that he appeared to Peter, and then to the Twelve.

Verses 3–11 record statements "received" by Paul. Verses 3–5 give the fundamentals of the gospel. Verses 6–8 lists some of the appearances of Christ, and this is followed by Paul's declaration of his apostleship (vv. 9–11)

The good news, the gospel, has a twofold foundation: the promises of the Old Testament Scriptures and the historical facts of Christ's death and resurrection. Jesus died on the cross, shed His blood, gave His life for our sins, on account of our sins, and in our place (cf. Rom. 4:25; 5:8; 1 Pet. 3:18). He did this according to the Scriptures. When we look back into the Old Testament we see a rich typology in the priesthood and sacrifices that reminds us that "the wages of sin is death" (Rom. 6:23), and that the blood of the sacrifice represents the life poured out in death (Lev. 17:11). So as Isaiah prophesied, God's suffering Servant had no sin of His own but "He was pierced for *our* transgressions" and became a guilt offering for us, satisfying the claims of God's law and justice (Isa. 53:5,10).[4] On the cross Jesus said, "'It is finished,'" and died (John 19:30). His work for our redemption was complete. Only one thing more needed to be done: He was raised for our justification (see Rom. 4:25). "The miracle of the Resurrection is foundational to Paul's Christology."[5] The literal, bodily resurrection of Jesus Christ is the bold proclamation to the universe that His death was efficacious and that indeed the hosts of darkness had been conquered and that in triumph the victorious Christ had risen from the grave,[6] making His resurrection the guarantee of ours.[7] This too was according to the Scriptures. Isaiah 53:11 prophesied that He would see the outcome of His sufferings and be satisfied.[8] "The Dead Sea Scrolls add that He will see the light of life, which was indeed fulfilled in his resurrection."[9] His appearances to Peter and the rest of the

[4]William W. Menzies and Stanley M. Horton, *Bible Doctrines: A Pentecostal Perspective* (Springfield, Mo.: Logion Press, 1993), 100.

[5]Vernon Purdy, "Divine Healing," in *Systematic Theology*, ed. Stanley M. Horton, rev. ed. (Springfield, Mo.: Logion Press, 1995), 512.

[6]The Gk. perfect tense indicates He is still alive.

[7]Horton, *Our Destiny*, 69.

[8]See also Pss. 2:7; 16:10–11; 17:15; 110:1; Hos. 6:2 ("on the third day" in their way of counting would include parts of days, as also Matt. 12:40).

[9]Stanley M. Horton, *Isaiah*, vol. 12 of *The Complete Biblical Library: The Old Testament* (Springfield, Mo.: World Library Press, 1995), 421.

Twelve (including Matthias) made them primary witnesses to His resurrection (as well as to His teachings).

> **6After that, he appeared to more than five hundred of the brothers at the same time, most of whom are still living, though some have fallen asleep. 7Then he appeared to James, then to all the apostles, 8and last of all he appeared to me also, as to one abnormally born.**

The appearance of Jesus to "more than five hundred of the brothers" (and sisters, since women were among His followers) probably took place in Galilee. This is important because most of these witnesses were still living at the time Paul wrote this letter to the Corinthians.[10] They could still go and check the truth of what Paul was saying. He would not have dared mention such appearances if they were not true. James the brother of Jesus was still alive also and so were most of the other apostles (James the brother of the apostle John had been martyred [Acts 12:2]). Jesus appeared to them again just before His ascension. Paul does not mean that He appeared only to the apostles in that appearance. The Gospels show that others were present as well (Luke 24:33).

That Jesus appeared to Paul "last of all"(on the Damascus Road [Acts 9:3–6]) means Paul was the last to be a firsthand witness to the resurrection of Jesus and therefore the last to be commissioned by Jesus as an apostle. The New Testament apostles did include others besides the Twelve (see comments on 9:3–5). "As direct witnesses and messengers of the risen Lord, they built the foundation of the church of Jesus Christ, a foundation that can never be added to or altered. Thus, these apostles can have no successors."[11] However, apostolic ministry continues today as "a church-building, fellowship-building work, exercised with accompanying miracles that are the work of the Spirit"[12] (cf. Eph. 4:11).

10When Paul refers to death as sleep, he is referring to the body. He knew that as soon as he was away from the body at death, he would be present with the Lord (2 Cor. 5:6–9; Phil. 1:23). Moses and Elijah at the Mount of Transfiguration knew what was going on and understood that Jesus' "departure" (Gk. *exodos*, the death, resurrection, and ascension) would mean something to them (Luke 9:31).

11Donald Stamps, ed., *The Full Life Study Bible* NIV, The New Testament (Grand Rapids: Zondervan Bible Publishers, 1990), 355.

12Stanley M. Horton, *What the Bible Says About the Holy Spirit* (Springfield, Mo.: Gospel Publishing House, 1976), 266.

"Abnormally born" (Gk. *ektrōmati*) is the ordinary word for a miscarriage, which we usually think of as coming before the due date for a birth; Paul here means his apostleship was given later. It may be that Paul's enemies used it of him in a contemptuous way, and Paul humbly accepts it.[13]

> **9For I am the least of the apostles and do not even deserve to be called an apostle, because I persecuted the church of God. 10But by the grace of God I am what I am, and his grace to me was not without effect. No, I worked harder than all of them—yet not I, but the grace of God that was with me. 11Whether, then, it was I or they, this is what we preach, and this is what you believed.**

Paul could never forget that he persecuted the *ekklēsia,* the assembly of God's people, who had become both His people and citizens of His heavenly kingdom. Neither could he forget the grace of God, the unmerited favor that was given him when Jesus stopped him on the Damascus Road and commissioned him as the apostle to the Gentiles, that is, to the nations of the world (Acts 9:15). That grace was effective in him and through him, because he responded in a faith and obedience that caused him to work harder than any of the other apostles.

But whether the Lord was using Paul or the others, they all preached the same gospel. Paul in Galatians tells how he went to Jerusalem to the Christian leaders and "set before them the gospel" that he preached among the Gentiles. James, Peter, and John gave him and Barnabas "the right hand of fellowship when they recognized the grace given to [them]" (Ga. 2:2,9). Thus, the gospel Paul preached is the same gospel recorded in our four Gospels, what Acts 2:42 calls "the apostles' teaching."

B. The Reality Of The Resurrection Of The Dead 15:12–58

1. The Resurrection Is Vital to Our Hope 15:12–19

> **12But if it is preached that Christ has been raised from the dead, how can some of you say that there is no resurrection of the dead? 13If there is no resurrection of**

---

[13]Gordon H. Clark, *First Corinthians: A Contemporary Commentary* (Nutley, N.J.: Presbyterian & Reformed Publishing Co., 1975), 258.

the dead, then not even Christ has been raised. [14]And if Christ has not been raised, our preaching is useless and so is your faith.

Emph.

Verse 12 continues where verse 2 left off. Some had turned against Paul and were not holding "firmly to the word" (v. 2) he preached. They had indeed "believed in vain," their faith, "useless." Even though they accepted the preaching that Christ had been raised from the dead (and was still alive), they were saying that there was no resurrection of the dead (that is, of dead believers). But Christ's resurrection and ours are part of one and the same plan of God. Jesus said, "'Because I live, you also will live'" (John 14:19). Jesus told Martha, "'I am the resurrection and the life. He who believes in me will live, even though he dies; and whoever lives [that is, is resurrected after he or she dies] and believes in me will never die'" (John 11:25–26). Thus, it would follow that if there is no resurrection of the dead, then Jesus was a liar and did not rise from the dead. If this were so, then all Paul's preaching was useless and meaningless, and so would be too the faith that responded to the preaching of the gospel.

[15]More than that, we are then found to be false witnesses about God, for we have testified about God that he raised Christ from the dead. But he did not raise him if in fact the dead are not raised. [16]For if the dead are not raised, then Christ has not been raised either. [17]And if Christ has not been raised, your faith is futile; you are still in your sins. [18]Then those also who have fallen asleep in Christ are lost.

perished

Not only was Christ a liar if the dead are not raised, but Paul and the apostles were false witnesses, not only to the Resurrection but to the very nature of God, and were actually bearing witness against God.

Our faith, our salvation, depends upon the objective, literal fact that Jesus rose from the dead. If He did not rise, then the Cross is meaningless, His death and the shedding of His blood did not atone for our sins, and we are still guilty sinners doomed to an eternal hell. Furthermore those who have died with their faith in Jesus are already lost—forever without hope.

We can apply the reverse of this. Those who deny that Jesus was literally, objectively raised from the dead are denying the fundamental truth of the gospel. They are making the Bible, Jesus, the apostles, and God himself false witnesses. But they are the false witnesses and have no right to call themselves Christians. Whatever faith they may claim to have is meaningless.

19 If only for this life we have hope in Christ, we are to
be pitied more than all men.

A popular song once said, "If I am dreaming, let me dream on." I have heard some people say, "The Christian life is the best and happiest life, so even if it is not true, it is good to be a Christian." But the apostle Paul would have none of that. When he said we are "to be pitied" more than all men, or "more miserable" (as the Gk. may mean), he did not mean we feel miserable. To Paul, it would be a miserable thing to believe something that is not true, and anyone who does so is to be pitied. Paul was not willing to be among those whose minds were blinded to the truth (cf. 2 Cor. 4:4).

2. Christ's Resurrection And The Final Consummation 15:20–28

20 But Christ has indeed been raised from the dead, the
firstfruits of those who have fallen asleep. 21 For since
death came through a man, the resurrection of the
dead comes also through a man. 22 For as in Adam all
die, so in Christ all will be made alive.

Triumphantly Paul declares the answer: "Christ has indeed been raised from the dead." His resurrection is an accomplished fact. Using two figures of speech, he calls Jesus the "firstfruits" of those "fallen asleep," that is, those who have died and are in Christ. The firstfruits were the first installment of the harvest and were presented to the Lord with thanksgiving in anticipation of the good harvest to come. Paul means "the resurrection of the dead is not simply something future." It began in Christ's resurrection.[14] Thus, believers who have died have a living relationship with Jesus.

This gives us comfort when we are faced with the death of believers (cf. Rom. 8:11; 1 Pet. 1:3–4). Both Jesus and Paul "used 'sleep' simply as a figure . . . to indicate that death was not to be feared but was an entrance into quietness and rest, which Jesus also identified with paradise."[15] There they enjoy His presence until the time when He comes to destroy the armies of the Antichrist and establish His

[14] Horton, *Our Destiny,* 68–69.
[15] Ibid., 55–56.

millennial kingdom (Rev. 19:11–21).

The resurrection of Jesus is significant for us also because He died and rose again as a man, a human being (Gk. *anthrōpou*), having identified himself with humankind. This was necessary because death came into the human race through the sin of a man, a human being. Because of Adam's sin everyone was cut off from the blessings of the Garden of Eden and all in some way inherit the corruption of sin.[16] All are "by nature the children of wrath" (Eph. 2:3, KJV). Consequently, "all sinned" (Rom. 5:12) and are subject to divine punishment. But because God so loved the world that He sent His unique, special Son, if we believe, we shall not perish but have eternal life (John 3:16). For eternal life, there must be resurrection, "so in Christ all will be made alive." He wants to restore all that humankind lost through the fall. He will do even more, for we shall have new bodies, and instead of a garden with one tree of life, we shall dwell in a city with many trees of life (Rev. 22:2).

Some take "all will be made alive" to be comprehensive, as in Acts 24:15, which speaks of resurrection of both "just and unjust" (KJV). This would mean a third resurrection.[17] While it is true that the wicked dead will be raised to face the Great White Throne judgment, Paul rather has in mind here "all who are united to Christ in the covenant of grace"[18] (cf. vv. 45–49).

> **[23]But each in his own turn: Christ, the firstfruits; then, when he comes, those who belong to him. [24]Then the end will come, when he hands over the kingdom to God the Father after he has destroyed all dominion, authority and power. [25]For he must reign until he has put all his enemies under his feet. [26]The last enemy to be destroyed is death.**

---

[16]"It may be that while Adam heard the command not to eat of the tree directly from God, Eve heard it only through her husband (Gen. 2:17; cf. 2:22). Hence, Adam was more responsible before God, and Eve was more susceptible to Satan (cf. John 20:29). This may explain Scripture's emphasis on Adam's sin ...when actually Eve sinned first." Bruce R. Marino, "The Origin, Nature, and Consequences of Sin," in *Systematic Theology,* ed. Horton, 259–60.

[17]Wilbur B. Wallis, "The Problem of an Intermediate Kingdom in 1 Corinthians 15:20–28," *Journal of the Evangelical Theological Society* 18, no. 4 (fall 1975): 235.

[18]Roger Nicole, "Covenant, Universal Call and Definite Atonement," *Journal of the Evangelical Theological Society* 38, no. 3 (September 1995): 405. See also Horton, *Our Destiny,* 235.

Paul treats the resurrection of Jesus and of the believers as a unit (what Rev. 20:5 calls "the first resurrection") by comparing it to a harvest. "Christ is the 'firstfruits of the harvest.' The main body of the harvest comes 'in [its]own turn' at the time of His coming to meet us in the air. Then [as Rev. 20:4 indicates] the gleanings of the harvest will be those martyred during the Tribulation; they will make the first resurrection complete."[19] Not until after the Millennium will the rest of the dead be resurrected to come before the Great White Throne (Rev. 20:5,12).[20]

Some take *eita to telos,* "Then the end will come," to mean that the final end, the final goal, comes immediately after the resurrection and rapture, leaving no room for a millennium. However, the fact that *eita* in verse 24 follows *epeita* in verse 23 indicates a time sequence between the Second Coming and the end. The Greek aorist subjunctive of "after he has destroyed all dominion" indicates that the destruction is prior to His handing over the Kingdom to God the Father at the end: "The delivering over follows the subjugation. This is confirmed by the parallel construction of verse 28."[21] Thus Christ's reign clearly takes place during the Millennium after His second coming.

Psalms 8:6 and 110:1 prophesy a royal reign as well. Zechariah (10:6,8–9,12) promises a future return of the Israelites to their land. These passages all call for a fulfillment in the Millennium.[22] The word "must" (Gk. *dei,* v. 25) indicates purpose. Christ must reign so that His enemies may be destroyed.[23] This implies He will "fulfill all of God's purposes in creation and redemption. He will right all wrongs. Martyrs and others who were condemned unjustly in this life will be vindicated and blessed."[24]

Revelation 19:20 makes it clear that the Antichrist will be cast into the lake of fire at Christ's second coming. Paul recognizes this as well

---

[19]Horton, *Our Destiny,* 188. Paul calls it literally the "outresurrection out from among the dead" (Phil. 3:11), implying "some of the dead will be left in their graves after the believers are raised and caught away to meet the Lord in the air." The main body of the harvest will also include the OT saints (Isa. 26:19–21; Ezek. 37:12–14; Dan. 12:2–3).

[20]Paul spoke of *tēn exanastasin,* "the outresurrection," out from among the dead (Phil. 3:11).

[21]Wallis, "Problem," 230.

[22]Horton, *Our Destiny,* 202–03.

[23]Cf. Ps. 110:1; Matt. 22:44.

[24]Horton, *Our Destiny,* 211.

(2 Thess. 2:8), and he notes that the saints will reign (1 Cor. 4:8; cf. Rev. 5:10). Then after the Millennium, Satan will be released for a short time; this will bring the final destruction of Satan and those who persisted in following him. It will bring the end of death as well, for death and Hades will be thrown into the lake of fire (Rev. 20:10,13–15). This will be the final defeat of "the last enemy," death. There will be no death in the new heavens and the new earth, for the lake of fire will be outside of them.[25]

> **27For he "has put everything under his feet." Now when it says that "everything" has been put under him, it is clear that this does not include God himself, who put everything under Christ. 28When he has done this, then the Son himself will be made subject to him who put everything under him, so that God may be all in all.**

Paul now applies Psalm 8:6 to Jesus as the one who truly fulfills what God purposed for humankind and as the one in whom we find fulfillment (cf. Heb. 2:6–8). God's putting "everything" under Jesus' feet obviously does not include God the Father. Jesus will still be the Son, subordinate to the Father even though equal with Him. Jesus' reign in the Millennium and the final destruction of Satan and death will complete the Son's messianic mission[26] and will lead to God the Father's being "all in all"—with everything and everyone in the new heavens and the new earth in perfect harmony with Him. We may have a foretaste of this when we witness the unity in diversity of charismatic operations within the church. Compare the "splendid paradox of Ephesians 3:18: only *'together with all the saints,'* together with all the different gifts, will we be able to know the unknowable: the width, length, height and depth of the love of the one Christ, the fullness of God."[27]

In other words, God being all in all does not mean pantheism, or losing one's individual personality by being dissolved in a great Brahman or Atman as Hindu philosophy teaches. God becomes all in all so we believers are glorified and become the fullness of the unique persons God intended us to be. In the New Jerusalem we shall all have

---

25Ibid., 231.

26J.J. Lias, *The First Epistle to the Corinthians* (Cambridge, England: University Press, 1899), 151.

27Jean-Jacques Suurmond, "Christ King: A Charismatic Appeal for an Ecological Lifestyle," *Pneuma* 10, no. 1 (spring 1988): 27.

a place. There will be wonderful variety and diversity, but instead of the fragmentation and brokenness so common today, the unity of the body of Christ will be perfect and complete.

Our relationship with Christ and the Father will be forever full of joy and peace. The fact "the Son himself will be made subject to" the Father indicates also that the kind of mediation between God and humankind that Christ carries out now (and will carry out in the Millennium) will no longer be necessary. Consequently, the subjection of the Son to the Father is "an administrative subjection . . . the Son is in no way inferior to the Father."[28] Our fellowship will be complete and there will be nothing between.

3. A Challenge To Believe In The Resurrection 15:29–34

29Now if there is no resurrection, what will those do who are baptized for the dead? If the dead are not raised at all, why are people baptized for them?

Paul further challenges those who deny bodily resurrection by pointing to a practice that some carried out. Paul does not explain why people were "baptized for the dead." He simply wants them to see that such a baptism, which pictures death and resurrection, is meaningless if there is no resurrection. One suggestion is that certain new converts died before they could be baptized. Their pagan relatives wanted to give them a heathen funeral, but another Christian was baptized in their stead to tell the world that this is what the dead believer would have done. This would be a means of claiming the body for Christian burial. It was probably a short-lived local practice By the time of John Chrysostom (A.D. 345–407) some were saying Paul meant they were being baptized for themselves because they were dead in sins. Others have taken it to mean a present baptism of trial and suffering.[29]

30And as for us, why do we endanger ourselves every hour? 31I die every day—I mean that, brothers—just as surely as I glory over you in Christ Jesus our Lord. 32If I fought wild beasts in Ephesus for merely human reasons, what have I gained? If the dead are not raised, "Let us eat and drink, for tomorrow we die."

---

[28]Timothy Munyon, "The Creation of the Universe and Humankind," in *Systematic Theology*, ed. Horton, 249.

[29]Lias, *First Epistle to the Corinthians*, 151.

Paul lived a life of constant danger (cf. 2 Cor. 11:23–28). Though he did teach dying to sin, that does not fit the context of danger here. By dying "every day" Paul meant he risked his life every day. He dared to do so for two reasons. First, because he knew that if he was killed he would lose nothing of what he was really looking for, to be forever with the Lord (1 Thess. 4:17). Second, he wanted others to come to Christ, just as he gloried over the fact the Corinthian believers were now in Christ Jesus because of his witness.

Luke does not record in Acts any fighting with wild animals in Ephesus. At the same time, he records only one shipwreck and Paul mentions three others (2 Cor. 11:25). Some suppose, however, that Paul is referring to a mob that acted like wild beasts. Paul as a Roman citizen would not have been thrown to wild beasts (which would have meant his death, as was the case with later martyrs).[30] (Note how his Roman citizenship protected him: Acts 16:37; 22:25).

Paul's point is still that all his suffering would have been without any divine reason or purpose, without any hope of reward, if there is no resurrection. In fact, life itself would be meaningless. They might as well follow the example of the unrepentant people of Isaiah's day who, seeing no hope for the future, said, "'Let us eat and drink, for tomorrow we die'" (see Isa. 22:13). That is, we might as well enjoy the brief time we have in this life.[31]

> **33Do not be misled: "Bad company corrupts good character." 34Come back to your senses as you ought, and stop sinning; for there are some who are ignorant of God—I say this to your shame.**

Those who were denying the resurrection were misleading the people. The Corinthian believers needed to disassociate themselves from these false teachers. We do not know who Paul was quoting when he said "'Bad company corrupts good character'";[32] however, the idea is found in Proverbs 22:24,25, which points out that those who associate with bad company risk learning their ways and becoming ensnared.

These false teachers were also encouraging sin, so often the case with false teachers, even today. The Corinthians should have had

---

[30]Donald S. Metz, "1 Corinthians," in *The Beacon Bible Commentary* (Kansas City, Mo.: Beacon Hill Press, 1968), 7:466; Fee, *First Epistle to the Corinthians*, 770–71.

[31]Horton, *Isaiah*, 169.

[32]It may have come from Menander's *Thais*, though it probably had become a popular saying. See Fee, *First Epistle to the Corinthians*, 773.

enough good sense to see that this was wrong and stop sinning. However, Paul recognized that the real reason they were associating with false teachers and falling into sin was that they were "ignorant of God"; they did not know Him in a real and personal way and thus lacked spiritual discernment (as the Gk. *agnōsian* indicates). Paul said this to put them to shame. Surely they had heard the truth and had the opportunity through Christ to enter into the depths of the knowledge of God (cf. Heb. 10:19–22).

4. The Resurrection Body 15:35–54

**35But someone may ask, "How are the dead raised?
With what kind of body will they come?" 36How foolish! What you sow does not come to life unless it dies.
37When you sow, you do not plant the body that will
be, but just a seed, perhaps of wheat or of something
else. 38But God gives it a body as he has determined,
and to each kind of seed he gives its own body.**

Paul anticipates another question. The question probably arose from the fact that the body that is buried decays: "To dust you will return" (Gen. 3:19). Because they didn't understand how the dead could be raised, they had given up the whole idea of resurrection. But death is not the end. Further, we need a body to be what God created us to be. To show continuity and to show that the new body will be greater than the one that dies, Paul compares sowing a seed in the ground: The outer hull dies, but the life that is within it springs up into a whole plant, just as God intended. Likewise, there will be a continuity between our present bodies and our new bodies, but our new bodies will be as much different from our present bodies as a wheat plant is from bare grain.

We can see a little of what this means "by comparing the raising of Lazarus, still wrapped in graveclothes (John 11:44), and the resurrection of Jesus, who rose up through the wrappings, leaving them behind (John 20:5–8)."[33] We will also be different from each other, just as the different varieties of plants are different from each other.

**39All flesh is not the same: Men have one kind of flesh,
animals have another, birds another and fish another.
40There are also heavenly bodies and there are earthly bodies; but the splendor of the heavenly bodies is**

---

[33]Horton, *Our Destiny*, 72.

one kind, and the splendor of the earthly bodies is
another. 41The sun has one kind of splendor, the moon
another and the stars another; and star differs from
star in splendor. 42So will it be with the resurrection of
the dead. The body that is sown is perishable, it is
raised imperishable; 43it is sown in dishonor, it is raised
in glory; it is sown in weakness, it is raised in power;
44ait is sown a natural body, it is raised a spiritual body.

To emphasize further that our resurrection bodies will be not only different but unique, so that there will still be tremendous variety in what our bodies will be like, Paul points to differences in the world of nature and in the brilliance of the objects in the sky. God loves variety. The sun, moon, stars, and the whole creation shows that. He will not change. There will be variety in our resurrection bodies.

All of our resurrection bodies will be glorious and powerful, however. Our new bodies will be "imperishable," not subject to the decay that begins usually with our teeth and gradually spreads to other bodily parts and functions. Our new bodies will be full of the glory we shall share with our Lord. Gone will be all "dishonor" (or humiliation) and all "weakness."

Though Jesus was not restored to the fullness of His former glory until after the Ascension, when He arose from the tomb His body was no longer torn, beaten, and bloody. "He arose healthy, able to walk to Emmaus. . . . This would imply also that babies and the elderly will not be resurrected in exactly the same form as when they died [cf. Phil. 3:20–21]. Each will indeed be the same individual, the same person, but in a form that will be mature and healthy."[34]

Another important contrast is the fact our present bodies are earthly, "natural" (Gk. *psuchikon*), and our new bodies will be "spiritual" (Gk. *pneumatikon*). This means "Holy Spirit dominated." It does not mean they will be "consisting of spirit" or that they will be immaterial, ethereal, or lacking in physical density. Jesus showed His disciples that His resurrection body was not ghostly, though it was of a different order, a supernatural order, suited for both earth and heaven. He was able to ascend into the heavens without benefit of a space suit. So our new bodies will be designed to fit not only the Millennium, but the eternal state.

---

[34]Ibid., 72,74.

44bIf there is a natural body, there is also a spiritual body. 45So it is written: "The first man Adam became a living being"; the last Adam, a life-giving spirit. 46The spiritual did not come first, but the natural, and after that the spiritual. 47The first man was of the dust of the earth, the second man from heaven.

Our present natural bodies have capacities, abilities, passions, and emotions adapted to the present earthly order. They have the same limits Adam had after the Fall. In contrast our resurrection bodies will have Spirit-given supernatural qualities of power and glory. We will still be finite beings, dependent wholly on God, but our bodies will be perfect instruments that will enable us to respond to His Spirit in new and wonderful ways.

The contrast is taken further: "'The first man Adam,'" became a living being when God breathed into him the breath of life (plural in the Heb., probably indicating Adam had both physical and spiritual life in the beginning); "the last Adam," Christ, then became "a life-giving Spirit." This "may mean He gives life from the spiritual realm where He is now reigning in glory."[35] It also refers to His giving life in the resurrection.

In God's plan the order calls for the natural to come first "and after that the spiritual." Adam was made of the dust of the earth. He did not have preexistence. Jesus came down from heaven and identified himself with humankind as a real man, but declared that He was indeed "from heaven" and then went back to heaven (John 3:13; 6:33,38).

48As was the earthly man, so are those who are of the earth; and as is the man from heaven, so also are those who are of heaven. 49And just as we have borne the likeness of the earthly man, so shall we bear the likeness of the man from heaven.

We have our present earthly bodies because of the earthly man, Adam, and as long as we are on this earth we are limited by the same physical limits. God created humankind in His own image and likeness. The image was still there after the Fall (Gen. 9:6). Adam had a son "in his own likeness, in his own image" (Gen. 5:3). So we have "borne the likeness of the earthly man," with bodies that, since the Fall, have shown the deterioration caused by sin. But the resurrected believers will bear the image of the man from heaven, and be "of heav-

[35]Horton, *What the Bible Says About the Holy Spirit*, 236.

en," like Jesus. He is the last Adam, and through Him we have a new start (cf. Eph. 4:24; Col. 3:10). "This does not suggest, even remotely, that believers will be glorified as Jesus was when He returned to His exalted position as very God in heaven . . . yet it suggests . . . that we will experience an ongoing glorification throughout eternity (cf. Phil. 3:21)."[36]

> **[50]I declare to you, brothers, that flesh and blood cannot inherit the kingdom of God, nor does the perishable inherit the imperishable.**

It is necessary for our bodies to be different, because our present bodies of flesh and blood are subject to corruption and cannot inherit the coming Kingdom. They are not suited for it. I heard someone tell of a vision where a sinner had a vision of heaven. He saw no barriers. The grass and the fruit trees looked beautiful. But when he tried to walk on the grass it was like walking on sword's points. When he tasted the fruit it burned his tongue like acid. He was not prepared to enjoy heaven and ended up in hell. Unless we are changed we cannot inherit and enjoy the coming Kingdom.

These perishable, decaying bodies are not prepared to enjoy the imperishable glories, beauties, and powers of heaven. Our bodies need to be changed.

> **[51]Listen, I tell you a mystery: We will not all sleep, but we will all be changed—[52]in a flash, in the twinkling of an eye, at the last trumpet. For the trumpet will sound, the dead will be raised imperishable, and we will be changed. [53]For the perishable must clothe itself with the imperishable, and the mortal with immortality. [54]When the perishable has been clothed with the imperishable, and the mortal with immortality, then the saying that is written will come true: "Death has been swallowed up in victory."**

To those who will inherit the Kingdom, Paul now tells "a mystery," something that had not been revealed previously. "We will not all sleep" (die); some believers will still be alive when Jesus comes again. "But we will all be changed" at the time of the resurrection and Rapture. The change will be sudden, accomplished in a split second

---

[36]Robert L. Brandt and Zenas J. Bicket, *The Spirit Helps Us Pray* (Springfield, Mo.: Logion Press, 1993), 198.

when "the last trumpet" sounds. It will also be final, for it will bring the perfection that God has promised.

"Paul uses the word 'last' here to indicate the close of the Church Age. He goes on to say, '*The* trumpet will sound.' He does not indicate that it is the last in a series. It sounds before the wrath of God falls on the earth. It summons the believers and is called the trumpet of God [1 Thess. 4:16]. At the same time, calling it 'last,' meaning the final one for this age, does not rule out the sequence of seven *angelic* trumpets coming later during the Tribulation."[37]

The raising of the dead as imperishable is a necessity, for how could a body subject to decay be immortal? Imperishability and immortality are both necessary for our new bodies to be suited to the eternal future God has prepared for us. Then, quoting from Isaiah, Paul celebrates the fact that death will be "'swallowed up in victory,'" for there will be no more death for believers. Isaiah prophesied this in a day when the Assyrians were causing many deaths and many tears (Isa. 25:8). Isaiah understood the promise as taking away all disgrace from God's people. "It implies the work of Christ and the restoration that will come when Jesus returns to establish his Millennial Kingdom."[38] It also means that the God who is Spirit (John 4:24; 1 Tim. 1:17) and who lives in "unapproachable light" (1 Tim. 6:16) will then be approachable in a new way.[39] In the New Jerusalem, also, the dwelling of God will be "'with men [redeemed people], and he will live with them. They will be his people, and God himself will be with them and be their God. He will wipe every tear from their eyes. There will be no more death or mourning or crying or pain, for the old order of things has passed away'" (Rev. 21:3–4).

5. Victory Through Christ 15:55–58

55"Where, O death, is your victory? Where, O death, is
your sting?" 56The sting of death is sin, and the power
of sin is the law. 57But thanks be to God! He gives us
the victory through our Lord Jesus Christ.

For the believer, though death is still "the last enemy" (15:26), it cannot be victorious over us.

37Horton, *Our Destiny,* 125.

38Horton, *Isaiah,* 191.

39Russell E. Joyner, "The One True God," in *Systematic Theology,* ed. Horton, 120–21.

> Jesus' victory over the devil has set free "those who all their lives were held in slavery by the fear of death" (Heb. 2:14–15). Death is no longer to be feared! "God has said 'Never will I leave you; never will I forsake you.' So we say with confidence, 'The Lord is my helper; I will not be afraid. What can man do to me?'" (Heb. 13:5–6). Death has [indeed] lost its sting![40]

The present tense of "gives . . . the victory" means He is giving the victory now and He will keep on giving the victory as we keep on trusting Him and fighting the battle against sin and evil. For the believer, "To live is Christ and to die is gain" (Phil. 1:21). Death can only mean a gain in our relationship with Christ: more of Him. Death will also bring a rest (literally, a "ceasing") of earthly labors and sufferings as we enter into glory (2 Cor. 4:17; cf. 2 Pet. 1:10–11; Rev. 14:13).

> **58Therefore, my dear brothers, stand firm. Let nothing move you. Always give yourselves fully to the work of the Lord, because you know that your labor in the Lord is not in vain.**

This hope and assurance of Christ's return and our resurrection to glory and power is something that should have a very practical effect in all of our lives. Paul's heart of love goes out to the Corinthians as dear brothers (and sisters). Because of this glorious truth he can encourage them to stand firm in the midst of all the persecutions, false doctrines, and everything else that was going on. They must let nothing move them from their firm stand for the Lord. But this does not mean standing idle. They will show they are standing firm for the truth not by arguing but by giving themselves fully to the work of the Lord. They can afford to do this for they know all their hard work is "not in vain," not useless, not without reward—nor will ours be.

Study questions for this section may be found in appendix B.

[40]Horton, *Our Destiny*, 41.

VIII. CONCLUDING INSTRUCTIONS 16:1–24

A. The Collection For God's People 16:1–4

[1]Now about the collection for God's people: Do what I told the Galatian churches to do. [2]On the first day of every week, each one of you should set aside a sum of money in keeping with his income, saving it up, so that when I come no collections will have to be made.

Paul now takes up the matter of a "collection for God's people," probably in answer to another question in their letter to him. Those of God's people he has in mind are the poor saints in Jerusalem (v. 3). He does not want the Corinthians to think he is putting all the responsibility on them or that he is asking them to do something other assemblies are not doing. So he tells them he is giving them the same instructions he gave to the Galatian believers. In his letter to the Galatians (probably written prior to this) Paul tells about his eagerness to "remember the poor" (Gal. 2:10). Acts 11:27–30 records Agabus predicting a famine and the people of Antioch responding by sending Paul and Barnabas with a gift. Now there was another opportunity to help the stricken saints in Jerusalem. So Paul tells the Corinthians what he told the Galatians.

What Paul directed them to do calls for the regular weekly setting aside of a sum of money as God has prospered them. The Greek is literally, "Let each of you by himself set aside storing up something in keeping with his gains." "By himself" means "at home."[1] That they are to do this specifically on "the first day" of the week seems significant. Other mentions of the first day, such as the gathering at Troas (Acts 20:27), taken together with Jesus' resurrection on the first day of the week, suggest that Christians met for worship on Sunday. There is evidence also that Jewish Christians went to the synagogues on Saturday to witness and then gathered for their own worship and encouragement on the first day of the week. Paul's point, however, is that by sav-

[1]Gordon D. Fee, *The First Epistle to the Corinthians* (Grand Rapids: Wm. B. Eerdmans, 1987), 813.

ing up weekly they would have more to give than if only one collection were to be made when he came to them.

> **3Then, when I arrive, I will give letters of introduction to the men you approve and send them with your gift to Jerusalem. 4If it seems advisable for me to go also, they will accompany me.**

Paul was very careful about finances. He wanted to be sure that the gift, which would be a heavy load of silver coins, was properly protected and taken care of, so that it would reach the poor in Jerusalem that it was intended for. Therefore, he wanted them to select more than one person—"men you approve" (and trust)—and send them with their gift (Gk. *charin,* "gracious gift") to Jerusalem.

Paul did not intend to pick up their offering and deliver it. Instead, he would write "letters of introduction." If they thought it "best," then he would "be glad to travel with them" (v. 4, *The Message*). Their presence would make the gift more personal and would help to make the Jewish Christians in Jerusalem appreciate not only the gift but fellowship with Gentile believers as well. Their presence would also make sure that Paul would be above suspicion with respect to whether he took all the credit for it or the Jerusalem believers got all that had been collected. (See Rom. 15:25; 2 Cor. 1:16, which show Paul did accompany them with the gift.)

B. Paul's Expectation To Come To Corinth 16:5–9

> **5After I go through Macedonia, I will come to you—for I will be going through Macedonia. 6Perhaps I will stay with you awhile, or even spend the winter, so that you can help me on my journey, wherever I go. 7I do not want to see you now and make only a passing visit; I hope to spend some time with you, if the Lord permits. 8But I will stay on at Ephesus until Pentecost, 9because a great door for effective work has opened to me, and there are many who oppose me.**

Paul was in Ephesus when he wrote this letter. He wanted the Corinthian believers to know that they still had considerable time to set aside money for the gift to the poor in Jerusalem, so he explains his travel plans. He would stay in Ephesus "until Pentecost," which was probably several months away.

See Acts 19:1 to 20:1 for Luke's description of the "great door for effective work" and the many adversaries that Paul speaks of here. God was doing many extraordinary miracles through Paul. A number who practiced sorcery believed and brought their scrolls (of magic formulas, etc.) and burned them. So many believed that the sale of silver images dropped off and the silversmiths stirred up a riot.

Paul expected to go next to Macedonia, where he would spend the summer and fall, and then go to Corinth to spend the winter. He wanted to spend considerable time with them and he hoped they would be able to help him on his journey. This probably did not mean he expected a money offering for himself (see 2 Cor. 11:7). More likely he hoped for traveling companions.

That he says "wherever I go" and "if the Lord permits" show that Paul was careful not to make plans that the Lord couldn't change. The Book of Acts shows how he was sensitive to the guidance and checks of the Holy Spirit and of Jesus (e.g., Acts 16:6–7).

C. Concern For Timothy And Apollos 16:10–12

10If Timothy comes, see to it that he has nothing to fear while he is with you, for he is carrying on the work of the Lord, just as I am. 11No one, then, should refuse to accept him. Send him on his way in peace so that he may return to me. I am expecting him along with the brothers.

The word "if" (Gk. *ean*) in this case means that Timothy should be expected to come, but the time is indefinite, so the idea is "whenever Timothy comes."[2] Paul had already said he was sending him (4:17), but it may be that Timothy would have some stops on the way.

What Paul wanted the Corinthian believers to do was to welcome Timothy, realize he was a faithful and true worker for the Lord, just as Paul was, and take care of him. It may be that Paul sensed there might be some opposition to Timothy, just as their letter showed there was some opposition to him.

The request to send Timothy on his way "in peace" means that they would consider his needs and well-being (see the Acts 19:22 mention

[2]William F. Arndt and F. Wilbur Gingrich, *A Greek-English Lexicon of the New Testament and Other Early Christian Literature* (Chicago: University of Chicago Press, 1957), 210.

of Erastus, who was probably the leader of those who went with him). Paul's mention of "the brothers" indicates some other believers would be traveling with Timothy, perhaps for encouragement and protection. Paul wanted them all to come back safely to him while he was still in Ephesus.

12Now about our brother Apollos: I strongly urged him to go to you with the brothers. He was quite unwilling to go now, but he will go when he has the opportunity.

Now Paul is taking up another question in response to his letter from the Corinthians, which may have asked him to encourage Apollos to come back to Corinth. In view of the discussion of 3:4–9, Paul considered him a fellow worker for the Lord, so Paul did urge him to go "with the brothers" (probably the three mentioned in verse 17). That Apollos was not willing to go at that time shows that Paul did not try to use "apostolic authority" to tell him what to do. We can be sure he was willing to let the Holy Spirit guide him. However, Apollos did say he would come when he had opportunity. He was not insensitive to the needs of an assembly where God had previously used him.

"Our brother Apollos" is better simply "Brother Apollos." Paul had good relationships and good fellowship with him in the Lord. There is nothing unscriptural about addressing fellow believers as Brother and Sister.[3]

D. A Challenge To Faith, Courage, And Love 16:13–14

13Be on your guard; stand firm in the faith; be men of courage; be strong. 14Do everything in love.

With five imperatives Paul sums up the exhortations he gave earlier in this letter. They needed to be alert, watchful, on guard against false teachers, the temptations of the world, and the old sinful nature. They needed to take a firm stand in the faith and for the faith, for the truth of the gospel. They needed to show manly characteristics such as bravery, or courage (the Greeks used this term even of old men whose hope in life was being renewed and of women who took a strong stand).

---

[3]Cf. Rom. 16:1 where a woman deacon of the church in Cenchrea is addressed as "sister Phoebe." (Paul calls her a *diakonon,* which in Gk. is masculine, referring to the office of deacon.)

They needed to grow strong. Paul later wrote that he prayed to the Father "that out of his glorious riches he may strengthen you with power through his Spirit in your inner being" (Eph. 3:16). But all this courage and firm stand for the gospel must not be displayed the same way the world takes its stand on issues (such as those so against abortion that they bomb abortion clinics or murder abortionists). We must "never let down from the holy calling of Christian life."[4] But everything must be done in love. "Everything" must be more than what was specifically dealt with in chapters 12 to 14. It must include their response to all the questions and problems that Paul dealt with earlier in this letter.

E. Recognition For The Household Of Stephanas 16:15–18

15You know that the household of Stephanas were the first converts in Achaia, and they have devoted themselves to the service of the saints. I urge you, brothers,
16to submit to such as these and to everyone who joins in the work, and labors at it.

Paul has a special concern that the Corinthian believers "submit to" the household of Stephanas, that is, yield to them voluntarily in love. He gives two reasons: They were the first (Gk. *aparchē,* "firstfruits") converts in Achaia (Greece). Paul personally baptized them (1:16). Calling them "firstfruits" indicates that they were the first of a harvest of souls (which they helped to bring in). Paul implies that they were leaders and remained true to the gospel in the midst of the false ideas and false teachings that were being circulated.

There was another reason for submitting to their leadership in love. The people of the household of Stephanas "devoted themselves" (Gk. *etaxan heautous,* "appointed themselves") to the service of the saints. That is, without anyone's urging, they gave themselves to serve the saints in a practical way. They and others like them who continually worked together with them—not just going along but working hard, laboring in the work of the Lord and in the ministry of the Word—deserved to have the Corinthian believers voluntarily subject themselves to them.

---

[4]Donald S. Metz, "1 Corinthians," in *The Beacon Bible Commentary* (Kansas City, Mo.: Beacon Hill Press, 1968), 7:480.

[17]I was glad when Stephanas, Fortunatus and Achaicus arrived, because they have supplied what was lacking from you. [18]For they refreshed my spirit and yours also. Such men deserve recognition.

Stephanas (Gk. "crowned") himself had arrived from Corinth along with Fortunatus (Lat., "fortunate" or "blessed") and Achaicus (Lat., from Gk. "belonging to Achaia"), two other believers, the Latin form of whose names possibly indicate that they were Roman citizens like Paul.[5]

They probably brought the letter mentioned in 7:1, and they ministered to Paul in some way, perhaps bringing gifts. The fact that they "supplied what was lacking" means they made up for their absence, or they represented the Corinthians in their absence. This seems to be a gentle rebuke to the Corinthians. These three brothers supplied the affection that Paul so desired from the Corinthians but which must have been lacking in their letter. The three "refreshed" Paul's spirit by their coming, and the fact he was blessed should refresh the spirits of the Corinthians as well. Paul commands the Corinthians to recognize them (the Gk. verb is imperative), something they well deserved.

F. Concluding Greetings And Benediction 16:19–24

[19]The churches in the province of Asia send you greetings. Aquila and Priscilla greet you warmly in the Lord, and so does the church that meets at their house. [20]All the brothers here send you greetings. Greet one another with a holy kiss. [21]I, Paul, write this greeting in my own hand.

Most, if not all, of the seven churches of the Roman province of Asia (in Asia Minor) mentioned in the Book of Revelation were founded while Paul was in Ephesus (Acts 19:10,26). He did not found them personally, for he "had discussions daily in the lecture hall of Tyrannus" (Acts 19:9), and he implies he was continually in Ephesus for the two years that he did this (Acts 20:18–21). But Ephesus was a center where people came from other parts of the province and were

---

[5]Fee suggests they were members of the household of Stephanas, possibly slaves or freedmen, perhaps coming on business to Ephesus, so the church asked them to carry the letter and be an official delegation representing them. Fee, *First Epistle to the Corinthians,* 831–32.

converted. Then they went back to their home cities and began winning people to the Lord, so assemblies were established. They all sent greetings to the Corinthian believers.

Then Paul included special greetings that were deep and warm from Priscilla and Aquila. Priscilla (also called Prisca) was a name used by upper-class Romans. In four of six mentions, she is named before her husband (see Acts 18:1–3,18,26; Rom. 16:3; 1 Cor. 16:19; 2 Tim. 4:19). Aquila (Lat. "eagle") was a slave name, probably a Jew captured by the Roman army in one of their military campaigns. Romans considered it a religious thing to set slaves free and set them up in business or with a trade. Apparently Aquila won his master's daughter to the Lord, was set free, married her, and they became tentmakers. In A.D. 49 the Roman Emperor Claudius made an edict banishing all Jews from Rome. The edict was lifted in A.D. 50, but Priscilla and Aquila remained in Corinth plying their tentmaking trade. When Paul first came to Corinth he worked and lived with them. When Paul left they went with him as far as Ephesus (Acts 18:18–19), where they instructed and encouraged Apollos (Acts 18:24–26). They were still there when Paul wrote this letter. Later, they returned to Rome (Rom. 16:3). But in Paul's second imprisonment they must have been with Timothy, probably at Ephesus (2 Tim. 4:19). As always, Priscilla and Aquila were active in their service for the Lord, so their home became a place where an assembly of believers met. This assembly sent greetings as well. So did all the other brothers and sisters in Ephesus.

In view of these warm greetings Paul urged the Corinthian believers to greet one another with "a holy kiss," a kiss that showed they shared the love of the Lord and respected one another as members of God's family. This was a common custom in those days. Later we read of men kissing men on the cheek and women kissing women as greetings in the Early Church.

Paul dictated this letter to a scribe (cf. Rom. 16:22). Some suggest this may have been Sosthenes. In any case, Paul added the final greeting in his own handwriting, as he always did (see Col. 4:18; 2 Thess. 3:17; Philem. 19). He drew attention to this because some had forged letters of false doctrines in his name (2 Thess. 2:2).

22If anyone does not love the Lord—a curse be on him. Come, O Lord!

Paul did want the people to love him, but he was much more concerned that they love the Lord. Anyone who does not love the Lord has broken the first and greatest commandment. When Jesus asked Peter, "'Do you love me?'" Jesus responded to his profession of love by saying, "'Feed my sheep'" (John 21:17). Jesus expected love to be followed by obedience to Him and ministry to others. Paul now adds that those who do not love the Lord with that kind of obedient response and ministry deserve a curse (Gk. *anathema*). This means they deserve to be under God's divine judgment (cf. Gal. 1:8–9; 2 Thess. 3:14).

Then Paul expresses a longing for the Lord to come, using the Aramaic expression *Marana Tha,* "Our Lord, come!" It was a phrase that the Early Church shouted again and again: It expressed loyalty to Jesus as their present Lord and it also expressed hope and desire of His future lordship, to be manifested fully when He comes back to earth (cf. Rev. 22:20).[6]

23The grace of the Lord Jesus be with you. 24My love to all of you in Christ Jesus. Amen.

As a final benediction Paul prays that the "grace of the Lord Jesus" would be with the Corinthians. He began this letter speaking of grace and peace. He concludes with grace. "Grace . . . is the single word that most fully expresses what God has done and will do for his people in Christ Jesus."[7] Then Paul adds an expression of his love for all the Corinthians who are "in Christ Jesus." He wants them to know that even though he had to give some strong rebukes and warnings in this letter, he still loved them and recognized them as being the body of Christ.

Study questions for this section may be found in appendix B.

---

[6]Stanley M. Horton, *Our Destiny: Biblical Teachings on the Last Things* (Springfield, Mo.: Logion Press, 1996), 76.

[7]Fee, *First Epistle to the Corinthians,* 839.

SECOND CORINTHIANS

INTRODUCTION TO SECOND CORINTHIANS

Timothy's visit to Corinth (1 Cor. 16:10) apparently did not have much effect on the situation that 1 Corinthians deals with. Paul was very concerned about their response to 1 Corinthians and to Timothy's visit. In addition, men who claimed to be apostles came to Corinth and denied Paul's apostleship and authority. At least one believer accepted their arguments and turned against Paul, urging others to do the same. This so troubled Paul that he left Ephesus and went to Corinth for a brief, unsuccessful, unpleasant visit (2 Cor. 2:1; 12:14; 13:1–2; see map, appendix A). He promised to return (2 Cor. 1:16), but decided to postpone his visit lest it cause even more pain (2 Cor. 1:23; 2:3; 13:2). Back in Ephesus he was in danger of his life (2 Cor. 1:8–11). He then wrote a severe letter "out of great distress and anguish of heart and with many tears" (2 Cor. 2:4; 7:8), sending it to them by Titus.

After the riot in Ephesus, he left for Macedonia (Acts 20:1) by way of Troas (2 Cor. 2:12–13). He was so disappointed when he did not meet Titus there as expected, that he did not minister there, even though he had opportunity. So he went on to Macedonia. There he did meet Titus, who encouraged him with news of repentance on the part of most of the believers in Corinth. The church as a whole were again responsive to Paul's apostolic authority and had dealt with the man who was causing the trouble (2 Cor. 2:5–11; 7:5–13).

Paul's joy over this news and his continuing concern over the troubles of the church prompted him to write 2 Corinthians, probably from Philippi (see 2 Cor. 11:9; Phil. 4:15). In it he defends his ministry and apostleship, encourages the Corinthians to finish raising funds for the poor saints in Jerusalem, and warns against false apostles. He also prepares them for his third visit. The letter was sent by Titus (8:6), probably in A.D. 56.[1]

Some scholars contend that 2 Corinthians 10 to 13 is the severe letter or part of it (see 2 Cor. 2:3–4; 7:8,12). However, there is much against this view. Nothing in these chapters suggests "anguish of heart

[1]For a discussion of the date see D. A. Carson, D. J. Moo, and Leon Morris, *An Introduction to the New Testament* (Grand Rapids: Zondervan Publishing House, 1992), 223–31.

and . . . many tears." Nor does the mention of a third visit fit. The severe letter was written to try to make a painful visit unnecessary. Second Corinthians 12:14–21 lets us know that even though the church as a whole had repented, some opposition still existed. Paul would deal with it on his third visit even if it had to be painful.[2]

[2]Everett F. Harrison, *Introduction to the New Testament* (Grand Rapids: Wm. B. Eerdmans, 1982), 285–86. Others suppose chapters 10 to 13 represent an even later letter. Victor Paul Furnish, *II Corinthians* (Garden City , N.Y.: Doubleday & Co., 1984), 35. Fisher points out that recent scholars are more likely to accept the unity of the epistle. Fred Fisher, *Commentary on 1 and 2 Corinthians* (Waco, Tex.: Word Books, 1975), 271. See also F. F. Bruce, *1 and 2 Corinthians* (Grand Rapids: Wm. B. Eerdmans, 1983), 166–70, 250. James Hernando also argues for the integrity of the book "in its present canonical form." James Hernando, "2 Corinthians," in *Full Life Bible Commentary* (Grand Rapids: Zondervan Publishing House, in press).

SECOND CORINTHIANS OUTLINE

I. Paul vindicates his conduct 1:1–2:11

- A. Grateful recognition of God's goodness 1:1–14
  - 1. Greetings 1:1–2
  - 2. Encouragement in suffering 1:3–11
    - a) Shared comfort and suffering 1:3–7
    - b) Deliverance from deadly peril 1:8–11
  - 3. Paul's holy, sincere conduct 1:12–14
- B. Paul's plan to visit Corinth 1:15–2:4
  - 1. Two visits were planned 1:15–22
    - a) Paul's visit postponed 1:15–17
    - b) Paul's claim to be consistent 1:18–22
  - 2. Paul's reason for not coming 1:23–2:4
    - a. Good reasons 1:23–24
    - b. Paul's love for the Corinthians 2:1–4
- C. Forgiveness for one who has caused grief 2:5–11

II. Paul's ministry under the new covenant 2:12–4:18

- A. An open door at Troas 2:12–13
- B. Led and sent by God 2:14–17
- C. A glorious ministry of the Spirit 3:1–18
  - 1. A ministry of power and life 3:1–6
  - 2 A ministry better than that of the Law 3:7–18
- D. An honest, Christ-centered ministry 4:1–18
  - 1. A genuine ministry 4:1–2
  - 2. An effective ministry 4:3–15
  - 3. A ministry sustained by hope 4:16–18

III. Paul's goals 5:1–6:13

- A. To please the Lord 5:1–15
  - 1. The Spirit guarantees a new body 5:1–5

2. Living by faith 5:6–8
3. The judgment seat of Christ 5:9–10
4. Motivated by fear and love 5:11–15

B. A ministry of reconciliation 5:16–6:13
1. A new creation 5:16–17
2. Christ's ambassadors 5:18–21
3. Now is the day of salvation 6:1–2
4. Paul's sufferings 6:3–10
5. Asking for a loving response 6:11–13

IV. APPEALING TO THE CORINTHIANS 6:14–7:16

A. Do not be partners with unbelievers 6:14–7:1
1. A call for separation 6:14–18
2. Inward holiness needed 7:1

B. Encouragement brought by Titus 7:2–16
1. Paul's right conduct 7:2–4
2. Paul in Macedonia 7:5–7
3. The effect of Paul's letter 7:8–13a
4. Titus's happiness 7:13b–16

V. ENCOURAGEMENT TO GIVE GENEROUSLY 8:1 TO 9:15

A. The example of the Macedonian churches 8:1–7
1. Macedonian generosity 8:1–5
2. Titus urged to encourage generosity 8:6–7

B. Jesus' example 8:8–9

C. Finish the work 8:10–15

D. The character of Titus and his companions 8:16–24

E. A generous gift was promised 9:1–5

F. Sowing and reaping 9:6–15

VI. PAUL'S APOSTOLIC OFFICE AND AUTHORITY 10:1–13:14

A. Paul's authority will be exercised 10:1–6

B. Paul's conduct as an apostle 10:7–11

C. Paul's boasting 10:12–12:10

1. The limits on Paul's boasting 10:12–18
2. Paul's exposes false apostles 11:1–4
3. Paul's apostolic status 11:5–6
4. Paul's refusal to accept pay 11:7–12
5. False apostles denounced 11:13–15
6. Paul's suffering 11:16–18
7. Paul compares himself with his opponents at Corinth 11:19–33
8. Paul's vision of paradise 12:1–6
9. Paul's thorn in the flesh 12:7–10

D. Paul's unselfish concern for the Corinthians 12:11–21

E. A renewed warning 13:1–10

F. Concluding greeting 13:11–14

I. PAUL VINDICATES HIS CONDUCT 1:1–2:11

A. Grateful Recognition Of God's Goodness 1:1–14

1. GREETINGS 1:1–2

1Paul, an apostle of Christ Jesus by the will of God, and Timothy our brother, To the church of God in Corinth, together with all the saints throughout Achaia: 2Grace and peace to you from God our Father and the Lord Jesus Christ.

In this second letter to the assembly of God in Corinth Paul again identifies himself as an apostle, "a sent one" of Jesus the Messiah: God's anointed Prophet, Priest, and King. Jesus himself sent Paul as His representative, His ambassador, by "the will of God," not his own. Paul implies that knowing God's will puts a great responsibility on believers to obey God and carry out His will. "Timothy our brother" (Gk. *Timotheos, ho adelphos,* "Timothy the brother"), or, as we would say, "Brother Timothy" is with him. As a fellow believer, a brother in the family of God, a coworker (but not an apostle), he joins Paul in greeting the assembly. Paul, however, was the sole writer of the letter.

He wanted it read not only by the church (Gk. *ekklēsia,* "assembly of citizens") in Corinth but by all the saints (Gk. *hagiois,* i.e., the holy believers)[1] in all the assemblies in Achaia, that is, in Greece. However, his attention in this letter is focused on the situation in the Corinthian assembly, God's *ekklēsia* in Corinth.

He combines the Gentile greeting of "grace to you" with the Jewish greeting of "peace to you." But we can be sure he had in mind the grace (unmerited favor and graciousness) of God that is ours through Jesus and the peace (including health and well-being) of God that Jesus gives. God the Father and Jesus as Lord join together on an equal plane as the givers. The believers are in a new relationship with God and Christ as they confess Jesus as Lord (cf. John 20:28; Acts 10:36;

---

[1]"Saint" in the NT never means someone is perfect or superior or a miracle worker. It simply means one belongs to the Lord, has begun a new life in Christ, and is headed in the right direction as one worships and serves Him (see Lev. 20:7–8;. Ezra 8:28; Jer. 2:3 for the OT background).

Rom 10:9,12; 1 Cor. 12:3; Phil. 2:11; Rev. 17:14; 19:16). Grace then brings peace, for their can be no real peace apart from the grace of God.[2]

2. Encouragement In Suffering 1:3–11

a) Shared Comfort And Suffering 1:3–7

[3]Praise be to the God and Father of our Lord Jesus Christ, the Father of compassion and the God of all comfort, [4]who comforts us in all our troubles, so that we can comfort those in any trouble with the comfort we ourselves have received from God.

Paul draws attention first to God, giving praise to Him while recognizing that Jesus humbled himself in his incarnation and called Him God, as well as Father.[3] Since Paul was very disturbed when he did not find Titus in Troas (2:13), he needed comfort, that is, encouragement. The word "comfort" occurs ten times in verses 3–7 (a total of twenty-nine times in 2 Cor.). All are from the Greek root *parakaleō,* which has the idea of help and encouragement.[4] God is the source and giver of every kind of encouragement and help (cf. Ps. 103:2–5,13).

God's encouragement comes first as we recognize that God is the Father of Jesus who is both the Christ (Messiah, "Anointed One") and our Lord and Master. This recognition should remind us that God's love sent Jesus to die for us and that Jesus is now our risen, ascended Lord, the Anointed King who will come again and fulfill all of God's plan. The love that sent Jesus to die for us while we were still sinners (Rom. 5:8,10) shows that God is also the Father who is full of compassion,[5] as well as the Father (and constant source) of all kinds of help and encouragement. We can depend on Him in all our troubles, including whatever pressures, suffering, mental anguish, difficulties, even persecutions, that come our way. But God does not comfort us

---

[2]R. C. H. Lenski, *The Interpretation of St. Paul's First and Second Epistles to the Corinthians* (Minneapolis: Augsburg Publishing House, 1963), 810.

[3]In the Gospels when Jesus referred to God as His Father, He never included anyone else. When He told His disciples to pray "'Our Father'" (Matt. 6:9), He did not include himself. God the Father is the Father of Jesus in a unique, special way.

[4]The "Comforter" (Gk. *paraklētos*) as a title of the Holy Spirit is from the same root.

[5]As the Gk. plural ("mercies," v. 3, KJV) indicates.

to make us comfortable, or encourage us just to make us feel good.

Paul suffered a great deal (11:16–29; 12:10), but he was always ready to encourage others. Everyone around us today has troubles, pressures, and difficulties. Christians in many parts of the world suffer severe persecution. God helps and encourages us so we can help and encourage others. He wants us to become channels of what we receive from Him to other believers who so desperately need help. We can do this through prayer, the gifts of the Spirit, and by giving practical help wherever possible. God does not intend for us to keep to ourselves anything we receive from Him. Just as God stands beside us to encourage us even in severe testing, so we should stand beside others who are being tested.

5For just as the sufferings of Christ flow over into our
lives, so also through Christ our comfort overflows. 6If
we are distressed, it is for your comfort and salvation;
if we are comforted, it is for your comfort, which pro-
duces in you patient endurance of the same sufferings
we suffer. 7And our hope for you is firm, because we
know that just as you share in our sufferings, so also
you share in our comfort.

Paul now applies this to his relationship with the assembly of believers in Corinth. Christ's sufferings ended when He said, "'It is finished'" (John 19:30). But the same attitudes that sent Jesus to the cross caused unbelievers and false believers to bring an overflow of suffering to Paul and his associates not only in Corinth but also in the Roman province of Asia (vv. 8–9). Thus he could speak of "the fellowship of sharing in his [Christ's] sufferings" (Phil. 3:10; cf. John 15:20–21; Acts 14:22; Rom. 8:17–18, 36; Col. 1:24). The sufferings, however, were balanced by the overflowing comfort and encouragement that comes through Christ.

Paul and his company endured all this suffering and distress in order to win people to Christ and establish the church in Corinth. Now he wants them to be encouraged by the gospel and receive the salvation that includes not only being born again but being saved from the coming wrath of God, a salvation that includes all the promises of God and our eternal destiny of blessing and joy with Him. The comfort Paul received he passed on to them so they could endure patiently and steadfastly, in obedient faith, the same sufferings that he and his company suffered. The Corinthians too would suffer as they took their stand for Christ and spread the gospel.

First Corinthians shows Paul knew their weaknesses, but now he expresses a firm, confident hope for them: firm because behind it is the faithfulness and compassion of God. They share in Paul's sufferings in that they are serving Christ in the midst of opposition. But they also share in the same comfort and encouragement that comes through Christ. Paul wants them to see how close their ties are, both to him and to Christ. We too are to be partners with the whole body of Christ in both Christ's sufferings and in His comfort or encouragement. He helps us, not by removing the troubles and afflictions, but by enabling us to endure them.

b) Deliverance From Deadly Peril 1:8–11

**8We do not want you to be uninformed, brothers,
about the hardships we suffered in the province of
Asia. We were under great pressure, far beyond our
ability to endure, so that we despaired even of life.
9Indeed, in our hearts we felt the sentence of death.
But this happened that we might not rely on ourselves
but on God, who raises the dead.**

To emphasize the theme of comfort and encouragement in the midst of troubles, Paul has some personal information he wants to inject here for the congregation at Corinth. He suffered in Corinth. He suffered even more intensely in the province of Asia, which must mean especially in Ephesus. Acts 19:1 to 20:1 tells of his ministry there: After three months, some members of the synagogue obstinately "refused to believe and publicly maligned the Way" (Acts 19:9). These unbelievers must have continued to put Paul under pressure. Then after two years of daily discussions in the lecture hall of Tyrannus and many extraordinary miracles, the silversmiths stirred a riot because the sale of their silver images of the goddess Artemis was falling off. Paul's life, however, was not threatened on that occasion. Some believe there were other threats and pressures that the Book of Acts does not tell us about.[6] Perhaps Paul was even imprisoned for a time.[7] Paul gives no details, but it is clear he was in real danger, such

---

[6]J. J. Lias, *The Second Epistle to the Corinthians* (Cambridge, England: University Press, 1897), 28.

[7]Victor Paul Furnish, *II Corinthians* (Garden City, N.Y.: Doubleday & Company, 1984), 123.

danger that he really felt like a prisoner under "the sentence of death."[8] What Paul wanted the Corinthians to know was that God allows things to happen that bring you to the end of yourselves in order to teach you to rely on God. The God who raises the dead will not forsake us. He still loves us and wants us to trust in Him.

[10]He has delivered us from such a deadly peril, and he will deliver us. On him we have set our hope that he will continue to deliver us, [11]as you help us by your prayers. Then many will give thanks on our behalf for the gracious favor granted us in answer to the prayers of many.

Paul did trust in God and God delivered him from whatever the situation was that caused despair (v.8). This deliverance renewed his courage to go on in spite of opposition and danger. He set his hope on God, believing that God would continue to deliver him and his evangelistic party in their present circumstances and also in the future. The prayers of the Corinthians would also have a part. Their prayers would be a help, bringing a manifestation of God's gracious favor that many would be thankful for. Notice the repetition of the word "many." The prayers of many will cause many to give thanks to God for His goodness. (They knew Paul also prayed for them [cf. Phil. 1:3–6]). Paul was concerned that the Corinthians recognize that the work of God needs to involve the body of believers as a whole, not only those in a local church or a city.

3. Paul's Holy, Sincere Conduct 1:12–14

[12]Now this is our boast: Our conscience testifies that we have conducted ourselves in the world, and especially in our relations with you, in the holiness and sincerity that are from God. We have done so not according to worldly wisdom but according to God's grace.

Paul's chief reason for writing this letter was to defend his ministry from false charges. Though Titus brought an encouraging report about the repentant attitude of the majority of the Corinthian believers, some still criticized Paul and his ministry severely. Paul felt he must defend his ministry lest these unfounded accusations hinder the spread of the gospel.

---

[8]R. P. C. Hanson, *The Second Epistle to the Corinthians: Christ and Controversy* (London: SCM Press, 1967), 28.

Paul had good reason for boasting. Ordinarily the Bible speaks of boasting as a sin because it comes from false pride. But Paul proceeds to boast, not because of pride or self-exaltation, but with a heart full of praise to God as well as with concern for the church and for the cause of Christ (cf. 10:17; 1 Cor 15:10). In good conscience he could say that his conduct, everything he did, reflected single-minded dedication to God (true holiness) and a godly sincerity that was transparent. Never did he depend on fleshly wisdom (the wisdom of unregenerate people, worldly philosophers, cf. 1 Cor. 2:1–5). He showed this holiness and sincerity "in the world," that is, outside the church, and even more abundantly toward the Corinthians in the church.

13For we do not write you anything you cannot read or understand. And I hope that, 14as you have understood us in part, you will come to understand fully that you can boast of us just as we will boast of you in the day of the Lord Jesus.

Paul next defends his letters. Some were criticizing him—saying that he did not mean what he wrote, suggesting that possibly he had some ulterior motive. He responds with a word play. What they read (Gk. *anaginōskete*) is the same thing that they should understand (Gk. *epiginōskete*), or acknowledge, as exactly what he meant. He was sincere and his motives transparent.

Some only acknowledged Paul in part, that is, not fully recognizing his apostolic authority. Paul hoped that they would finally recognize him and his associates again just as they did when he first came to Corinth and established the church. They boasted in the sense of glorifying God for Paul and his associates. Let them come again to that place; for none of them had changed. Paul expected the Corinthians not to change in their relationship to Christ; he would be able to glorify God because of them in the day when Jesus comes again and they are all joined together in the company of the redeemed (cf. Phil. 4:1; 1 Thess. 2:19–20).

B. Paul's Plan To Visit Corinth 1:15–2:4

1. Two Visits Were Planned 1:15–22

a) Paul's Visit Postponed 1:15–17

15Because I was confident of this, I planned to visit you first so that you might benefit twice. 16I planned to visit you on my way to Macedonia and to come back to

you from Macedonia, and then to have you send me
on my way to Judea. 17When I planned this, did I do it
lightly? Or do I make my plans in a worldly manner so
that in the same breath I say, "Yes, yes" and "No, no"?

Because Paul was confident of their glorifying God because of him, he had planned (or wished, the Gk. does not mean a fixed decision[9]) to visit them so they might have two opportunities for spiritual benefit from his ministry (cf. Rom. 1:11–12). However, some Corinthians had a problem because he had not followed the itinerary he had announced in his first letter (1 Cor. 4:19; 16:5–6). Some were denouncing Paul for this even though he had made his plans with the full intention of carrying them out. He was not saying yes and meaning no, as so many worldly people do. He had already visited them twice, once to evangelize the city and establish the church, once for a short, painful visit (2:1). This time he hoped for a double benefit (Gk. *charin,* "grace"), or occasion for joy (Gk. *charan,* as some ancient authorities read). However, when he met Titus and heard how the Corinthian believers had changed their attitude (7:6–13), he changed his mind and postponed the visit.

b) Paul's Claim To Be Consistent 1:18–22

18But as surely as God is faithful, our message to you is
not "Yes" and "No." 19For the Son of God, Jesus Christ,
who was preached among you by me and Silas and
Timothy, was not "Yes" and "No," but in him it has
always been "Yes." 20For no matter how many promises
God has made, they are "Yes" in Christ. And so through
him the "Amen" is spoken by us to the glory of God.

Paul's concern was not over his itinerary, but over the gospel. Some were not only criticizing his change in plans, they were saying that Paul was not dependable and therefore they could not depend on the gospel he preached. So Paul declares that there was no contingency or uncertainty in the message, for behind the message is the faithfulness of God.[10] God has made many promises. They have their enduring "'Yes' in Christ." That is, Christ has put the "'yes'" to all of them for all time. Paul, Silas, and Timothy put the "'amen'" (Heb. "truly") to

---

[9]Philip Edgcumbe Hughes, *Paul's Second Epistle to the Corinthians* (Grand Rapids: Wm. B. Eerdmans, 1973), 50.

[10]"As God is faithful" is not an oath as some take it to be. It is simply a recognition of the nature of God.

them as they proclaimed the glory of God on their first visit to Corinth (Acts 18:1–18). Truly, God receives glory when we see His promises fulfilled.

> **[21]Now it is God who makes both us and you stand firm in Christ. He anointed us, [22]set his seal of ownership on us, and put his Spirit in our hearts as a deposit, guaranteeing what is to come.**

To further defend his integrity Paul uses four participles that describe God's faithfulness: God is the one who (1) makes us stand firm in Christ, (2) anoints us, (3) seals us, and (4) gives us His Spirit as a deposit. Paul did not claim that his sincerity and reliability were due to anything in himself (see also v. 12). Nor did he put the Corinthian believers on a different level. The power and ability to stand firm in Christ (Gk. *eis Christon,* "into Christ," a progressive experience) came to all from God himself. Not only are the promises ours through Christ; God, by His Spirit, has done a threefold work in us that makes us stand firm in Christ.[11] The anointing, the seal of ownership, and His Spirit in our hearts as a deposit all describe what takes place at the baptism in the Holy Spirit. Anointing refers to receiving the same Spirit that Jesus (the Messiah, "Anointed One") received after His baptism (cf. Isa. 61:1–2; Luke 3:22; 4:18–21).[12] The seal was an external mark of identification, or sign of ownership, of a purchased possession. On the Day of Pentecost and throughout the Book of Acts the seal, the external sign, was speaking in other tongues.[13] The deposit refers to the Spirit and his gifts as a first installment of what we shall have in its fullness when Jesus comes again (see Eph. 1:13–14, where

---

[11]The three aorist tenses in Gk. indicate the distinct, specific action of the Holy Spirit at a definite time in their experience. Frank G. Carter, "II Corinthians," in *The Beacon Bible Commentary* (Kansas City, Mo.: Beacon Hill Press, 1968), 7:511. They not only make us stand firm, they confirm us in Christ. See James Hernando, "2 Corinthians," in *Full Life Bible Commentary* (Grand Rapids: Zondervan Publishing House, in press). Hernando prefers to see the confirming and the putting the Spirit as a deposit or pledge to refer to God's saving activity.

[12]OT prophets, priests, and kings were anointed with special oil, which was a type, representing the Spirit's work in preparing them for service (e.g., 1 Sam. 16:1,13).

[13]See Assemblies of God, "The Initial Physical Evidence of the Baptism in the Holy Spirit," in *Where We Stand* (Springfield, Mo.: Gospel Publishing House, 1990), 145–55.

the sealing comes after the believing as a distinct act; see also Rom. 8:23; 1 Pet. 1:4–5).[14]

2. Paul's Reason For Not Coming 1:23–2:4

a) Good reasons 1:23–24

[23]I call God as my witness that it was in order to spare you that I did not return to Corinth. [24]Not that we lord it over your faith, but we work with you for your joy, because it is by faith you stand firm.

Paul now returns to his reason for not visiting Corinth as he had planned to. He calls on God as the witness to his sincerity. Figuratively, he could have come "with a whip" (1 Cor. 4:21), but he wanted to spare them that. He wanted them to understand his love and concern for them. His purpose was not to act like a dictator, lording it over their faith. Only one is our Lord, the Apostle and High Priest whom we confess (Heb. 3:1), the Shepherd and Overseer of our souls (1 Pet. 2:25). Jesus warned His disciples not to be like tyrants who like to lord it over people and show their power. He also set the example by His humble service (Luke 22:25–27). So Paul wanted to help the Corinthians, working with them to make them rejoice in their faith. He wanted them to stand firm by faith, not only by their faith in God, but by "the faith,"[15] the truth, the gospel—which, in fact, they were already doing.

b) Paul's Love For The Corinthians 2:1–4

[1]So I made up my mind that I would not make another painful visit to you. [2]For if I grieve you, who is left to make me glad but you whom I have grieved?

Paul deals further with his change of plans. He did not make a snap judgment. In chapter 1:15 he spoke of his wish to come. Now he explains that he made up his mind. The Greek implies he considered the entire situation carefully, as a judge would, and decided another visit at that point would be painful to him and to the Corinthians. It would not be for their best interests. Their deplorable conditions would only grieve him and he would have to cause grief to them by

[14]See Stanley M. Horton, *What the Bible Says About the Holy Spirit* (Springfield, Mo.: Gospel Publishing House, 1976), 236–39.

[15]The Gk. has the article: "the."

censuring them. This would deprive him of the joy he felt when he saw people come to Christ and serve Him. So he visited the Macedonian churches in order to delay his arrival at Corinth. He knew he had grieved them. He wanted them to make him glad. That is, he was expecting them to change before he came again. He loved them and his happiness depended on them. Their joy would be his joy (cf. Phil. 2:17–18).

**[3]I wrote as I did so that when I came I should not be
distressed by those who ought to make me rejoice. I
had confidence in all of you, that you would all share
my joy. [4]For I wrote you out of great distress and
anguish of heart and with many tears, not to grieve
you but to let you know the depth of my love for you.**

Paul had written a painful letter, not to hurt the Corinthians but to help them cause him to rejoice instead of being distressed.[16] Then they would share in his joy. The circumstances at the Corinthian church brought Paul "distress and anguish of heart." He had shed many tears writing a painful letter to them. He had written not to hurt them but to help them, which would cause him to rejoice instead of being distressed. Then they would share in his joy. Though he had to be severe in what he had written, he had done so out of a heart of love (Gk. *agapē,* a high, holy, selfless love), and he wanted them to know that. Because he loved them, he rebuked them severely in order to restore them to faith and to a right relation to Christ and the gospel. We can be sure also that he wanted the Spirit to lead them and restore their joy.

C. Forgiveness For One Who Has Caused Grief 2:5–11

**[5]If anyone has caused grief, he has not so much griev-
ed me as he has grieved all of you, to some extent—
not to put it too severely. [6]The punishment inflicted on
him by the majority is sufficient for him. [7]Now instead,
you ought to forgive and comfort him, so that he will
not be overwhelmed by excessive sorrow. [8]I urge you,
therefore, to reaffirm your love for him.**

[16]Lenski contends that the painful letter was 1 Corinthians. Most scholars believe it was a letter written after 1 Corinthians and then lost. R. C. H. Lenski, *The Interpretation of St. Paul's First and Second Epistles to the Corinthians* (Minneapolis: Augsburg Publishing House, 1963), 874.

Most older commentators believe the person who had "caused grief" was the man who was involved immorally with his stepmother (1 Cor. 5:1).[17] However, it seems that Paul is referring to someone who had insulted him (11:4,20), probably a ringleader who opposed him, causing him and the congregation distress.[18]

It seems that the majority in the Corinthian assembly were grieved by what this person did and responded to Paul's urging that the person be disciplined. We are not told how the Corinthians disciplined him, but Paul said they had done enough. Now they needed to forgive, treat him kindly, and encourage him, reaffirming him publicly. The person must have repented, but felt so guilty he was in danger of suffering from severe depression. He also felt cut off from the community of believers. He needed to know they still loved him. Paul told the Galatians earlier, "Brothers, if someone is caught in a sin, you who are spiritual should restore him gently" (Gal. 6:1). Paul was always more concerned about restoration than about punishment. We too must remember that no matter what sin people commit they can be sure Jesus will forgive (1 John 1:7,9). We can always look to "Jesus Christ, the Righteous One"—He "who speaks to the Father in our defense" (1 John 2:1).

9The reason I wrote you was to see if you would stand the test and be obedient in everything. 10If you forgive anyone, I also forgive him. And what I have forgiven—if there was anything to forgive—I have forgiven in the sight of Christ for your sake, 11in order that Satan might not outwit us. For we are not unaware of his schemes.

"I wrote you" probably means "I have just written you" (in this present letter).[19] He was expecting them to stand the test and be obedient. He was expecting them to take the initiative and forgive those who had hurt Paul and hurt them.

Paul was ready to forgive whatever needed forgiveness as well. He was aware that whatever he did was in the sight of Christ, and that

[17]Philip Edgcumbe Hughes, *Paul's Second Epistle to the Corinthians* (Grand Rapids: Wm. B. Eerdmans, 1973), 63–65.

[18]Frank G. Carter, "II Corinthians," in *The Beacon Bible Commentary* (Kansas City, Mo.: Beacon Hill Press, 1968), 7:514–15. Victor Paul Furnish, *II Corinthians* (Garden City, N.Y.: Doubleday & Co., 1984), 163–68.

[19]Fred Fisher, *Commentary on 1 and 2 Corinthians* (Waco, Tex.: Word Books, 1975), 301. Others disagree, referring this to the previous letter. Hughes, *Second Corinthians,* 69–70.

Christ would see and be pleased when he forgave. For Christ is always ready to forgive (1 John 1:7,9).

Paul (and the Corinthian believers [v. 11]) knew too that Satan as the "adversary" (1 Pet. 5:8, KJV) is always looking for ways to outwit believers. One way he outwits us is to take advantage of an unforgiving spirit. Another way is to drive a person who feels guilt and sorrow away from the Lord when God's people do not seek to restore and encourage him. Forgiveness and restoration would make Satan's schemes ineffective.[20]

Study questions for this section may be found in appendix B.

II. PAUL'S MINISTRY UNDER THE NEW COVENANT 2:12–4:18

A. An Open Door At Troas 2:12–13

12Now when I went to Troas to preach the gospel of
Christ and found that the Lord had opened a door for
me, 13I still had no peace of mind, because I did not
find my brother Titus there. So I said good-by to them
and went on to Macedonia.

Paul now returns to the subject of his change in plans. He wanted the Corinthian believers to know that the change was not caused by any lack of love for them. He went to Troas with one purpose: to preach the good news about Jesus Christ. The Lord had opened a door of opportunity for him to do so, and it continued to be open (as the Gk. perfect tense indicates). This suggests there was good response to the gospel—that people were saved and the church was established. But Paul also expected to find Titus there. When he didn't, he had no peace of mind (Gk. *anesin,* "release" or "freedom" in his own spirit) to stay at Troas. This was because of his concern for the assembly in Corinth. So he said good-bye to the believers in Troas and went to Macedonia, still intending to go toward Corinth.

Paul interrupts his thought here and continues in 7:5, where he takes up with what happened when he arrived in Macedonia.

[20]James Hernando, "2 Corinthians," in *Full Life Bible Commentary* (Grand Rapids: Zondervan Publishing House, in press).

B. Led And Sent By God 2:14–17

[14]But thanks be to God, who always leads us in triumphal procession in Christ and through us spreads everywhere the fragrance of the knowledge of him. [15]For we are to God the aroma of Christ among those who are being saved and those who are perishing. [16]To the one we are the smell of death; to the other, the fragrance of life. And who is equal to such a task?

Paul digresses to defend his ministry (including that of his associates). Even though Paul did not have a vision or direct word from God to go to Macedonia, as he did on his previous (second) journey (Acts16:9,10), he knew God was always leading him and his company and he gives God thanks for this.

Some writers interpret the "triumphal procession" as headed by the resurrected, ascended Christ, victoriously leading those taken captive by the triumph of His redemption and giving them as gifts to the Church (Eph. 4:7–8,10–13).[1]

The idea of a triumphal procession does not mean Paul was feeling triumphant, however. Scott Hafemann considers 2:14 to 3:3 as "part of the 'theological heart'" of 2 Corinthians.[2] He interprets "leads us in triumphal procession" (Gk. *thriambeuonti*) to describe a Roman general, in a triumphal procession of his troops, putting his conquered enemies on display as he leads them to their death. As a former enemy of Christ, Paul was being led by Jesus to death.[3] In leading him, Christ's purpose was to reveal himself. Suffering and weakness were essential to God's plan for spreading the gospel.[4] Thus, Paul was being crushed as rose petals might be crushed in order to bring out their fragrance. So all Paul's troubles only made it possible for him to show the "fragrance of the knowledge of [Christ]" (which we find now in the Bible) to everyone everywhere he went. He became a sweet fragrance of Christ directed to God, among both those "being saved" and those "perishing," lost, headed for eternal death. That is, Paul gave the same message to all, but they had to make a choice. To some it became an

---

[1]James Hernando, "2 Corinthians," in *Full Life Bible Commentary* (Grand Rapids: Zondervan Publishing House, in press).

[2]Scott J. Hafemann, *Suffering and Ministry in the Spirit: Paul's Defense of His Ministry in II Corinthians 2:14—3:3* (Grand Rapids: Wm. B. Eerdmans, 1990), 1–2.

[3]Ibid. 7–34.

[4]Ibid., 62.

aroma of life that brought life, to others an aroma of death that condemned to eternal death.

By asking "who is equal to such a task," Paul meant that these results did not come because of his sufficiency, competency, qualifications, or worthiness. No one can produce such results because of who or what they are. They come because of who Christ is. When we are doing His work, our sufficiency is of God.

17Unlike so many, we do not peddle the word of God for profit. On the contrary, in Christ we speak before God with sincerity, like men sent from God.

Paul proclaimed his sincerity and purity of motives further by comparing himself and his fellow workers with those who use the Word of God as a means of "profit," or gain for themselves. They are like peddlers who put good wheat on top of a sack of chicken feed or water down the milk they are selling. That does not mean preachers should not be paid well (see 1 Tim. 5:17–18 where "honor" includes the idea of "honorarium"). But some were like Greek teachers who took pride in having important and wealthy people as their disciples. Those who make it their chief concern to enrich themselves and cheapen or corrupt the message to attract people to themselves deserve to be condemned.[5]

In contrast, Paul, in a right relationship to Christ and in the sight of God, spoke Spirit-inspired truth and acted with godly sincerity and pure motives. His whole ministry was truly apostolic.

C. A Glorious Ministry Of The Spirit 3:1–18

1. A Ministry Of Power And Life 3:1–6

1Are we beginning to commend ourselves again? Or do we need, like some people, letters of recommendation to you or from you? 2You yourselves are our letter, written on our hearts, known and read by everybody. 3You show that you are a letter from Christ, the result of our ministry, written not with ink but with the Spirit of the living God, not on tablets of stone but on tablets of human hearts.

[5]Ibid., 124. See also Jerry L. Sumney, *Identifying Paul's Opponents* (Sheffield, England: Journal for the Study of the New Testament Press, 1990), 132.

Beginning here and carrying on through 6:10, Paul again deals with those who oppose him and doubt his credentials. His concern is not for himself, but for the gospel he preached and for the assurance of those who believed it. Paul had written on this subject before (1 Cor. 4 and possibly in the painful letter) and would write more.

Some were accusing him of praising or exalting himself. Some of his opponents were intruders who came with letters of recommendation and wanted letters of recommendation when they left. This was a common custom. But it is implied that the letters they came with were unreliable. Even so, some Corinthians apparently were then asking Paul for letters of recommendation that would prove his apostleship. Paul did use letters of recommendation (see Rom. 16:1–2; 1 Cor. 16:10–11; Col. 4:10). However, he is incredulous that the Corinthians should ask this of him. He did not need letters of recommendation either to the Corinthians (that is, from the elders in Jerusalem) or from them (that is, as a means of opening further doors of ministry). What the Holy Spirit had done in their lives, saving them, transforming them, filling them, made them precious to his own heart and mind. The change in their lives was obvious to everyone (cf. Matt. 5:14). Paul did not need any further recommendation of his ministry.

By comparing what God has done for them by His Spirit in their hearts to what He did on the tablets of stone for Moses, Paul emphasizes that the work of the Holy Spirit is both supernatural and personal. What God had done for them should have been enough to show them that Paul was sent from God and that his gospel was the truth of God. For the Corinthians themselves as a whole were the permanent and impressive letter, Christ's letter of recommendation, for Paul and his ministry (cf. 1 Thess. 2:19). What better letter could he have! What a contrast to the intruders' ways of promoting themselves!

> **4Such confidence as this is ours through Christ before God. 5Not that we are competent in ourselves to claim anything for ourselves, but our competence comes from God. 6He has made us competent as ministers of a new covenant—not of the letter but of the Spirit; for the letter kills, but the Spirit gives life.**

Those who doubted the validity of Paul's credentials needed to know that Paul's confidence was not self-confidence, nor did it come from the applause people might give. It came from his relationship with Christ before God. Christ was the One who gave Paul the right to rely on God. God was the One who gave Paul his credentials. Paul, no doubt, had in mind his call on the Damascus Road where he had met the risen, glorified Jesus (Acts 9:3–7). There Jesus said, "'I have appeared to you to appoint you as a servant and as a witness of what you have seen of me and what I will show you. I will rescue you from your own people and from the Gentiles. I am sending you to them to open their eyes and turn them from darkness to light, and from the power of Satan to God, so that they may receive forgiveness of sins and a place among those who are sanctified by faith in me'" (Acts 26:16–18).

Paul did have natural abilities and was trained in the Old Testament Scriptures under the outstanding rabbi Gamaliel (Acts 22:3). But none of that gave him the competency to preach the gospel. It all came from God and Christ, including his being filled with the Holy Spirit (Acts 9:17). Thus he could say, "Therefore I glory in Christ Jesus in my service to God. I will not venture to speak of anything except what Christ has accomplished through me in leading the Gentiles to obey God by what I have said and done—by the power of signs and miracles, through the power of the Spirit" (Rom. 15:17–19). New Testament ministry must be done through the power of the Spirit.

God also gave him and his fellow workers the competency they had as ministers of a new covenant, the covenant put into effect by the death of Jesus and the shedding of His blood (Heb. 9:11–28).[6]

The new covenant was prophesied in Jeremiah 31:31–35 (cf. also Ezek. 11:19), which both Hebrews 8:8–12 and 10:15–17 quote. Though it was given first to Israel, the New Testament shows it includes all who believe in Jesus. It is a not merely a prescribed written code as the Ten Commandments were, but something written on our hearts and minds as the Holy Spirit inspires our spirits. The law gave precepts to follow, but it gave no power to accomplish them. It called for death to the offender (Deut. 30:15–18), and even gave sin the opportunity to deceive and, through the commandment, bring death (Rom. 7:10–11). God allowed this so that the law, which was "holy, righteous and good" (Rom. 7:12), might become the means of showing that sin is "utterly sinful" (Rom 7:13; cf. 1 Cor. 15:56). The new covenant, because of Jesus, brings life and power from the Spirit of God to the believer (John 3:17; Rom. 3:20,24; 5:20–21). The old

---

[6]Paul may be implying that the false apostles were old covenant ministers, that is, Judaizers. Philip Edgcumbe Hughes, *Paul's Second Epistle to the Corinthians* (Grand Rapids: Wm. B. Eerdmans, 1973), 96.

covenant was written on cold, dead stone. But the Spirit of the living God puts His instructions in our minds and writes them on our hearts (Jer. 31:33). Even more, God promised a new heart and a new spirit and the indwelling of the Holy Spirit (Ezek. 36:26–27). Now the Spirit helps believers under the new covenant to do the things that are pleasing to God.

By saying that God made him and his companions "competent as ministers of a new covenant—not of the letter" Paul was contrasting the old covenant blazoned on stone and the new covenant "of the Spirit." He did not mean that the literal sense of Scripture is something deadening and to be avoided. Nor did he mean we should look for some "spiritual" meaning or interpretation. Much damage has been done by people spiritualizing or allegorizing the plain, literal truths of the Bible. Paul goes on to further describe the "letter," that is, the law, as "the ministry that brought death" (v. 7).

2. A Ministry Better Than That Of The Law 3:7–18

7Now if the ministry that brought death, which was engraved in letters on stone, came with glory, so that the Israelites could not look steadily at the face of Moses because of its glory, fading though it was,
8will not the ministry of the Spirit be even more glorious?
9If the ministry that condemns men is glorious, how much more glorious is the ministry that brings righteousness!
10For what was glorious has no glory now in comparison with the surpassing glory.
11And if what was fading away came with glory, how much greater is the glory of that which lasts!

Looking back at Exodus 19 to 21 we see the Ten Commandments given in the midst of tremendous sights and sounds—"thunder and lightning, with a thick cloud over the mountain, and very loud trumpet blast. . . . Mount Sinai was covered with smoke, because the Lord descended on it in fire. The smoke billowed up from it like smoke from a furnace, the whole mountain trembled violently, and the sound of the trumpet grew louder and louder" (Exod. 19:16,18–19). Then when Moses came from Mount Sinai with stone tablets engraved by God himself, his face was so radiant with God's glory that the people were afraid to come near him (Exod. 34:29–35). Moses then put a veil over his face so they would not see that the glory was fading (v. 7).

Though the Law given through Moses was a means by which the Israelites could learn to walk with God, its judgments on their failures were severe. Thus Paul calls the ministry of the Law a "ministry of death" (v. 7, NASB). It was something like a thermometer. A thermometer can measure heat, but it cannot generate heat. So the Law could measure their righteousness (or unrighteousness), but could not help them become righteous. No wonder Paul calls the ministry of the Spirit "even more glorious" than the ministry of the Law: The Spirit can clothe us with Christ's righteousness and help us to do the good things and live in the right ways God wanted for His people when He gave the Law. The Law was not something bad. It was "holy, righteous and good" (Rom. 7:12). In fact, it was "spiritual" (Rom. 7:14). But because of humankind's weakness, the Law brought condemnation and death. In contrast, God sent Jesus not "'to condemn the world, but to save the world'" (John 3:17). That is the reason the temporary, fading glory that accompanied the giving of the Law cannot compare with the permanent glory that accompanies the spread of the gospel in the power of the Holy Spirit—including His gifts and blessings.

> **12Therefore, since we have such a hope, we are very
> bold. 13We are not like Moses, who would put a veil
> over his face to keep the Israelites from gazing at it
> while the radiance was fading away. 14But their minds
> were made dull, for to this day the same veil remains
> when the old covenant is read. It has not been
> removed, because only in Christ is it taken away.
> 15Even to this day when Moses is read, a veil covers
> their hearts. 16But whenever anyone turns to the Lord,
> the veil is taken away.**

Our hope in the gospel with its proclamation of a better covenant and a greater glory is a sure hope, a steadfast hope, an anchor of the soul (Heb. 6:19). Paul had such confidence in the truth of the gospel and in the God of hope (Rom. 15:13) that he did not hesitate to proclaim it, boldly speaking freely and openly. Moses had put a veil over his face to keep Israel from seeing that the glory was "fading away." But the glory of the old covenant did fade. Nevertheless Paul, on the other hand, put no hindrances to the glory of the gospel, nor did he have anything to cover or conceal.

The covering of Moses' face with a veil was not the only time the glory was fading. Looking back over the history of Israel we see that it was full of ups and downs. Too often they backslid and turned to the worship of other gods, gods that encouraged immorality instead of holiness (cf. Rom. 1:21–23). Their minds were dulled, hardened by sin and unwillingness to believe and obey. Thus, it was their own fault that when the old covenant (including the entire Old Testament) was read, they did not understand. There was "a veil cover[ing] their hearts." When the books of Moses were read in the synagogues, the truth could not penetrate their inner being and change them. That veil continued over the hearts of the Jews until they turned to the Lord Jesus. As soon as they were saved, born again, baptized by the Holy Spirit into the body of Christ, the veil was taken away. The Old Testament became a new book to them, and they could see God's plan in it that led up to the coming of Jesus. Paul certainly experienced this after he met Jesus on the Damascus Road.

> **17Now the Lord is the Spirit, and where the Spirit of the**
> **Lord is, there is freedom. 18And we, who with unveiled faces all reflect the Lord's glory, are being transformed into his likeness with ever-increasing glory, which comes from the Lord, who is the Spirit.**

Those in Christ have the veil taken away from the heart and mind so they can have the freedom to serve God and reflect the Lord's glory, the glory of Christ (4:4; cf. Rom. 8:29; Heb. 1:3). This is a process where we are changed from one degree of glory to another as we are being transformed into His likeness, or as one writer puts it, "into transparent symbols of the self-giving Creator."[7] This is the sanctifying work of the Holy Spirit and will be complete when Jesus comes again (1 John 3:2; Rev. 22:4).

By saying "the Lord is the Spirit" Paul was identifying the Spirit with Christ, not in personal identity but "in redemptive action (Gal. 3–5; Rom. 6–8). The Spirit is self-effacing in His presentation of Christ so as not to detract from the Lord (John 15:26; 16:13)."[8]

---

[7]Jean-Jacques Suurmond, "The Meaning and Purpose of Spirit-Baptism and the Charisms," *EPTA Bulletin* 9, no. 4 (1990): 114.

[8]Frank G. Carter, "II Corinthians," in *The Beacon Bible Commentary* (Kansas City, Mo.: Beacon Hill Press, 1968), 7:529. Some, however, take the Spirit here to be the Spirit in contrast to the letter, with Christ working in the power of the Spirit. Still others say Paul may mean that the Lord Jesus in this passage is the Spirit, so that "Moses' turning to the Spirit was equivalent to his turning to Christ." R. P. C. Hanson, *The Second Epistle to the Corinthians: Christ and Controversy* (London: SCM Press, 1967), 40.

D. An Honest, Christ-Centered Ministry 4:1–18

1. A Genuine Ministry 4:1–2

1Therefore, since through God's mercy we have this ministry, we do not lose heart. 2Rather, we have renounced secret and shameful ways; we do not use deception, nor do we distort the word of God. On the contrary, by setting forth the truth plainly we commend ourselves to every man's conscience in the sight of God.

Though God made him competent as a minister of the new covenant (3:6), Paul never forgot that he did not deserve to have this new covenant ministry. He was persecuting Christians, opposing Christ, with no intention of serving Him or preaching the gospel when he was stopped by Him (cf. 1 Tim. 1:12–16). The Book of Acts records his experience on the Damascus Road three times (Acts 9:3–19; 22:3–16; 26:9–18).

So overwhelmed was he by the unmerited favor and mercy of God that changed him and the whole course of his life and ministry that thinking about it always gave him courage to go on, no matter what happened. Nothing could make him lose heart, or "shrink back," from the ministry God had given him.[9] His suffering only confirmed that he was a true follower of Christ (see Acts 9:16).

Probably in response to the accusations of his enemies, Paul says the change in his own heart caused him to refuse to use any secret, shameful, or deceptive ways.[10] The light that shone around him on the Damascus Road was followed by the light of Christ in his heart and the illumination of the Holy Spirit on God's Word. So there was no way that Paul would twist, adulterate, dilute, or distort it. Nor would he present the truth of the gospel in a way that only the initiated or the educated could understand. He presented it fully, but simply and plainly. His conscience was clear, and by the power of the Spirit he wanted every person's conscience to perceive that he was giving the

---

[9]Victor Paul Furnish, *II Corinthians* (Garden City, N.Y.: Doubleday & Co., 1984), 217.

[10]See 12:16, which may imply that Paul's enemies accused him of being "a crafty trickster." Philip Edgcumbe Hughes, *Paul's Second Epistle to the Corinthians* (Grand Rapids: Wm. B. Eerdmans, 1973) 123.

truth "in the sight of God," that is, just as God wanted it given (cf. 1 Thess. 2:13). Although Paul rejects his opponents' way of recommending themselves, he "is forced to commend himself"[11] for the sake of the truth. His example encourages us to keep our consciences clear before God.

2. An Effective Ministry 4:3–15

3And even if our gospel is veiled, it is veiled to those who are perishing. 4The god of this age has blinded the minds of unbelievers, so that they cannot see the light of the gospel of the glory of Christ, who is the image of God.

Paul previously spoke of the a veil over the hearts of Jews when the law of Moses was read in the synagogues. Now he recognizes that a veil might hinder "those who are perishing" (on their way to hell) when the gospel is proclaimed.[12] This would include both Jews and Gentiles. If they thought Paul's preaching of the gospel was vague or had some hidden meaning, it was their unbelief that put a veil over their minds. Their minds were blinded by "the god of this age," that is, by Satan (cf. John 12:31; 14:30; 16:11; Eph. 2:2; 1 John 5:19).

Jesus encountered the same problem with unbelieving Pharisees. He said that His language was not clear to them, that they were unable to hear what He was saying, because they belonged to their father the devil and wanted to carry out his desire. "'He was a murderer from the beginning, not holding to the truth, for there is no truth in him. When he lies, he speaks his native language, for he is a liar and the father of lies'" (John 8:44). Those who worship anyone or anything other than the true God (the Trinity of Father, Son, and Holy Spirit) are really worshiping Satan and allowing him to be their god by letting him direct and control their lives. Satan keeps them in darkness so they cannot see the light of the good news, that is, the glory of the full revelation of Christ's divine nature and character as the perfect image of God (cf. Col. 1:15; Heb. 1:1–5)—"being in very nature God" (Phil. 2:6). Through Him all believers are delivered from the

---

[11]Jerry L. Sumney, *Identifying Paul's Opponents* (Sheffield, England: Journal for the Study of the New Testament Press, 1990), 134.

[12]Paul calls it "our gospel" not because it was different in content from what the other apostles preached (see Gal. 1:11; 2:1–9), but because they were the ones preaching it.

power of Satan and darkness of this evil age. Christians are living in the light of Christ and of the age to come (Gal. 1:4; Eph. 2:1–7; Col. 1:13).

By calling Satan "the god of this age," the Bible reveals that his time and power are limited (see Rev. 20:10). What a contrast to the eternal glory of Christ who reveals to us the full glory of God!

> **5For we do not preach ourselves, but Jesus Christ as Lord, and ourselves as your servants for Jesus' sake. 6For God, who said, "Let light shine out of darkness," made his light shine in our hearts to give us the light of the knowledge of the glory of God in the face of Christ.**

If the gospel was veiled to some, it was not because it had its origin in Paul's mind or because it was a mere human set of ideas. Paul and his fellow workers had no desire to set themselves up as people who wanted others to give them devotion. They proclaimed Christ as divine Lord, worthy of all their worship and praise. Paul and his company were just servants or "slaves" (Gk. *doulous*)— of Christ first (Rom. 1:1; Phil. 1:1; Titus 1:1) and then of the Church, given by Jesus as slaves to do His will by helping the Church for His sake and in His stead (cf. Eph. 4:11–14).[13]

They could bring blessing to the Church because of what God had done for them. They knew by experience—Paul, for example, on the road to Damascus—that the same God who created physical light (Gen. 1:3) caused "his [own] light" (which must mean spiritual light) to shine in their inner being and their minds. This makes believers lightbearers (cf. Matt. 5:15). The purpose of this light was to illuminate the knowledge of God's glory "which is radiant on the face of Christ" (v.6, Weymouth). Thus, Jesus is the continuing Revealer of that light and glory in contrast to Moses whose face soon lost the glory (3:13).

The reference to the light in Genesis 1:3 implies further that God uses His spiritual light to make us new creations in Christ, which Paul knew from personal experience.

Christianity is more than a new way of life, more than following a good example or high ideals. It is union with a new Person, our Lord Jesus Christ. We become part of His Body, the Church, and continue in vital relationship with Jesus by faith.

> **7But we have this treasure in jars of clay to show that this all-surpassing power is from God and not from us.**

13"Your servants" does not mean they belonged to them, i.e., the Corinthians, but were given to serve them.

Paul knew the glory. He also knew the suffering his ministry often involved. His knowledge of the glory of God in Christ is a priceless treasure. People in those days would hardly think of putting jewels in jars of mere clay. But we who have the light of Christ still live in frail human bodies in a sinful world.[14]

God does not change our bodies now, but has chosen to leave us in human weakness so that it will be obvious to all that the greatness of His power manifest through His servants is "from God and not from us." God used Paul for many miracles, but he himself remained physically weak and unimpressive.

> **8We are hard pressed on every side, but not crushed;**
> **perplexed, but not in despair; 9persecuted, but not**
> **abandoned; struck down, but not destroyed.**

Clay jars were fragile. When I was helping to excavate the ruins of Dothan we uncovered several thousand broken pieces of clay jars on every level of the city. It was rare to find a jar that was intact. Paul, however, wanted the Corinthians to know that no matter what happened, the treasure in the clay jar of his body kept him from being broken by circumstances or by enemies.

In four ways Paul emphasizes that the power of God overcame his weakness in his ministry. (1) Troubles pressed hard on every side (or, in every way), but because of the incomparable power of God, they could not crush him—which can also mean they could not even restrict him from spreading the gospel. (2) He did not always understand what and why things were happening, being perplexed by many problems, but he was never in the kind of despair that doubted God.[15] (3)He was persecuted (the Gk. includes the ideas of being driven out and of being pursued from place to place; cf. Acts 14:5–6; 17:13), but he was not abandoned. The Lord did not forsake him, neither did his fellow workers leave him in the lurch. (4) He was struck down by his enemies, but not destroyed, or ruined.

> **10We always carry around in our body the death of**
> **Jesus, so that the life of Jesus may also be revealed in**

---

[14]The term "formed" (Gen. 2:7) was often used of a potter forming a jar. Paul may have had this in mind when he called our bodies jars of clay. (Cf. also Rom. 9:20–21; Isa. 29:16; 45:9; 64:8; Jer. 18:6).

[15]The Gk. has a wordplay *aporoumenoi all' ouk exapouroumenoi:* "perplexed but not utterly perplexed" or "bewildered, we are never at our wits' end" (NEB).

our body. [11]For we who are alive are always being given over to death for Jesus' sake, so that his life may be revealed in our mortal body. [12]So then, death is at work in us, but life is at work in you.

By saying he always carried in his body the death, or the putting to death, of Jesus, Paul meant that the same kind of sufferings that brought about the death of Jesus were present in his body. Then, because Jesus died for him Paul was constantly willing to risk his life for Jesus and for what He died for—the salvation of lost souls. The beatings and stonings left scars so that Paul could say "I bear on my body the marks of Jesus" (Gal. 6:17). Yet in it all he was able to reveal the resurrection life of Jesus in his body. Even when he was stoned and left for dead, he arose, healed, and continued his missionary journey (Acts 14:19–20).

In verse 11 Paul repeats the same idea. Though he and his fellow workers were still living, they were repeatedly being handed over to death because of their relationship to Jesus (cf. Phil. 2:30; note those who tried to avoid this, Gal. 6:12). The testimony they gave to judges, governors, and kings demonstrated the life of Christ that was present in their flesh that was mortal (subject to death). Later, Paul wrote to the Romans: "As it is written [Ps. 44:22]: 'For your sake [i.e. God's] we face death all day long; we are considered as sheep to be slaughtered.' No, in all these things we are more than conquerors through him who loved us" (Rom. 8:36–37).

Though death was thus working in Paul and his fellow workers because of the troubles and persecutions they endured, at the same time they were encouraged because through them the Spirit ministered life to those who accepted their message of the gospel.

[13]It is written: "I believed; therefore I have spoken." With that same spirit of faith we also believe and therefore speak, [14]because we know that the one who raised the Lord Jesus from the dead will also raise us with Jesus and present us with you in his presence. [15]All this is for your benefit, so that the grace that is reaching more and more people may cause thanksgiving to overflow to the glory of God.

Paul quotes from Psalm 116:10, where the psalmist, inspired by the Spirit (2 Tim. 3:16; 2 Pet. 1:21), speaks of the faith that caused him to call on the Lord. The psalm as a whole gives praise to the Lord for deliverance from death. Paul was moved to express the same Spirit-given, Spirit-inspired faith, as he continued to speak the truth of the gospel. The psalmist spoke after deliverance from death. This paralleled Jesus' rising from the dead. Paul looked ahead to deliverance from death, because the God who raised Jesus from the dead will raise not only Paul and the Corinthian believers, but all of us who believe. Together with Paul and all the saints we will be presented by Jesus to God (cf. 1 Thess. 4:14–18).

All that Paul suffered and all the preaching of the hope of eternal glory, Paul says, was for the benefit of the Corinthian believers. He wants God's grace to cause more and more people to turn to Him, so that grace abounding through them will cause more "thanksgiving to overflow" to God's glory.

3. A Ministry Sustained By Hope 4:16–18

**16Therefore we do not lose heart. Though outwardly
we are wasting away, yet inwardly we are being
renewed day by day. 17For our light and momentary
troubles are achieving for us an eternal glory that far
outweighs them all. 18So we fix our eyes not on what
is seen, but on what is unseen. For what is seen is temporary, but what is unseen is eternal.**

Because of the divine light and the hope of resurrection and being with Christ, Paul does not let human limitations cause him to lose heart (or "shrink back"[16]). He knows Christ in him as "the hope of glory" (Col. 1:27). But he also knows that in this present life nothing can stop the process of aging. Our bodies are gradually wasting away, dying. The physical sufferings Paul endured for Christ certainly did not slow down that process. But Paul did not let this discourage him, because every day he experienced inward renewal (cf. Rom. 12:2; Col. 3:10).

All the hardships he endured (see 11:23–29) he calls "light and momentary," compared with the eternal "weight" of glory that makes them all seem insignificant. God is causing all our troubles to achieve that incomparable abundance of glory for us (or, in us), even as He is now recreating us in Christ (4:6). This also is the work of the Holy Spirit (cf. 5:5). With His help we can endure the trials and suffering as we look ahead to what God has promised.

---

[16]Furnish, *II Corinthians,* 261.

The glory that will be ours is not yet seen while we are in these mortal bodies. But we, like Paul, must keep it in view, fixing our eyes on it instead of giving our attention to our present troubles (this will help us to be ready when Jesus comes; cf. 1 John 3:2–3). Although our troubles are real to us now, they are temporary. The glory is real and eternal. We shall enter into it all when Jesus comes again.

Study questions for this section may be found in appendix B.

III. PAUL'S GOALS 5:1–6:13

A. To Please The Lord 5:1–15

1. The Spirit Guarantees A New Body 5:1–5

[1]Now we know that if the earthly tent we live in is destroyed, we have a building from God, an eternal house in heaven, not built by human hands.

Because Paul recognized that outwardly we are wasting away, he could call the present human body an "earthly tent." It is suited for the present life, but it is a frail, temporary dwelling capable of being destroyed. Since Paul did not know when Jesus might return, nor did he know when death might occur, he said "if" the tent is destroyed. But though he was facing death constantly, he did not fear the destruction of "the earthly tent" because he knew something better awaited him (and us)—a new body in heaven that he compares to an "eternal house." To make sure we understand he is talking about a house created by God himself, he adds it is "not made with hands" (v. 1, KJV). (See 1 Cor. 15:35–54.)

Some believe God has already prepared a spiritual body for us.[1] Paul, however, indicated in a previous letter that the new body suited for both earth and heaven is given us at the time of the resurrection and Rapture (1 Cor. 15:52; 2 Cor. 5:4; see also Phil. 3:21; 1 Thess. 4:15–17). Paul's point here is that once we receive the new body that clothes our resurrected body, it is ours forever.

---

[1]R. P. C. Hanson, *The Second Epistle to the Corinthians: Christ and Controversy* (London: SCM Press, 1967), 45.

[2]Meanwhile we groan, longing to be clothed with our heavenly dwelling, [3]because when we are clothed, we will not be found naked. [4]For while we are in this tent, we groan and are burdened, because we do not wish to be unclothed but to be clothed with our heavenly dwelling, so that what is mortal may be swallowed up by life.

to be Rightly clothed,

While we are in this body we groan because of our sufferings, sufferings that are the result of the fall, sufferings we all must share to some degree (Rom. 8:22–23). We groan too because we know a better body will be ours in the resurrection; and if we have the same vision Paul had of the glory to come, we long with intense desire to be free from the weaknesses of our present body. The present body is mortal, subject to death, in fact, gradually dying. The new body will be immortal and incorruptible, not subject to death or decay.

Many Greeks considered the body a prison from which death sets us free. Gnostics "might regard such 'nakedness' as desirable";[2] Paul, however, is not anxious to be "found naked." "Naked" could mean "without an upper garment," but here it means without a body.[3] He recognizes that we need a body for the full expression of our personality and nature. The Greek can mean the new body will be put on over us "like an overcoat"[4] "in a flash, in the twinkling of an eye" (1 Cor. 15:52). But death is still an enemy (1 Cor. 15:26), and though nakedness between death and the resurrection is not desirable, Paul is comforted by the assurance that to be "absent from the body" is to be "present with the Lord" (v. 8, KJV).

[5]Now it is God who has made us for this very purpose and has given us the Spirit as a deposit, guaranteeing what is to come.

Though we groan in this body, longing for the resurrection and the coming age, we are encouraged by the hope that God stirs in us by His Spirit. God's purpose is to prepare us for our mortality being swallowed up by life.

---

[2]F. F. Bruce, *1 and 2 Corinthians* (Grand Rapids: Wm. B. Eerdmans, 1983), 203.

[3]Some suggest that "naked" refers to the possibility of not deserving the resurrection (cf. Rev. 3:4; 6:11; 7:9 where some take the white robes to be spiritual bodies given to the martyrs as their reward). See Hanson, *Second Epistle to the Corinthians,* 45.

[4]Bruce, *1 and 2 Corinthians,* 203.

The Spirit is a "deposit," or rather, a first installment, "guaranteeing" our future resurrection and giving us assurance of the coming age (see 1:22; Rom. 8:1–11; 1 Cor. 15:36–38). In a sense, the baptism in the Holy Spirit and the life in the Spirit is a demonstration to us of the faithfulness of God. We now have the first installment of what we shall have in its fullness when Jesus comes again (cf. Phil. 1:6).

2. Living By Faith 5:6–8

6 Therefore we are always confident and know that as
long as we are at home in the body we are away from
the Lord. 7 We live by faith, not by sight. 8 We are confi-
dent, I say, and would prefer to be away from the body
and at home with the Lord.

Paul's confidence is in his personal relationship with Christ and in his inner relationship with the Holy Spirit. He knows that as long as Christians maintain this relationship they do not need to fear death. While we are in the present body we are distant from the glorified Christ, so we must live "by faith, not by sight," for He ascended to the right hand of the Father in heaven (Acts 2:33; cf. 1:9). We can indeed have communion with Jesus by faith now. When we leave this body, however, we shall be present with the Lord, in an even closer relationship with Him; our faith will become sight (cf. Phil. 1:21, 23), "for we shall see him as he is" (1 John 3:2).

3. The Judgment Seat Of Christ 5:9–10

9 So we make it our goal to please him, whether we
are at home in the body or away from it. 10 For we must
all appear before the judgment seat of Christ, that
each one may receive what is due him for the things
done while in the body, whether good or bad.

Because of the assurance that we shall be with the Lord, we should "make it our goal [and our ambition] to please" the Lord. This involves really working at pleasing Him regardless of whether our efforts bring continued life or death.

An important reason for living to please the Lord is the coming "judgment seat of Christ," where all believers must appear and where God will reveal the true character of our deeds to us (cf. Rom. 14:12; 1 Cor. 3:12–15). Then each will receive what is due, depending on whether the deeds were "good or bad."[5] This means we are saved to serve, saved to do good deeds, saved to be salt that has an effect on the world around us. As believers, as R. P. C. Hanson pointed out, we cannot "ignore the inequalities and injustices of this world in order to concentrate wholly upon securing . . . happiness in the next."[6]

4. Motivated By Fear And Love 5:11–15

**11Since, then, we know what it is to fear the Lord, we
try to persuade men. What we are is plain to God, and
I hope it is also plain to your conscience. 12We are not
trying to commend ourselves to you again, but are
giving you an opportunity to take pride in us, so that
you can answer those who take pride in what is seen
rather than in what is in the heart. 13If we are out of
our mind, it is for the sake of God; if we are in our right
mind, it is for you.**

Paul now resumes the defense of his new covenant ministry as an apostle. Some were still misunderstanding him. Some apparently questioned his integrity. He responds by saying that in his apostolic ministry he is motivated by the "fear of the Lord," whom he will face at the Judgment Seat. This fear is not terror but holy awe and reverence that makes him see the importance and consequences of his actions and causes him to continually seek to persuade people to accept the gospel.

His motives and his character—all that he is—is "plain to God" now, just as it will be at the Judgment Seat. He hopes that his life is transparent enough for them to see it too. If they do, their conscience will properly evaluate him and his ministry and trust him.

He wants to give them a valid reason to be proud so they can reply to outsiders who take pride in "what is seen" (external appearances), rather than in the reality that is in the heart. Their boasting in appearances is wrong. Forms of the Greek *kauchaomai* ("boast") and its cognates are so frequent in this letter that is seems that "the matter of the legitimate versus illegitimate boasting was an important part of the

---

[5] Sinners will not be resurrected until after the Millennium and they will face the judgment of the Great White Throne (Rev. 20:12–14). See Stanley M. Horton, *Our Destiny: Biblical Teachings on the Last Things* (Springfield, Mo.: Logion Press, 1996), 83–88; 221–24.

[6] Hanson, *Second Epistle to the Corinthians*, 46–47; cf. Rom. 14:10; 1 Cor. 3:12–15.

dispute between Paul and his Corinthian rivals."[7]

Whatever people say about Paul, his only desire is to serve God and His people. If he is out of his mind (probably worshiping and praying in the Spirit), he is not insane as unbelievers might think (cf. Mark 3:21; Acts 26:24); it is for God. If he is in his right mind, speaking in their language, it is for them.

[14]For Christ's love compels us, because we are convinced that one died for all, and therefore all died.
[15]And he died for all, that those who live should no longer live for themselves but for him who died for them and was raised again.

In addition to the fear of God, Christ's love for all motivates Paul. Love that was demonstrated by Christ's death on Calvary's cross and imparted to us by the Holy Spirit (Rom. 5:5) must be the compelling motive of the Christian. If we really believe John 3:16 we have no choice but to love everyone and seek their salvation.

That salvation is available to all because Jesus died for all. When He died on the cross, He took the place of all, not only as our Representative, but as "the incorporated Head of the human race," so that "in principle" all died.[8] Thus, all who believe in Jesus share in the benefits of His death as they die to the old life, are born again by the Spirit, given life from above, and are united to Christ. (Water baptism symbolizes and declares this; Rom. 6:3–4.) Thus, all believers have a "fresh start . . . and so share the life He now possesses (verse 17)."[9] We must not forget, however, that we experience His life in us only as long as we cease to live the old, self-centered life "and begin to *live for him who for their sake died and was raised to life.*"[10] (See Gal. 2:20; 6:14.)

B Ministry Of Reconciliation 5:16–6:13

1. A New Creation 5:16–17

[16]So from now on we regard no one from a worldly point of view. Though we once regarded Christ in this

[7]Victor Paul Furnish, *II Corinthians* (Garden City, N.Y.: Doubleday & Co., 1984), 28. See also Jerry L. Sumney, *Identifying Paul's Opponents* (Sheffield, England: Journal for the Study of the New Testament Press, 1990), 129.

[8]Hanson, *Second Epistle to the Corinthians,* 50.

[9]Margaret E. Thrall, *The First and Second Letters of Paul to The Corinthians* (Cambridge, England: University Press, 1965), 149.

[10]Ibid.

way, we do so no longer. 17Therefore, if anyone is in Christ, he is a new creation; the old has gone, the new has come!

The point of view of the old creation, including its standards, values, and view of wisdom and power, is quite different from that of the new creation in Christ. The disciples applied worldly standards to their understanding of Jesus before Peter's great confession (Matt. 16:13–17). So Paul, as a Pharisee before his conversion, had a wrong conception of the Messiah. He probably looked for a political Messiah.[11] He thought Jesus was a blasphemer and he was filled with a zeal to destroy Christians (Acts 9:1,21; 22:4,19; 26:9; Gal. 1:13,23). "Now love had taken the place of that zeal as the controlling force at the center of his being."[12] Now he judged Jesus by the revelation that He was "declared with power to be the Son of God by his resurrection from the dead" (Rom. 1:4).

We learn from this that the standards of Paul's opponents are worldly, standards inappropriate for Christians. Paul wants the Corinthians to judge his apostleship by heavenly standards and to know him as they know Christ, according to the Spirit.[13]

Paul was a "new creation" in Christ. So is everyone who is in Christ, whether changed dramatically, like Paul, or quietly, perhaps like Timothy (2 Tim. 3:14,15), simply turning to Jesus in faith and accepting Him as Lord and Savior. "The 'in Christ' life of believers is central to the Pauline understanding of the nature of salvation. . . . Paul mentions that Christians are 'in Christ,' 'in Him,' or 'in the Lord' in all but one of his letters—164 times in all."[14]

2. Christ's Ambassadors 5:18–21

18All this is from God, who reconciled us to himself through Christ and gave us the ministry of reconciliation: 19that God was reconciling the world to himself in Christ, not counting men's sins against them. And he has committed to us the message of reconciliation.

11Bruce, *1 and 2 Corinthians,* 208.

12Paul Barnett, *The Second Epistle to the Corinthians* (Grand Rapids: Wm. B. Eerdmans, 1997), 288.

13Ibid., 293.

14Melvin E. Dieter, "The Wesleyan Perspective," in Melvin E. Dieter et al., *Five Views on Sanctification* (Grand Rapids: Zondervan Publishing House, 1987), 34.

[20]We are therefore Christ's ambassadors, as though God were making his appeal through us. We implore you on Christ's behalf: Be reconciled to God.

The Epicurean philosophers Paul met in Athens (Acts 17:18) taught that the gods were far away and had no interest in human beings.[15] The Bible makes it clear that every human being has a relationship with God, one of either fellowship or rebellion. Because of the Fall the world as a whole is in rebellion and needs to be reconciled to God so that fellowship can be enjoyed.

"All this" that is from God refers especially to His work of reconciling us to himself through Christ's death (cf. Rom. 5:10) and to everything that is involved in our new life in Christ (cf. Gal. 2:20). God's part has been done, completed at the cross before anyone accepted it (see Rom. 5:8–10). Now we who have been reconciled have the responsibility to call people to be reconciled (cf. Rom. 5:11). Like Paul, we stand between God and all humankind with God-given authority to bring them the message of reconciliation. "This passage is . . . one of the charters of the Christian ministry in the New Testament"[16] (cf. Isa. 52:7; Rom. 10:15; Eph. 6:15).

[21]God made him who had no sin to be sin for us, so that in him we might become the righteousness of God.

Jesus was personally free from all sin (John 8:46; Heb. 4:15; 1 Pet. 2:22; 1 John 3:5), but God identified Him with sinful humankind, making Him one with us, so that when we are joined with Him we are not only identified with the righteousness of God but we become the righteousness of God in Christ (cf. Gal. 2:16–17; Phil. 3:9). We are therefore forgiven and free from condemnation (Rom. 8:1).

He did not become a sinner.[17] He remained the spotless Lamb of God on the cross.[18] (See Isa. 52:13 to 53:12 where He is the sin-bearer.) In the Old Testament the Hebrew *chatta'th* is used for both "sin" and "sin offering," for the sin offering is substitutionary for the sin. Thus

---

[15]Thrall, *First and Second Letters*, 151.

[16]Hanson, *Second Epistle to the Corinthians*, 49.

[17]The false idea that Jesus became a sinner and had to be "born again" in hell denies the truth of the Cross, that the shedding of Jesus' blood purchased our redemption (1 Pet. 1:18–19).

[18]Daniel B. Pecota, "The Saving Work of Christ," in *Systematic Theology*, ed. Stanley M. Horton, rev. ed. (Springfield, Mo.: Logion Press, 1995), 344.

God appointed Jesus to be a sin offering for us and in His death God judged our sin.

Then, because He hung on a wooden cross ("tree" in Deut. 21:23 can mean anything made of wood) He became a curse for us (Gal. 3:13). Thus, He bore the wages of sin (Rom. 6:23), and when He cried on the cross, "'It is finished'" (Gk. *tetelestai,* meaning it stands finished and nothing needs to be added to His sacrifice for sin; John 19:30), the price for our redemption was fully paid. His resurrection then demonstrated that the power of sin and death was broken and God in Christ has triumphed. Thus, in Christ we both stand in His righteousness before God and are becoming the righteousness of God in Him. This can mean our righteousness comes from God or it expresses God's righteousness. Paul probably had both in mind.

3. Now Is The Day Of Salvation 6:1–2

1As God's fellow workers we urge you not to receive God's grace in vain. 2For he says, "In the time of my favor I heard you, and in the day of salvation I helped you." I tell you, now is the time of God's favor, now is the day of salvation.

As God's fellow workers, who belong to Him as well as work for Him, and as Christ's ambassadors (5:20), Paul and his company urge the Corinthians not to receive God's grace to no purpose.[19] The Corinthians had indeed received God's grace, including His salvation through Christ, but they must not suppose that salvation is maintained automatically. It is possible to "let it go for nothing" (v. 1, NEB). This could happen if they turned back to their old ways or if they listened to super-spiritual critics or to false apostles who were teaching a different gospel (cf. 11:4; Gal. 2:21). We need to live according to the new life given us (cf. John 15:2; God takes away branches that do not bear fruit).

Then Paul quotes Isaiah 49:8 and applies it to the Corinthians. They are living in the time in which prophecy is being fulfilled. It is God's day, God's time. Paul does not discount the importance of the future age or the last things. But they must recognize that their pre-

---

[19]Though Paul is defending his apostleship here, we do not need to limit the ministry of reconciliation to apostles. God has given other ministries to the Church (Eph. 4:11). Paul Barnett, *The Second Epistle to the Corinthians* (Grand Rapids: Wm. B. Eerdmans, 1997), 320–21.

sent age is the final age before the millennial age. Now is the day when God makes possible reconciliation to himself through Christ. "Now is the day of salvation" (cf. Heb. 3:12–15). As we approach the end of the age we too must apply Paul's remarks to our time so that we also do not receive the grace of God "in vain" (Gk. *eis kenon,* "into emptiness," that is, to no purpose, without effect, without reaching its goal). Nothing would be sadder than to have once received the grace of God but in the end be lost. It is no wonder that Paul warned Christians often (cf. Rom. 8:12–13; Gal. 5:19–21; Eph. 5:5–6; Heb. 2:1–4; 6:4–6; 10:26–31).

4. Paul's Sufferings 6:3–10

3We put no stumbling block in anyone's path, so that our ministry will not be discredited. 4Rather, as servants of God we commend ourselves in every way: in great endurance; in troubles, hardships and distresses; 5in beatings, imprisonments and riots; in hard work, sleepless nights and hunger;

Paul wants the Corinthians to be reconciled to him, but he knows that they cannot be reconciled until they acknowledge his apostleship, his pure motives, and his godly, righteous life.[20]

Paul did not want to give any unnecessary offense to the culture of the people he was seeking to win to Christ. Nor did he want to make improper self-commendation a stumbling block to the Corinthians, which might cause them to receive God's grace in vain and fall away from the truth. He commends himself only as a servant (slave) of God should.

In contrast to his opponents who were exalting themselves, Paul draws attention to his sufferings and weakness. They claimed that apostles should have an impressive bearing and demonstrate the power of God in spectacular ways. "Paul, on the other hand, contends that apostles can be unimpressive to the average observer" and "show God's power by being able to endure trials and hardships (i.e. being 'weak') and, in the process, bring others to the gospel."[21]

Paul lists his sufferings in three sets of three: (1) troubles, hardships, and distresses—all of which put pressure on him and could have

---

[20]Jerry L. Sumney, *Identifying Paul's Opponents* (Sheffield, England: Journal for the Study of the New Testament Press, 1990), 137.

[21]Ibid., 147.

crushed him; (2) beatings, imprisonments, and riots—that is, persecutions by both Jews and Gentiles because of his bold preaching of the gospel; and (3) hard work, sleepless nights, and hunger (that is, "fasting," probably as self-discipline). All of these he suffered willingly, remembering how Jesus suffered for him.

**6in purity, understanding, patience and kindness; in
the Holy Spirit and in sincere love; 7in truthful speech
and in the power of God; with weapons of righteousness in the right hand and in the left;**

In the midst of all his hardships Paul continued to cultivate qualities of purity, including sincerity as well as integrity in financial matters; understanding, especially in his bringing people to the knowledge of God through the gospel; patience, using self-control in dealing with difficult people and difficult circumstances; and kindness, like the kindness, goodness, and generosity of God (cf. Rom. 2:4).

"In the Holy Spirit" means the Holy Spirit was the source of the graces that sustained Paul as well as the agent who ministered His gifts through Paul.[22] These gifts in Paul's ministry were accompanied by sincere, genuine, unhypocritical love (cf. Rom. 12:9; 1 Cor. 13). They lined up with a faithful presentation of the Word of truth, the gospel, in the power of God.[23] The power of God enabled him to endure all the difficulties and obey God in all his ministry.

The power of God also enabled him to use "weapons of righteousness." This probably refers to Paul's adherence to righteous principles in his life and ministry,[24] whether things were going well or not, as the following apologetic antitheses indicate. These weapons of inward righteousness "in the right hand and in the left" means he was fully equipped to face whatever came his way.

**8through glory and dishonor, bad report and good
report; genuine, yet regarded as impostors; 9known,
yet regarded as unknown; dying, and yet we live on;
beaten, and yet not killed; 10sorrowful, yet always
rejoicing; poor, yet making many rich; having nothing,
and yet possessing everything.**

---

[22]Kenell H. Easley, "The Pauline Usage of Pneumati as a Reference to the Spirit of God," *Journal of the Evangelical Theological Society* 27, no. 3 (September 1984): 304.

[23]Barnett, *Second Epistle,* 329.

[24]Cf. Rom. 6:13.

Paul shows how effective those weapons were by summarizing what he went through in his ministry by pairs of opposite ideas: He experienced glory from God and dishonor from people. His enemies gave a bad report; some of his converts gave a good report (cf. 1 Thess. 1:9). God knew he was genuine, even though his opponents regarded him and his company as impostors (or deceivers), leading people astray by distorting the truth.[25] His ministry made him known, but those who called him an impostor said he was unknown (not known by then as a genuine apostle). He was dying in the sense that he was continually threatened by death, but he still lived on (as when he was stoned and left for dead [Acts 14:19–20]). He experienced sorrow, for even some of the Corinthians caused him grief. Yet nothing could take away his sense of the Lord's presence and the eternal hope which produced a deep joy. He humbled himself by willingly becoming poor, just as Christ did (Phil. 2:6–8). He worked hard in his tentmaking in order to give many the riches of the gospel and the grace of God. Though he had a lifestyle that did not depend on possessions ("having nothing"), yet he possessed all things: all the blessings of salvation in the present (Eph. 1:3) as well as the assurance of eternal blessings in the future.

All these contrasting experiences show that Paul did not look at his life and ministry the way the world (and some of the Corinthians) did. He rejoiced in the midst of sorrow and suffering. In all these things he was more than conqueror (cf. Rom. 8:37).

5. Asking For A Loving Response 6:11–13

[11]We have spoken freely to you, Corinthians, and opened wide our hearts to you. [12]We are not withholding our affection from you, but you are withholding yours from us. [13]As a fair exchange—I speak as to my children—open wide your hearts also.

Paul previously made a plea for the Corinthians to respond to God's grace (6:1). Now he makes an impassioned appeal for them to respond to his own love and affection for them. His mouth continued to speak to them, wanting them to listen. His heart was "opened wide" and remained so (as the Gk. indicates). The word "heart" was used to express both thought and feeling. His love was that of a good undershepherd bringing Christ's love to the flock.

---

[25]Barnett, *Second Epistle,* 331.

Some Corinthians may have felt Paul did not love them. The truth was that some of them were withholding their love from him and his companions. As a spiritual father who brought them to the Lord and to a new birth by the Spirit, he appeals to them as deserving "a fair exchange" from his "children." He wants them to open their hearts wide like his. He wants to feel their affection, as any good pastor would.

Study questions for this section may be found in appendix B.

IV. APPEALING TO THE CORINTHIANS 6:14–7:16

A. Do Not Be Partners With Unbelievers 6:14–7:1

1. A Call For Separation 6:14–18

14Do not be yoked together with unbelievers. For what
do righteousness and wickedness have in common?
Or what fellowship can light have with darkness?
15What harmony is there between Christ and Belial?
What does a believer have in common with an unbe-
liever? 16What agreement is there between the temple
of God and idols? For we are the temple of the living
God. As God has said: "I will live with them and walk
among them, and I will be their God, and they will be
my people." 17"Therefore come out from them and be
separate, says the Lord. Touch no unclean thing, and I
will receive you." 18"I will be a Father to you, and you
will be my sons and daughters, says the Lord
Almighty."

Because Paul knew the hearts of some of the Corinthians were closed to him, he follows his plea with exhortations to remove hindrances that close their hearts and minds to the truth. Though Paul had warned them to "flee from idolatry" (1 Cor. 10:14), they were still too involved in the pagan society around them. So Paul digresses again from 6:14 to 7:1, in order to remind them that God wants a holy people, a separated people. To emphasize this, Paul asks five rhetorical questions. Surely there is no common ground shared by righteousness and unrighteousness, no fellowship between light and darkness, no harmony between Christ and Belial (a name applied to both Satan and the Antichrist),[1] nothing in common between believers and unbelievers, no agreement between the temple of God and idols. God wants us to be separated from all evil, from every unclean thing.

For the Corinthians this meant especially separation from unconverted unbelievers involved in pagan worship.[2] Just as an ox and a donkey would be unevenly yoked when plowing and would be mismated if anyone attempted to crossbreed them (cf. Deut. 22:10; Lev. 19:19), so a believer and an unbeliever would be mismated. God wants to see fellowship in Christian marriages and in all our close relationships, including business partnerships and our worship. Fellowship between the righteousness of Christ which clothes the believer, and the wickedness (Gk. *anomia,* "lawlessness," a frame of mind that leads to lawless deeds) of an unbeliever is impossible. This, of course, does not mean that circumstances for working with unbelievers are nonexistent (cf. 1 Cor. 5:9–10). Physically we are still in this world. It is spiritually that we must be, and remain, separate. We do not belong to the world (John 15:19); we are not "of the world" (John 17:14). Worldly ideas and worldly corruption are to have no influence on us.

We must especially remember that the Church as a body is the temple of the living God (Gk. *naos,* the inner sanctuary, the place where God manifests His presence; see 1 Cor. 3:16–17; Eph. 2:22). But each individual is also His temple (1 Cor. 6:19). He is the living God, the one true God, and His worship leaves no room for compromise with the worship of lifeless idols, which are mere nothings.

We, like Israel, have the promise that God's purpose is to live with His people, walking among us, and showing himself to be our God (see Lev. 26:11–12; Ezek. 37:26–27; 43:7; cf. also Zech. 2:10–11; 1 Pet. 2:9–10). Therefore, because He is doing this, God calls believers to separate themselves from worldly lusts and from pagan cults, which today would include New Age doctrines and anything connected with the occult. We are not even to touch any defiled thing. Why? Because we have the promise that God will receive us and will be a Father to

---

[1]F. F. Bruce, *1 and 2 Corinthians* (Grand Rapids: Wm. B. Eerdmans, 1983), 214–15.

[2]Barnett, *Second Corinthians,* 342, 345.

us, making us His sons and daughters.[3] This puts a responsibility on us to live consistently as His sons and daughters. It calls on us to obey and worship Him as our loving heavenly Father as well. We have a responsibility to maintain our relationship with Him, avoiding anything that comes between us and Him.

2. Inward Holiness Needed 7:1

[1]Since we have these promises, dear friends, let us purify ourselves from everything that contaminates body and spirit, perfecting holiness out of reverence for God.

As a climax to this digression that began at 6:14 Paul reminds the Corinthians of the promises just mentioned, promises that include all that God's gracious salvation will provide when Jesus comes again. These promises should encourage them to get rid of everything that contaminates the physical body and their own spirit (including attitudes and desires and any of the habits of the old life and the influences of pagan ideas and worship; cf. Rom. 8:12–13; Gal. 5:16). This will enable them to perfect holiness, that is make holiness their goal and keep working toward it.[4] We will do the same if we truly reverence the God who said """Be holy, because I am holy""" (Lev. 11:44) and "'I am the Lord who makes you holy'" (Lev. 22:32).

B. Encouragement Brought By Titus 7:2–16

1. Paul's Right Conduct 7:2–14

[2]Make room for us in your hearts. We have wronged no one, we have corrupted no one, we have exploited no one. [3]I do not say this to condemn you; I have said before that you have such a place in our hearts that we would live or die with you. [4]I have great confidence in you; I take great pride in you. I am greatly

---

[3]Vv. 17–18 quote words and phrases from various prophets (cf. Isa. 43:6; 52:11; Jer. 31:9; 32:38; 51:45; Ezek. 11:17; 20:34,41; Hos. 1:10; Zeph. 3:20).

[4]"Perfecting" (Gk. *epitelein*) means to bring to a goal. The term is always repetitive in the NT. See Frank G. Carter, "II Corinthians," in *The Beacon Bible Commentary* (Kansas City, Mo.: Beacon Hill Press, 1968), 7:566.

encouraged; in all our troubles my joy knows no bounds.

Paul knows he is still being misunderstood. So he again appeals to the Corinthians to love and trust him (see 6:13). Now he lets them know he is worthy of their love and trust. Whatever his opponents have said against him is false. The Corinthians have no reason to withhold their love, for he has not wronged, corrupted, or exploited any of them. All he wants is their spiritual advancement.

Lest they misunderstand his purpose, he says also that he is not condemning them. His heart is so full of love for them that he would live and die with them. That is, Paul knew that persecutors might cause his death; but he was committed to live for Christ. They too faced the same possibility of death and needed the same commitment. Because he saw that commitment, he had great confidence and great pride in them. More than that, he was encouraged in all his troubles, possibly because some Corinthians did open their hearts to him. Thus his joy was abundant, overflowing. Paul never let difficulties rob him of joy and thankfulness.

2. Paul In Macedonia 7:5–7

5For when we came into Macedonia, this body of ours had no rest, but we were harassed at every turn—conflicts on the outside, fears within. 6But God, who comforts the downcast, comforted us by the coming of Titus, 7and not only by his coming but also by the comfort you had given him. He told us about your longing for me, your deep sorrow, your ardent concern for me, so that my joy was greater than ever.

Because Titus did not meet him in Troas, Paul was so disappointed that he went to Macedonia, hoping to meet him there. In Macedonia, probably at Philippi,[5] Paul found opposition and persecution. These conflicts (probably including both persecution from unbelievers and quarrels within the church) brought fears or foreboding (cf. 2:12–13). He may also have had foreboding about the outcome of Titus's visit to Corinth. He had sent Titus with a stern, rebuking letter that he was afraid might not have been well received. But this fear changed when Titus came and brought encouragement from the Lord. Paul recog-

[5]Paul Barnett, *The Second Epistle to the Corinthians* (Grand Rapids: Wm. B. Eerdmans, 1997), 368–69.

nized then that it is God's nature to comfort the downcast, those who are discouraged, depressed, and afflicted (Isa. 40:1; 49:13; 51:3,12, 19; 52:9; 61:2; 66:13; cf. Pss. 113:6; 138:6; Zeph. 3:12).

Titus also brought good news of how the Corinthians had encouraged him. As a result of Paul's painful letter that Titus had brought them (a letter now lost), their attitude toward Paul had changed. Now they longed for Paul, wanting to restore relationships with him. Their repentance was shown by deep sorrow. They were deeply concerned about Paul. This change brought even greater joy to Paul.

3. The Effect Of Paul's Letter 7:8–13a

**[8]Even if I caused you sorrow by my letter, I do not
regret it. Though I did regret it—I see that my letter
hurt you, but only for a little while—[9]yet now I am
happy, not because you were made sorry, but
because your sorrow led you to repentance. For you
became sorrowful as God intended and so were not
harmed in any way by us.**

The letter that caused sorrow was the painful letter delivered by Titus (already mentioned in 2:3). Paul did regret having to cause them sorrow, but he no longer regretted it. Instead, he rejoiced because the letter was effective. It caused repentance on the part of the Corinthian believers and prepared the way for the reconciliation Paul asks for in this letter. Thus, their sorrow was a sorrow that God wanted to see. God was the one who prompted Paul to write the painful letter, so the outcome was that the Corinthians were hurt only for a little while. So Paul did them no harm by the letter.

**[10]Godly sorrow brings repentance that leads to salva-
tion and leaves no regret, but worldly sorrow brings
death. [11]See what this godly sorrow has produced in
you: what earnestness, what eagerness to clear yourselves, what indignation, what alarm, what longing,
what concern, what readiness to see justice done. At
every point you have proved yourselves to be innocent
in this matter.**

The Corinthians proved their sorrow was godly by how they reacted to Paul's letter. What a contrast there is between godly sorrow and worldly sorrow. Godly sorrow brings repentance, a complete change of mind and attitudes. This leads to salvation, including all the blessings of the gospel. It leaves no regret, for the past sins are not only forgiven, they are gone (Isa. 1:18; 38:17; 43:25; Mic. 7:19; Acts 3:19; Heb. 10:17). Worldly sorrow, in contrast, may involve remorse, regret, and guilty feelings that do not go away. It ultimately brings death.

The proof of their godly sorrow was easy to see. It brought "earnestness," including moral integrity, sincerity, and commitment; "eagerness" to clear themselves; "indignation" toward the one who wronged Paul; "alarm," or fear and reverence for God (cf. Phil. 2:12); "longing" to see Paul and have fellowship with him; "concern" for the truth and for the gospel; and "readiness to see justice done." Now they had become "innocent," or blameless, because of their repentance and because of the righting of the wrong done to Paul (see 2:9).

> **[12]So even though I wrote to you, it was not on account of the one who did the wrong or of the injured party, but rather that before God you could see for yourselves how devoted to us you are. [13a]By all this we are encouraged.**

Paul wants them to know that he did not write the painful letter because of the person who did wrong, nor because of the effect of that wrong on Paul. Rather, he wanted them to see how much they cared for him in the presence of God.

All this (which was discussed in vv. 8–12) brought encouragement to Paul and made him rejoice.

4. Titus's Happiness 7:13b–16

> **[13b]In addition to our own encouragement, we were especially delighted to see how happy Titus was, because his spirit has been refreshed by all of you. [14]I had boasted to him about you, and you have not embarrassed me. But just as everything we said to you was true, so our boasting about you to Titus has proved to be true as well. [15]And his affection for you is all the greater when he remembers that you were all obedient, receiving him with fear and trembling. [16]I am glad I can have complete confidence in you.**

The report Titus brought was encouraging. More than that, Titus himself brought delight to Paul by his happiness. The Corinthian believers welcomed Titus, receiving him with fear and trembling. By their response and obedience they refreshed the spirit of Titus. Paul had assured Titus that they would. What Paul said in the painful letter was true. But the good things he said about them and the obedient response he expected proved true as well. This caused Titus to remember them with deep affection. If they had not welcomed Titus in this manner, Paul would have been embarrassed, ashamed of boasting about what he expected. But he did not expect to be embarrassed. He knew they believed the Word of God. He knew they were filled with the Holy Spirit. They were in Christ, and Christ was in them. Since they proved themselves by obedience and by the courage to right the wrongs the painful letter dealt with, he rejoices that he can have complete confidence in them.

Study questions for this section may be found in appendix B.

V. ENCOURAGEMENT TO GIVE GENEROUSLY 8:1–9:15

A. The Example Of The Macedonian Churches 8:1–7

1. Macedonian Generosity 8:1–5

1And now, brothers, we want you to know about the
grace that God has given the Macedonian churches.
2Out of the most severe trial, their overflowing joy and
their extreme poverty welled up in rich generosity. 3For
I testify that they gave as much as they were able, and
even beyond their ability. Entirely on their own, 4they
urgently pleaded with us for the privilege of sharing in
this service to the saints. 5And they did not do as we
expected, but they gave themselves first to the Lord
and then to us in keeping with God's will.

Paul next brings up the matter of the collection for the poor saints in Jerusalem (see 1 Cor. 16:1–3; cf. Acts 24:17; Rom. 15:25–27). During the previous year the Corinthians apparently lost interest in the project. Because he wanted to encourage them to continue giving, he told them of the grace God had given to the Macedonian assemblies[1]—grace that included not only salvation, but also the gifts of the Holy Spirit. They were suffering severe trials, or persecutions. (cf. 1 Thess. 2:14–15; 2 Thess. 1:4). Yet "out of . . . their extreme poverty," inspired by the Spirit, they gave sacrificially and with enthusiasm. Paul did not ask them to do this; they did it all on their own. They even begged Paul "for the privilege" of ministering in this way to the poor saints in Jerusalem (Rom. 15:26). Then they did far more than Paul expected. They were an inspiring example of "rich generosity."

They also did more than give money. "And they gave in a way we did not expect: They first gave themselves to the Lord and to us" (v. 5, NCV). They gave themselves to the Lord in renewed dedication to His will. Then they gave themselves to Paul and his company, thus recognizing Paul's apostleship and bonding with him in fellowship. They did this recognizing and depending on the will of God.

2. Titus Urged To Encourage Generosity 8:6–7

6So we urged Titus, since he had earlier made a beginning, to bring also to completion this act of grace on your part. 7But just as you excel in everything—in faith, in speech, in knowledge, in complete earnestness and in your love for us—see that you also excel in this grace of giving.

Titus had brought back a good report from Corinth. However, the believers there did not respond in giving the way the Macedonian believers did. Titus did make an appeal in Corinth for the collection, but it was only "a beginning." Now Paul was sending Titus to Corinth with this letter and an urgent plea that Titus be allowed to finalize the collection among them as an act manifesting God's grace.

From the good report Titus brought, Paul could say that grace overflowed in faith (probably shown by healings and miracles), speech (probably including prophecy, tongues, interpretation, and teaching), in knowledge (of God, His Word, and His purposes), in complete earnestness, and in their love for Paul.[2] Now he challenges them to overflow in the grace of giving, which is also a gift of the Spirit (Rom. 12:8).

---

[1]These would include the assemblies in Thessalonica, Philippi, and Berea (Acts 16:11 to 17:15).

[2]In view of 6:12, some (including the Jerusalem Bible) prefer the reading that speaks of Paul's love for the Corinthian believers. See Paul Barnett, *The Second Epistle to the Corinthians* (Grand Rapids: Wm. B. Eerdmans, 1997), 403 n. 64.

B. Jesus' Example 8:8–9

[8]I am not commanding you, but I want to test the sincerity of your love by comparing it with the earnestness of others. [9]For you know the grace of our Lord Jesus Christ, that though he was rich, yet for your sakes he became poor, so that you through his poverty might become rich.

Paul did not command the people to give. He did not want to pressure them, causing them to give out of a sense of obligation instead of voluntarily from a heart of sincere love. He was using the earnestness of the Macedonian believers as an example to encourage the Corinthians to give. But the real and most compelling motivation for giving comes from the supreme example of Jesus himself. He showed marvelous grace when He gave up all the riches of heaven and "became poor." He was born in a manger, lived in humble Nazareth, and had no place to lay His head during his ministry (Matt. 8:20). As Paul reminded the Philippians, "Your attitude should be the same as that of Christ Jesus: . . . taking the very nature of a servant . . . he humbled himself and became obedient to death—even death on a cross!" (Phil 2:5–8). He did this that we might now receive the riches of His salvation, His righteousness, and the Spirit's gifts as well as share in the riches of His glory throughout eternity.

C. Finish The Work 8:10–15

[10]And here is my advice about what is best for you in this matter: Last year you were the first not only to give but also to have the desire to do so. [11]Now finish the work, so that your eager willingness to do it may be matched by your completion of it, according to your means. [12]For if the willingness is there, the gift is acceptable according to what one has, not according to what he does not have.

Paul next advises them about the collection for the Jerusalem church. He reminds them that they were the first to give, the first to want to give. Then he urges them to "finish the work" by completing the collection. Then their initial willingness will be matched by willingness to complete it—out of what they have and are able to give. In other words, he is not implying they should go beyond their means as the Macedonians did. He wants to see the willingness to give out of what they do have, not out of what they do not have. He is not asking for a so-called faith promise, a promise to give something one does not yet have. What God wants to see is the willingness to give, not the amount (see 9:7).

[13]Our desire is not that others might be relieved while you are hard pressed, but that there might be equality. [14]At the present time your plenty will supply what they need, so that in turn their plenty will supply what you need. Then there will be equality, [15]as it is written: "He who gathered much did not have too much, and he who gathered little did not have too little."

Paul in his letters often anticipates questions. Here he is answering those who might wonder if it was right to impoverish themselves in order to help the Jerusalem believers.

Paul's answer is that he does not want them to be "hard pressed." What he wants to see is equality and fairness, where the one who has plenty supplies the needs of others, who in turn supply the need when they have plenty. To illustrate the principle of equality he refers to the manna in the desert, when no matter what the amount each gathered, their daily needs were met without either lack or surplus (Exod. 16:18). R. P. C. Hanson notes that Paul takes this as "a foretaste or prophecy of the self-adjusting love of Christ in His members which supplies the need of each without deficiency or embarrassment."[3]

D. The Character Of Titus And His Companions 8:16–24

[16]I thank God, who put into the heart of Titus the same concern I have for you. [17]For Titus not only welcomed our appeal, but he is coming to you with much enthusiasm and on his own initiative.

Paul had no doubts about the success of the mission of Titus. God put "the same concern," the same feeling, that Paul had for the Corinthians in the heart and mind of Titus. "There is no training program that can produce that kind of partnership."[4] It has to be God-

[3]R. P. C. Hanson, *The Second Epistle to the Corinthians: Christ and Controversy* (London: SCM Press, 1967), 69.

[4]Bard M. Pillette, "The Kind of Person Who Worked Best with Paul," *Emmaus Journal* 5, no. 2 (winter 1996): 157.

produced. God used not only Paul's teaching, but "his attitudes, discernment, and ethics" to influence those who joined him in ministry.[5] Thus Titus was happy to bring Paul's appeal for the collection to Corinth. In fact, he volunteered enthusiastically to do it because of his affection for the Corinthian believers.

> **18And we are sending along with him the brother who is praised by all the churches for his service to the gospel. 19What is more, he was chosen by the churches to accompany us as we carry the offering, which we administer in order to honor the Lord himself and to show our eagerness to help. 20We want to avoid any criticism of the way we administer this liberal gift. 21For we are taking pains to do what is right, not only in the eyes of the Lord but also in the eyes of men.**

To insure the success of the mission Paul was sending with Titus a special brother, praised by all the Macedonian churches and chosen by them (not by Paul).[6] He did not want anyone to think he was making a profit for himself. He also wanted the churches to know that the offering would be administered in a way that would honor the Lord, giving Him the glory. This would also show Paul's eagerness to help. Paul wanted the Jerusalem believers to know he honored them as well as the Lord. He was very careful to take forethought to do what is right in the eyes of the Lord and also in the eyes of the people (cf. 2:17; 4:2; 5:11). He knew that failure to be honest in administration of financial matters could ruin his ministry and turn people away from the Lord.

> **22In addition, we are sending with them our brother who has often proved to us in many ways that he is zealous, and now even more so because of his great confidence in you. 23As for Titus, he is my partner and fellow worker among you; as for our brothers, they are representatives of the churches and an honor to Christ. 24Therefore show these men the proof of your love and the reason for our pride in you, so that the churches can see it.**

To make sure that the Corinthians would have no reason to hesitate in their giving, Paul was sending with Titus a second unnamed brother of proven ministry and worth. He was a brother Paul could

---

[5]Ibid.

[6]The Gk. means they chose him by a show of hands.

trust, who had the same earnestness as Paul and his companions. This brother also had confidence in the Corinthian believers, so they in turn could receive him with confidence.

To emphasize this, Paul reminds them again of his relationship with Titus, among them as his partner and fellow worker. Then he repeats his commendation of the two Christian brothers chosen by the Macedonian churches as their "representatives" (Gk. *apostoloi,* "sent ones" or, in this case, official representatives of the churches that sent them), because they are an "honor" (Gk. *doxa,* "glory") to Christ. They shine brightly for Him against the dark background of the pagan society around them (cf. Phil. 2:15).[7]

Paul wanted the other churches to see the love of the Corinthian church. Behind this was his concern that the believers in Jerusalem see it. He wanted the Jewish believers and the Gentile believers to love one another and share with one another as part of the one body of Christ.

Paul also wanted his pride in the Corinthians to be demonstrated to the Macedonian assemblies. The Corinthians could do this by completing the collection. This was Paul's concern. He implemented this concern by "careful attention to thoughtful organization and prudent administration" as well as to teaching and prayer.[8]

E. A Generous Gift Was Promised 9:1–5

1There is no need for me to write to you about this service to the saints. 2For I know your eagerness to help, and I have been boasting about it to the Macedonians, telling them that since last year you in Achaia were ready to give; and your enthusiasm has stirred most of them to action. 3But I am sending the brothers in order that our boasting about you in this matter should not prove hollow, but that you may be ready, as I said you would be. 4For if any Macedonians come with me and find you unprepared, we—not to say anything about you—would be ashamed of having been so confident.

Paul almost apologizes for having to write to the Corinthian believers about this matter of the collection for the impoverished believers in Jerusalem. He remembers their initial enthusiasm, how he used

---

[7]Barnett, *Second Epistle to the Corinthians,* 427.
[8]Ibid., 428.

their example with pride to stir up the Macedonian assemblies to give, and how well most of Macedonian believers responded. But it was obvious that the enthusiasm of the Corinthian believers had waned. What would the Macedonian believers think if they came and found the Corinthians unprepared to give a generous offering! Paul would be ashamed of being so confident of their generosity, and so the Corinthians should be as well. Just as Paul had used the example of the Corinthian believers in a positive way to motivate the Macedonians, so now he was using the Macedonians in a positive way to encourage the Corinthians. Positive examples are usually more effective than negative examples.

5So I thought it necessary to urge the brothers to visit you in advance and finish the arrangements for the generous gift you had promised. Then it will be ready as a generous gift, not as one grudgingly given.

To avoid any such shame, Paul urged Titus and the two brothers with him to visit Corinth before Paul himself did in order to finish the arrangements for the generous gift the Corinthians had promised. But he still wants it to be a "generous gift" (Gk. *eulogian,* "a blessing" or "a gift that blesses"), as well as one given with love and enthusiasm, not given grudgingly. Paul was confident they would do this. Their generosity would not only preserve their reputation, but would also draw the assemblies in Greece and Macedonia together as they shared in this project.

F. Sowing And Reaping 9:6–15

6Remember this: Whoever sows sparingly will also reap sparingly, and whoever sows generously will also reap generously. 7Each man should give what he has decided in his heart to give, not reluctantly or under compulsion, for God loves a cheerful giver.

To encourage generosity Paul reminds them of a principle that every farmer should know. I remember a farmer in northern California who complained because his crops did not measure up to those of his neighbors. He had his soil tested, but it was the same as theirs. Then he found the difference. He was sowing half as much seed as his neighbors did. If farmers need to be reminded of this principle, so do we. Eventually, God will see to it that the generosity we cultivate in our giving is rewarded (cf. Prov. 11:18,25; 22:8; Gal. 6:7–9).

God, however, is not pleased with giving that is done "reluctantly or under compulsion." Each one should decide what he or she is able to give and give it cheerfully. The Greek *hilaron* does not mean "hilarious," however. It simply means we give because we are glad to give (cf. 1 Chron. 29:17). Thus we give neither legalistically nor reluctantly, but with the only compulsion coming from our hearts. This too can be a generosity motivated by the Holy Spirit (Rom. 12:8).

> **8And God is able to make all grace abound to you, so that in all things at all times, having all that you need, you will abound in every good work. 9As it is written: "He has scattered abroad his gifts to the poor; his righteousness endures forever."**

What God has done in making all kinds of grace abound is another important motive for giving (cf. Rom. 8:32). We do not need to fear that our generosity will hurt us, for God knows our needs and He will continue to supply. He wants to give us more than we need so we, like God himself, can overflow to all kinds of good works, even to helping other believers we do not know, just as the Corinthians did not know the Jerusalem believers personally.

The quotation in verse 9 is from Psalm 112:9,[9] which describes the acts of a righteous man. Some believe Paul is applying it to the righteous acts of God, since God is the subject of verses 8 and 10. God gives to the poor and His righteousness (including His faithfulness) endures forever.[10] However, most take it as the psalmist does and apply it to the righteous acts of the believer, which are "a part of that larger righteousness of God" by which we live and in which we "shall remain forever."[11] Often in the Old Testament righteousness is said to involve concern for the poor. Jesus also identified giving to the needy as acts of righteousness (Matt. 6:1–2). This is not contrary to the New Testament teaching of justification by faith apart from works. Rather, it indicates "that such mercy to the poor has a lasting, even permanent effect on the moral character of righteousness in one's life."[12]

---

[9]That is, from Ps. 111:9 in the Septuagint.

[10]Paul Barnett, *The Second Epistle to the Corinthians* (Grand Rapids: Wm. B. Eerdmans, 1997), 440.

[11]Victor Paul Furnish, *II Corinthians* (Garden City, N.Y.: Doubleday & Co., 1984), 449.

[12]James Hernando, "2 Corinthians," in *Full Life Bible Commentary* (Grand Rapids: Zondervan Publishing House, in press).

**10Now he who supplies seed to the sower and bread
for food will also supply and increase your store of
seed and will enlarge the harvest of your righteousness. 11You will be made rich in every way so that you
can be generous on every occasion, and through us
your generosity will result in thanksgiving to God.**

Now Paul draws on the Septuagint translation of Isaiah 55:10 and Hosea 10:12 to apply the metaphor of sowing and reaping further. God not only provides but increases what the believer has to sow. The Greeks used the word "supply" of a wealthy man providing generously for festal displays for the people of his city. Here is it used of God's generous provision, where the harvest is always greater than what is planted. For God also enlarges the harvest yielded by the believer's righteousness (that is, righteous acts; generosity that demonstrates Christ's righteousness).

In verse 11 Paul further applies this to the Corinthians' gift to the poor believers in Jerusalem. God is enriching the Corinthians so that through Paul their gift will bring thanksgiving to God from grateful Jerusalem believers.

**12This service that you perform is not only supplying the
needs of God's people but is also overflowing in many
expressions of thanks to God. 13Because of the service
by which you have proved yourselves, men will praise
God for the obedience that accompanies your confession of the gospel of Christ, and for your generosity in
sharing with them and with everyone else. 14And in
their prayers for you their hearts will go out to you,
because of the surpassing grace God has given you.**

This is not a "prosperity gospel," however. They are not to seek anything for themselves. Their only motive is to be able to give generously to the needy in order that God may be glorified.[13]

Their offering is a sacred service or ministry (cf. Rom. 15:27; Phil. 2:17). It will bring thanksgiving to God not only for their generosity, but also for their obedience that accompanies and demonstrates confessing Christ. Others will recognize that the Corinthians not only believe the gospel, but live it. As a result the hearts of the Jerusalem church, who receive their generosity, will go out to them as they pray.

13Barnett, *Second Corinthians,* 443.

For they will recognize the "surpassing grace" God has given to both them and the Corinthians. Paul wants the Corinthians' generosity to be "the spontaneous overflow of the grace which God has poured into their lives."[14]

15Thanks be to God for his indescribable gift!

When Paul speaks of God's grace, he is always overwhelmed. So he interjects thanks to God for the gift of His grace, the "indescribable gift": the gift of Christ (cf. John 3:16; 2 Cor. 8:9). In Him we see all the grace of God manifest. This concludes his challenge to the Corinthians to give generously. (See Rom. 5:15; 6:23; 11:33; Eph. 3:18–19; Col. 2:9; Heb. 6:4.)

Study questions for this section may be found in appendix B.

VI. PAUL'S APOSTOLIC OFFICE AND AUTHORITY 10:1–13:14

Though Titus brought good news about the attitude of the majority of the Corinthian believers, Paul, in chapters 11 to 13, again deals with his opponents who claim to be apostles (10:7; 11:5,13). They were still there trying to cause trouble and discredit him. These Jewish Christians, who came from outside, in an arrogant way were taking credit for the establishment of the assemblies in Greece (10:12–18; 11:18,20,22). They were preaching a different gospel, probably one that makes Christianity a form of Judaism. They probably made Moses more important than Jesus. They were also slandering Paul's character and ministry.[1]

A. Paul's Authority Will Be Exercised 10:1–6

1By the meekness and gentleness of Christ, I appeal to you—I, Paul, who am "timid" when face to face with you, but "bold" when away! 2I beg you that when I

[14]F. F. Bruce, *1 and 2 Corinthians* (Grand Rapids: Wm. B. Eerdmans, 1983), 228.

[1]Some scholars believe chaps. 10–13 were originally a separate letter. For a good defense of the unity of 2 Corinthians see Paul Barnett, *The Second Epistle to the Corinthians* (Grand Rapids: Wm. B. Eerdmans, 1997), 450–56.

come I may not have to be as bold as I expect to be toward some people who think that we live by the standards of this world.

The repetition of "I . . . I, Paul" emphasizes that Paul's "personal character and commission are at issue (cf. Gal. 5:2; 1 The. 2:18; also 2 C. 12:16)."[2] False apostles were saying Paul was timid or weak when with them and only bold through his letters. To defend himself against this charge, Paul appeals to the example of the unassuming meekness and patient "gentleness of Christ": Though He endured abuse (Isa. 53:7), He was not weak or without authority (cf. Matt. 11:29). Paul hopes he will not have to be bold and show his authority against "some people" (i.e., the false apostles) when he comes to Corinth.

These detractors were also criticizing Paul, saying that he and his company[3] were living by the standards of this world. Paul has already denied this by saying he did not act by worldly wisdom (1:12).

[3]For though we live in the world, we do not wage war as the world does. [4]The weapons we fight with are not the weapons of the world. On the contrary, they have divine power to demolish strongholds.

Paul now pictures his apostolic ministry in terms of a military campaign.[4] He and his companions in ministry lived in the world (Gr. *en sarki,* "in the flesh," cf. "in jars of clay" 4:7). But he did not wage war as the world does (Gk. *kata sarka,* "according to the flesh," that is, limited by what is finite, human, earthly, or merely physical). No matter how weak or timid Paul might seem to be in the presence of the Corinthians, he did not have to put on a bold front or use the methods and weapons the world uses. When the Spirit anointed him he had weapons with "divine power" to demolish enemy strongholds. Those weapons are the Spirit and the Word. The "strongholds" were those clever arguments against the simple gospel of Christ that Paul preached as well as the attempts to destroy his ministry and bring his converts into spiritual bondage by his enemies' false doctrines.

---

[2]F. F. Bruce, *1 and 2 Corinthians* (Grand Rapids: Wm. B. Eerdmans, 1983), 229.

[3]Note the change from "I" to "we."

[4]This continues through v. 6 and is "by far the most elaborate instance of the use of military imagery in the Pauline letters. Cf. His reference to 'the weapons of righteousness' in 6:7b, and Phil. 2:25; 1 Thess. 5:8; Philem. 2." Victor Paul Furnish, *II Corinthians* (Garden City, N.Y.: Doubleday & Co., 1984), 457.

We can apply this to the forces of evil that would seek to destroy the Church by bringing in false doctrines, worldly ways, secular entertainment, and worldly display. The Word and the Spirit are still able to demolish the powers of darkness (see Eph. 6:14–18).

5We demolish arguments and every pretension that sets itself up against the knowledge of God, and we take captive every thought to make it obedient to Christ. 6And we will be ready to punish every act of disobedience, once your obedience is complete.

By preaching the true gospel in the power of the Holy Spirit Paul pulls down the clever-sounding philosophical arguments and systems, as well as the misleading pretensions set up by false apostles and prophets. Paul's purpose was to "take captive every thought" (including those of the false apostles) and make them obedient to Christ. We, too, need to be careful that human philosophies and false teachings do not influence our thinking. We need to bring "both mind and will into complete submission to, and therefore harmony with, the mind and will of Christ."[5]

Paul indicates too that he expects the assembly as a whole to put themselves fully into his hands in obedience to Christ. Then he will be better able to deal with the Corinthians who thought Paul lived "by the standards of this world" (10:2) as well as the rebels (the false apostles) who have come from outside.

B. Paul's Conduct As An Apostle 10:7–11

7You are looking only on the surface of things. If anyone is confident that he belongs to Christ, he should consider again that we belong to Christ just as much as he. 8For even if I boast somewhat freely about the authority the Lord gave us for building you up rather than pulling you down, I will not be ashamed of it.

Paul wants the Corinthians to look at the facts and think about what they know he has done. Everything his opponents were saying about him was superficial and didn't deal with reality. His opponents may have claimed they followed Jesus while he was still on earth. At least, they claimed a special relationship to Christ and denied that Paul had such a relationship (cf. those who said, "'I follow Christ,'" 1 Cor. 1:12).

---

[5]Philip Edgcumbe Hughes, *Paul's Second Epistle to the Corinthians* (Grand Rapids: Wm. B. Eerdmans, 1973), 353.

Paul indicates they abuse the authority they claim.[6] He affirms that he belongs to Christ just as much as his opponents do. If he were to boast more than he does he would still be telling the truth, so he would not be ashamed. The only purpose of the authority the Lord gave him was to build up, not to tear down. As the Lord's slave, he did tear down the strongholds of his opponents, but his purpose was only to build up the Corinthian believers.

He is confident that he will not be brought to shame (as a liar or empty boaster), that is, before the judgment seat of Christ (5:10).[7] His authority, like the gifts and fruit of the Spirit, was given to edify, to build up (2 Cor. 10:8; cf. 1 Cor. 14:26).

9I do not want to seem to be trying to frighten you with my letters. 10For some say, "His letters are weighty and forceful, but in person he is unimpressive and his speaking amounts to nothing." 11Such people should realize that what we are in our letters when we are absent, we will be in our actions when we are present.

Ironically, Paul says he was not trying to scare the Corinthians into submission with his letters. They must not think that he was. Paul's opponents compliment his letters but say that he is personally "'unimpressive'" in his demeanor and his speech. He was not the orator Apollos was (Acts 18:24). They imply that Paul is forceful in his letters because he is writing from a safe distance, but that when he comes he will not carry out his warnings. They imply also that the weakness of his person is inconsistent with his letters and this proved he lacked apostolic authority.

Paul, however, warns that when he comes he will show the same authority revealed in his letters. They can expect him to deal actively with the situation and discipline those who need it. He will be just as effective when present with them as when absent.

C. Paul's Boasting 10:12–12:10

1. The Limits On Paul's Boasting 10:12–18

12We do not dare to classify or compare ourselves with some who commend themselves. When they measure

[6]Jerry L. Sumney, *Identifying Paul's Opponents* (Sheffield, England: Journal for the Study of the New Testament Press, 1990), 158.

[7]Barnett, *Second Epistle to the Corinthians,* 473.

themselves by themselves and compare themselves with themselves, they are not wise. [13]We, however, will not boast beyond proper limits, but will confine our boasting to the field God has assigned to us, a field that reaches even to you.

With irony Paul rejects any comparison of himself with his opponents.[8] As *The Message* puts verse 12, "We're not, understand, putting ourselves in a league with those who boast that they're our superiors. We wouldn't dare do that." They were trying to make their achievements seem impressive by foolishly comparing "themselves with themselves." They refuse to recognize what God has done through Paul in connection with his commission to the Gentiles—given to him by Christ (Acts 9:15; Gal. 2:9). They say Paul should boast as they do and present the kind of proof of his apostleship they want him to—if he is a real apostle. But Paul will boast only within the limits of the ministry God has given him, which include Corinth. By saying this, Paul is implying that the false apostles are intruders who are hurting the assembly God sent him to establish.

[14]We are not going too far in our boasting, as would be the case if we had not come to you, for we did get as far as you with the gospel of Christ. [15]Neither do we go beyond our limits by boasting of work done by others. Our hope is that, as your faith continues to grow, our area of activity among you will greatly expand, [16]so that we can preach the gospel in the regions beyond you. For we do not want to boast about work already done in another man's territory.

Paul's boasting is not going too far, beyond proper limits, for he and his companions were the first to arrive in Corinth with the gospel. This was the farthest point he had reached in his missionary journeys up to this time. His hope was, however, to enlarge his work in Corinth and then go to regions beyond. In Paul's view this would include Illyricum, Rome, and Spain (see Rom. 15:19,23–24,28). But he would not be like the false apostles, for he would not claim that he was the first to bring the gospel into a territory that had actually been evangelized by another person.

[8]The Gk. has a wordplay here, *enkrinai ē sunkrinai*, "to rank among or to compare with."

**17But, "Let him who boasts boast in the Lord." 18For it is
not the one who commends himself who is approved,
but the one whom the Lord commends.**

Paul limits his boasting further by paraphrasing Jeremiah 9:24.[9] This is another reason why no one should boast about taking over something that is another person's responsibility.

Actually, any boasting or commending of one's self or one's ministry is not important. The only thing that counts is the Lord's commendation[10] (cf. Rom. 2:29; 1 Cor. 4:3–5; 2 Cor. 3:1–3). He will not give that commendation to those who are seeking to exalt themselves.

2. Paul Exposes False Apostles 11:1–4

**1I hope[11] you will put up with a little of my foolishness;
but you are already doing that. 2I am jealous for you
with a godly jealousy. I promised you to one husband,
to Christ, so that I might present you as a pure virgin
to him.**

Paul does more than defend himself. He wants to expose the false apostles in order to protect the Corinthian believers from their deceptions.

Paul speaks of "foolishness" because he has called the self-exaltation of the false apostles meaningless and empty (cf. 10:12). Now he feels it necessary to emphasize the claims of his own authority, which might sound as if he is doing the same thing. However, he does so not because he wants to commend himself, but because the false apostles are trying to change the fundamental teachings of the gospel and the Corinthians are in danger of accepting their authority instead of Christ's and the true gospel's.

Paul has a genuine concern for the Corinthian believers. His "jealousy" for them is not selfish but godly in that it is like God's and from God. God wants the best for His people, so Paul does not want them led astray by false teachers or false apostles.

Because Paul founded the assembly in Corinth he feels like a father

---

[9] Also paraphrased in 1 Cor. 1:31.

[10] The Greek for "approved," *dokimos,* means tested and approved, or tried and true, and thus accepted by the Lord.

[11] The words "to God" (v.1, KJV) are not in any Greek manuscript but were added by the British translators.

who wants to give his daughter in marriage as a pure virgin.[12] He brought them to Christ at their conversion, which he compares to an engagement promise of marriage, so Paul wants to present the entire assembly of believers to Christ as pure: free from moral sins and false doctrines (cf. Eph. 5:25–27).[13]

> **3But I am afraid that just as Eve was deceived by the serpent's cunning, your minds may somehow be led astray from your sincere and pure devotion to Christ. 4For if someone comes to you and preaches a Jesus other than the Jesus we preached, or if you receive a different spirit from the one you received, or a different gospel from the one you accepted, you put up with it easily enough.**

Paul has already said that the believer is a new creation and that the Christian life is a new way, so new that it is like a new world (5:17). He does not want the new creation to be spoiled the way Eve spoiled the first creation.[14] He knows that the influence of the false apostles could do just that.

With irony he recognizes that the Corinthians have been too tolerant of these false apostles, especially one of them who comes preaching another Jesus, one like Him, but probably denying His full deity or even His resurrection (see 1 Cor. 15:12–18). From these "apostles" the Corinthians could receive an entirely different spirit, probably a demon spirit, not the Holy Spirit they had actually received under Paul's ministry, for they would be receiving a very different gospel (cf.

---

[12]Fathers in those days were responsible for finding husbands for their daughters and for protecting them between the time they were engaged and the time of marriage. For Paul's relationship to other believers as a father cf. 1 Cor. 4:14–15; 2 Cor. 6:13; 12:14–15; Gal. 4:19; 1 Tim. 1:2; 2 Tim. 1:2; Philem. 10.

[13]For OT background of the marriage relationship as a metaphor for the relationship between God and His people, see Isa. 54:3,6; Jer. 3:1; Hos. 2:19–20. For the metaphor of Christ as the Bridegroom of the Church see Eph. 5:25–33. For a similar relation of each church, of each Christian, see 1 Cor. 6:13–17. Cf. Matt. 25:1–13; Mark 2:18–20; Rev. 19:6–9 for the closeness, inviolability of the union of Christians with the Savior. R. P. C. Hanson, *The Second Epistle to the Corinthians: Christ and Controversy* (London: SCM Press, 1967), 77.

[14]Some see the Church here as a second Eve betrothed to the second Adam, Christ (1 Cor. 15:45). J. J. Lias, *The Second Epistle to the Corinthians* (Cambridge, England: University Press, 1897), 110.

Gal. 1:6–9), different from the one they accepted (Gk. *edexasthe,* "welcomed") when Paul first proclaimed it in Corinth.

3. Paul's Apostolic Status 11:5–6

[5]But I do not think I am in the least inferior to those "super-apostles."[15] [6]I may not be a trained speaker, but I do have knowledge. We have made this perfectly clear to you in every way.

The false apostles were putting themselves forward as "'super-apostles,'" thus demeaning Paul.[16] But Paul did not accept their claims. They may have been well-trained orators, able to impress people with their vocabulary and style. Paul may have had them in mind when he wrote to the Romans that "such people are not serving our Lord Christ, but their own appetites. By smooth talk and flattery they deceive the minds of naive people" (Rom. 16:18). Though Paul was trained as a rabbi under Gamaliel (Acts 22:3), he was not trained in the artificial, flamboyant Greek style of oratory.[17] Paul, however, had something more important. He had knowledge from God that they did not have, as the Corinthian believers well knew. Paul had demonstrated this "in every way"; that is, by giving them powerful, anointed teaching in plain language—not in the deceptive "logic" and superficial rhetoric of the false apostles. Truth is more important than style or the "charisma" of the speaker.

4. Paul's Refusal To Accept Pay 11:7–12

[7]Was it a sin for me to lower myself in order to elevate you by preaching the gospel of God to you free of charge? [8]I robbed other churches by receiving support from them so as to serve you. [9]And when I was with you and needed something, I was not a burden to

---

[15]Sumney argues that these are not the Twelve Apostles. Jerry L. Sumney, *Identifying Paul's Opponents* (Sheffield, England: Journal for the Study of the New Testament Press, 1990), 159–61. *The Message* calls them "big-shot 'apostles.'" Paul is being sarcastic here, as the context shows.

[16]Some take the "'super-apostles'" to be James, Peter, and John who were "reputed to be pillars" (Gal. 2:9), and that Paul is simply saying he is not inferior to them. F. F. Bruce, *1 and 2 Corinthians* (Grand Rapids: Wm. B. Eerdmans, 1983), 236–37. However, the Jerusalem apostles would not have presented a different Jesus or a different gospel (cf. Gal. 2:2–10).

[17]Victor Paul Furnish, *II Corinthians* (Garden City, N.Y.: Doubleday & Co., 1984), 490.

anyone, for the brothers who came from Macedonia supplied what I needed. I have kept myself from being a burden to you in any way, and will continue to do so.

Paul turns again to the fact that he preached the gospel in Corinth "free of charge" (see 1 Cor. 9). In those days, even in the universities, the students paid fees directly to the teacher. Paul's opponents probably said that his failure to take contributions for himself was evidence that his teaching was of little value and that he was not a true apostle. With irony Paul asks if his failure to accept contributions was a sin. Apparently his adversaries were saying that this made Paul inferior to them. Paul, however, kept himself from being a burden to the Corinthians by supporting himself and his fellow evangelists by his tentmaking (Acts 18:3). Then some friends came from Macedonia (Acts 18:5) bringing offerings, especially from Philippi (Phil. 4:15). Paul accepted their gift, calling it "robbery" of other churches, because he was not ministering to them at the time. However, Paul would not change his method of evangelizing cities and starting churches.

**10As surely as the truth of Christ is in me, nobody in the
regions of Achaia will stop this boasting of mine.
11Why? Because I do not love you? God knows I do!
12And I will keep on doing what I am doing in order to
cut the ground from under those who want an opportunity to be considered equal with us in the things they boast about.**

Paul had already said that the mind of Christ is in him (1 Cor. 2:16). Now he says the truth of Christ was in him. It had become a part of his very nature, guiding and directing all that he said and did. Because of this, he would not let anyone "stop this boasting."

Paul's opponents also implied that Paul had no love for the Corinthians, and that was why he took no offerings for himself. They implied his lack of love made him not want to feel under obligation to them. Paul denies that emphatically. He loved them intensely, as God knew.

Paul probably thought the Corinthians would again press him to accept payment (as the false apostles did) when he came to them again. But he assures them he would continue to refuse "in order to keep those other 'apostles' from having any reason for boasting and saying that they work in the same way that we do" (v. 12, TEV).

5. False Apostles Denounced 11:13–15

**[13]For such men are false apostles, deceitful workmen,
masquerading as apostles of Christ. [14]And no wonder,
for Satan himself masquerades as an angel of light.
[15]It is not surprising, then, if his servants masquerade
as servants of righteousness. Their end will be what
their actions deserve.**

Because of the character of those "'super-apostles'" (v. 5), the Corinthians should not believe them in their boasting. They may have claimed Peter and John sent them. But Paul says they are "false apostles, deceitful workmen" putting on a false front.

He compares them with Satan, the deceiver, the adversary. Satan is not an "angel of light" (his realm is darkness; Acts 26:18), but he often masquerades as one. So they are not "servants of righteousness" even though they try to give that impression. It is probable that the righteousness they claimed and taught was a righteousness that depended on the law of Moses and denied the grace of Christ. They deserve judgment (cf. Rom. 2:6,8–9), and in the end their actions will bring it.

6. Paul's Suffering 11:16–18

**[16]I repeat: Let no one take me for a fool. But if you do,
then receive me just as you would a fool, so that I may
do a little boasting. [17]In this self-confident boasting I am
not talking as the Lord would, but as a fool. [18]Since many
are boasting in the way the world does, I too will boast.**

Paul has already started his boasting three times (10:1,8; 11:1); and then stopped to deal with the empty boasts of his opponents. Now he proceeds to carry his boasting through (see 11:1). He tells the Corinthians not to take him for a fool, though he knows some will do that. In irony, he says they should then receive him as they would any fool (for they were receiving the false apostles), allowing him to "do a little boasting."

He is still comparing himself with the false apostles, though he does not name them here. He simply refers to the "many" who are his opponents. They "operate with different standards" than Paul does.[18] But since they have been identifying with him, trying to claim apostleship, he will now return the favor and identify with them—by becoming a fool and boasting!

---

[18]Sumney, *Identifying Paul's Opponents*, 152.

Paul does not want the Corinthians to misunderstand him, however. He is not speaking the way the Lord would speak but in the "self-confident" way a fool would speak, "the way the world does" (Gk. *kata tēn sarka,* "according to the flesh"). But his purpose is to reveal their foolishness, "while at the same time positively expounding the authentic 'foolishness' of God's ways, which he, Paul, is following."[19]

7. Paul Compares Himself With His Opponents At Corinth 11:19–33

19You gladly put up with fools since you are so wise!
20In fact, you even put up with anyone who enslaves you or exploits you or takes advantage of you or pushes himself forward or slaps you in the face. 21To my
shame I admit that we were too weak for that! What anyone else dares to boast about—I am speaking as a fool—I also dare to boast about. 22Are they
Hebrews? So am I. Are they Israelites? So am I. Are they Abraham's descendants? So am I.

Ironically Paul notes that the Corinthians gladly put up with his opponents who were pushing themselves forward acting as superiors and trying to dominate the Corinthians. They let them enslave, exploit, take advantage, and even slap them in the face. Ironically Paul admits he was "too weak" to abuse them in that way. He implies the Corinthians are the real fools.

Whatever the false apostles could boast about, Paul could match and do more. Again, he recognizes that he is speaking like a fool, but he dares to do so, as we have seen, because of his concern for the Corinthian believers.

The false apostles must have boasted about their heritage. But Paul could match the best of them. He was a Hebrew, not a proselyte (convert) to Judaism, and not like Timothy with only one parent a Jew (cf. Phil. 3:5). He was an Israelite, part of the congregation of Israel, brought up under the Law. He was a descendant of Abraham, heir to the promises God gave him (cf. Rom. 9:4–5; Gal. 3:6–18). His background and training were as good as any of them. This may suggest that his opponents were Hellenistic-Hebrew Christians.[20]

---

[19]Paul Barnett, *The Second Epistle to the Corinthians* (Grand Rapids: Wm. B. Eerdmans, 1997), 530.

[20]Ibid., 534.

[23]Are they servants of Christ? (I am out of my mind to talk like this.) I am more. I have worked much harder, been in prison more frequently, been flogged more severely, and been exposed to death again and again. [24]Five times I received from the Jews the forty lashes minus one. [25]Three times I was beaten with rods, once I was stoned, three times I was shipwrecked, I spent a night and a day in the open sea, [26]I have been constantly on the move. I have been in danger from rivers, in danger from bandits, in danger from my own countrymen, in danger from Gentiles; in danger in the city, in danger in the country, in danger at sea; and in danger from false brothers.

The false apostles claimed to be "servants of Christ." No doubt, they claimed to have achieved great things. But Paul's service went far beyond what any of them had done or experienced. But the long list that follows is a record, not of brilliant victories, but of the fulfillment of promise of suffering Jesus made to him (Acts 9:16).

He said before that he spoke as a fool. Now he goes further and states that he is out of his mind (Gk. *paraphronōn*, "insane").

He says he was exposed to death again and again. Then he gives examples in verses 24–26. The Bible does not mention elsewhere Paul's receiving forty lashes minus one.[21] Acts tells us of one imprisonment at Philippi (Acts 16:15–40), of a beating with rods there (Acts 16:22–23),[22] of a stoning in Lystra (Acts 14:19), and of one shipwreck that occurred long after Paul wrote about the three others. Obviously, Luke in Acts was emphasizing key events that the Holy Spirit wanted him to record. But many other things also took place, and Paul refers to them here. Everywhere he went he faced dangers, not the least of which were "false brothers" (such as the false apostles in Corinth).

[27]I have labored and toiled and have often gone without sleep; I have known hunger and thirst and have often gone without food; I have been cold and naked.

His work was often toil under difficult circumstances. We do not

[21]Jewish custom was that the person doing the flogging was not responsible if the person died while receiving thirty-nine lashes. Forty lashes was considered to be fatal. Thus, if even one more lash was given and the person died, the flogger was exiled.

[22]Beating with rods was a Roman way of punishment and must have been done in cities that were Roman colonies.

know what caused him to go without sleep or why he was often hungry and sometimes thirsty.[23] He must have been cold in prison. By "naked," he meant he was without sufficient clothes (not nude, but with only the short tunic a slave might wear).

> **28Besides everything else, I face daily the pressure of**
> **my concern for all the churches. 29Who is weak, and I**
> **do not feel weak? Who is led into sin, and I do not**
> **inwardly burn?**

Despite these persecutions, dangers, and privations, Paul never forgot his primary purpose and mission: His concern, not just for the Corinthian believers but for all the assemblies he founded, pressed on him every day. Even in prison he kept in touch with them and felt their weakness. He burned with anger whenever any of them was tripped up and fell into sin. Physically and emotionally he suffered. His anxiety over the churches gave him the most pain of all.

> **30If I must boast, I will boast of the things that show my**
> **weakness. 31The God and Father of the Lord Jesus,**
> **who is to be praised forever, knows that I am not lying.**
> **32In Damascus the governor under King Aretas had**
> **the city of the Damascenes guarded in order to arrest**
> **me. 33But I was lowered in a basket from a window in**
> **the wall and slipped through his hands.**

Paul did not want the Corinthians to think he was a proud person. So he boasts of things that show his weakness. To declare the truth of what he says, he praises God as the Father of Jesus who is Lord.Acts 9:23–25 gives Luke's account of Paul's escape from Damascus. Luke indicates that Jews conspired to kill Paul. Here Paul indicates that the governor under King Aretas IV of Arabia (that is, of the Nabataean Arabs) gave the order. (King Aretas reigned from A.D. 9–39.) Some suggest that the governor may have been a Jew, since Jews were often put in official positions because kings respected their integrity.[24]

His disciples let him down in a large basket through a window of a house which had a room built on the city wall. I have seen similar rooms on the present city wall of Damascus.

---

[23]Food and drink were not provided in prisons. Paul probably lacked these things in cities where he was arrested but did not yet have supporters.

[24]Margaret E. Thrall, *The First and Second Letters of Paul to the Corinthians* (Cambridge, England: University Press, 1965), 175.

God knows Paul is not lying when he reminds the Corinthians of "a humiliating and undignified experience, in which he cut such a ridiculous figure that the mere thought of it killed any tendency to pride."[25] In all of these sufferings Paul was really saying what he later told the Philippians: "I want to know Christ and the power of his resurrection and the fellowship of sharing in his sufferings, becoming like him in his death, and so somehow, to attain to the resurrection from the dead. Not that I have already obtained all this, or have already been made perfect, but I press on to take hold of that for which Christ Jesus took hold of me" (Phil. 3:10–12). What a contrast to the pride and self-exaltation of the false apostles who were opposing Paul!

8. Paul's Vision Of Paradise 12:1–6

**1 I must go on boasting. Although there is nothing to be
gained, I will go on to visions and revelations from the
Lord. 2 I know a man in Christ who fourteen years ago
was caught up to the third heaven. Whether it was in
the body or out of the body I do not know—God
knows. 3 And I know that this man—whether in the
body or apart from the body I do not know, but God
knows— 4 was caught up to paradise. He heard inex-
pressible things, things that man is not permitted to tell.**

Because of his opponents Paul feels forced to "go on boasting." Apparently, they were claiming impressive visions and revelations. But Paul says such visions and revelations gain nothing; that is, they are not evidence of apostleship, nor do they help the congregation in general. This is not to deny the edifying value of the Holy Spirit's gift of revelation (1 Cor. 14:6,26,30). Rather, Paul is dealing with the claims of the false apostles. None of their visions could be any more impressive than the one the Spirit prompted him to tell about. Yet he is reticent about recounting the vision and puts it in the third person, though it is obvious that the "man in Christ" was Paul himself, as verse 7 shows. Probably he distanced himself from the vision because he did not want to use it as an apostolic credential and did not "want to be known as 'visionary,' but only as a weak and suffering apostle . . . through whom God's incomparable power is disclosed (4:7–15)."[26]

---

[25]Bruce, *1 and 2 Corinthians,* 244.

[26]Victor Paul Furnish, *II Corinthians* (Garden City, N.Y.: Doubleday & Co., 1984), 544.

He received the vision fourteen years before, which would be about A.D. 41, probably shortly after the Jerusalem leaders sent him to Tarsus (Acts 9:30). He was caught up (Gk. *hērpagē,* "snatched up unexpectedly") into the third heaven, which he also calls "paradise."[27] He probably thought of the first heaven as the atmosphere surrounding the earth, where the birds fly and where the clouds are; the second heaven as that of the stars; and the third heaven as the heaven of heavens, the highest heaven, the place where the throne of God and paradise are. The idea of seven heavens is not found in the Bible, though it was common in Zoroastrianism and became part of later Jewish and Christian theology.[28]

Paul was not sure whether he was in the body or out of the body. Only "God knows" that. But he knew he who had been humiliated by being let down in a basket was then caught up to a real place where he heard things he was "not permitted to tell." However, "not permitted" (Gk. *ouk exon*) can also mean "not possible." Thus, it may be that there are no human words adequate to express what he heard and saw. Some commentators take it that the words were "praises offered to God by the inhabitants of heaven."[29]

5I will boast about a man like that, but I will not boast about myself, except about my weaknesses. 6Even if I should choose to boast, I would not be a fool, because I would be speaking the truth. But I refrain, so no one will think more of me than is warranted by what I do or say.

Paul again recognizes that whatever boasting he might do would be true; however, the only thing he really wants to boast about is his weaknesses—including everything he suffered because of his faithful ministry of the gospel. Unlike his detractors, he wants people to see that all the power is of God (see 1 Cor. 2:4–5).

9. Paul's Thorn In The Flesh 12:7–10

7To keep me from becoming conceited because of these surpassingly great revelations, there was given

---

[27]"Paradise" is a term borrowed from the Persian and used in the Septuagint of the Garden of Eden (Gen. 2:8–10) and by Jesus of the place where He would be after His death on the cross (Luke 23:43). This can be understood to be heaven, for He committed His spirit into the Father's hands (Luke 23:46).

[28]Stanley M. Horton, *Our Destiny: Biblical Teachings on the Last Things* (Springfield, Mo.: Logion Press, 1996), 55.

[29]Margaret E. Thrall, *The First and Second Letters of Paul to the Corinthians* (Cambridge, England: University Press, 1965), 178.

**me a thorn in my flesh, a messenger of Satan, to tor-
ment me. [8]Three times I pleaded with the Lord to take
it away from me. [9]But he said to me, "My grace is sufficient for you, for my power is made perfect in weakness." Therefore I will boast all the more gladly about
my weaknesses, so that Christ's power may rest on
me. [10]That is why, for Christ's sake, I delight in weaknesses, in insults, in hardships, in persecutions, in difficulties. For when I am weak, then I am strong.**

This vision of the third heaven and paradise was only one of the "surpassingly great revelations" God gave Paul. To keep him from being conceited (like the false apostles, 11:20) or "unduly elated" (v. 7, NEB), a thorn in the flesh, a messenger (Gk. *angelos*) of Satan, was given to him (by God), not to punish but to torment or buffet him (implying something recurring).

There is no agreement concerning what the thorn in the flesh was.[30] Chysostom thought it referred to Alexander the coppersmith (2 Tim 4:14, KJV).[31] Others take it to be a Judaizer who followed Paul, causing him distress. Since it was "in [the] flesh," that is, in the body, most take it to be a sickness (Gal. 4:13–14; cf. 1 Cor. 2:3). Some take it to be recurring malaria, noting that he left the lower swampy regions of Galatia for higher ground on his first missionary journey. All we can be sure about is that God gave Satan permission to harass Paul, just as He gave permission to harass Job.

Three times Paul pleaded with the Lord to take away the thorn. The Lord (that is, Christ, for the Lord's power is identified as "Christ's power") replied that His grace was "'sufficient.'" It would always be with him. So would Christ's power be with him: rest on or in him (Gk. *episkēnōsēi,* "pitch its tent, take up its abode in"). Then, because of Paul's weakness, Christ could manifest His power in a more effective way. Paul's weakness, too, would make it all the more obvious that the mighty power was Christ's, not his. Thus, his weakness including his thorn was further evidence of his apostleship. So, "for Christ's sake" he welcomed and delighted in all kinds situations where he was

---

[30]The Gk. *skolops* can mean a pointed stake, thorn, spike, or splinter. It was used in the Septuagint of the Canaanites (Num. 33:55). It could also be translated "a thorn for the flesh" that is, causing him disadvantage in his "mortal existence." See Paul Barnett, *The Second Epistle to the Corinthians* (Grand Rapids: Wm. B. Eerdmans, 1997), 568–69.

[31]Chrysostom *Homilies on 2 Corinthians* Homily 26.

weak, including insults, hardships, persecutions, and difficulties. For when he was weak, then he was powerful with resurrection power given by the grace of Christ. Thus, his weakness became an asset, not a liability.

Christ's assurance that His grace is sufficient and that his power is perfected in weakness encourages us today. Instead of trying to control our own destiny, we must submit to God's will. Whenever we feel powerless, "whether bodily, relational, financial, or structural,"[32] we can say, "'Not my will, but yours be done'" (Luke 22:42). Then as we actively obey the Lord, we can claim His sufficient grace and experience His power "'made perfect in weakness.'"

D. Paul's Unselfish Concern For The Corinthians 12:11–21

11I have made a fool of myself, but you drove me to it. I ought to have been commended by you, for I am not in the least inferior to the "super-apostles," even though I am nothing. 12The things that mark an apostle—signs, wonders and miracles—were done among you with great perseverance. 13How were you inferior to the other churches, except that I was never a burden to you? Forgive me this wrong!

Because the Corinthians were accepting the teachings and claims of the false "'super-apostles,'" Paul felt driven to make a fool of himself by boasting. The Corinthian believers should have been commending Paul. Though he in himself was nothing, he was not at all inferior to the false "'super-apostles.'"

Paul implies his opponents were not manifesting the Holy Spirit in a proper way. But in Paul's ministry God had given apostolic signs, wonders, and works of miraculous power. Paul did not hold back, but with great endurance he continued to let God demonstrate these marks of an apostle (in the face of much opposition). We would say today that Paul's evangelism was indeed charismatic. More important, his conduct and character were Christlike.

Then with irony Paul asked why the Corinthians felt inferior to the other churches. Had he demeaned them by not being a burden to them? They must forgive him this wrong, this injustice!

32Barnett, *Second Epistle,* 574.

[14]Now I am ready to visit you for the third time, and I will not be a burden to you, because what I want is not your possessions but you. After all, children should not have to save up for their parents, but parents for their children. [15]So I will very gladly spend for you everything I have and expend myself as well. If I love you more, will you love me less?

On Paul's first visit he founded the assembly at Corinth. His second visit was painful (2 Cor. 2:1). Now he was ready to visit them a "third time." As their spiritual parent (cf. 1 Cor. 4:14–15) he did not want to burden them. He wanted them, not their possessions, not their money. In their culture parents made provision for their children, not the other way around. He would spend what he had as well as expend himself in kind to secure their love. He loved them so much. He wanted them to respond—something they were not doing. So he asks ironically whether his loving them more causes them to love him less.

[16]Be that as it may, I have not been a burden to you. Yet, crafty fellow that I am, I caught you by trickery! [17]Did I exploit you through any of the men I sent you? [18]I urged Titus to go to you and I sent our brother with him. Titus did not exploit you, did he? Did we not act in the same spirit and follow the same course?

Paul was not a burden to the Corinthians.[33] Yet some were saying that by sending Titus and another unnamed brother Paul was using trickery, using them to do what Paul personally had not done. But Titus did not exploit them. (The question about Titus calls for a negative answer. As the New Living Translation puts v. 18: "Did Titus take advantage of you? No, of course not!") Nor did he take money from them and slip it to Paul. "Titus left the same footprint, the same ethical impression" as Paul.[34] Thus, in no way did Paul abuse his relationship with the Corinthians.

[19]Have you been thinking all along that we have been defending ourselves to you? We have been speaking in the sight of God as those in Christ; and everything we do, dear friends, is for your strengthening.

---

[33]"I" in v. 16 is emphatic.

[34]Bard M. Pillette, "The Kind of Person Who Worked Best With Paul," *Emmaus Journal* 5, no. 2 (winter 1996): 157.

The Corinthians indeed had been thinking that Paul was defending himself. But Paul was not accountable to them. He was accountable only to God and Christ, and he was speaking before God and in Christ with one purpose—to strengthen them as his "dear friends" (Gk. *agapētoi,* "loved ones"), to bring them to a greater spiritual maturity.

20For I am afraid that when I come I may not find you as I want you to be, and you may not find me as you want me to be. I fear that there may be quarreling, jealousy, outbursts of anger, factions, slander, gossip, arrogance and disorder. 21I am afraid that when I come again my God will humble me before you, and I will be grieved over many who have sinned earlier and have not repented of the impurity, sexual sin and debauchery in which they have indulged.

Paul does not want to find the Corinthians involved in sins that will make it necessary for him to be severe. He remembers and specifies the things he had to deal with before: "quarreling"—rivalry, discord, strife; "jealousy"—or envy; "outbursts of anger"—or selfish indignation; "factions"—or contentions caused by self-seeking and selfish ambition; "slander"—or evil speech; "gossip"—or whisperings, secret tale-bearing; "arrogance"—or conceit; and "disorder"—or unruly commotions. He was afraid he might have to deal with these things again if they did not respond to this letter in loving obedience.

He did not want God to humble him by making him feel grieved over those who had not repented and changed their ways (cf. 11:29). He was especially concerned about those who had indulged in moral impurity, sexual sin (including adultery, homosexuality, prostitution, and union with prostitutes), and debauchery and might not have repented. If he should find these things he would be humiliated, humbled by God.

E. A Renewed Warning 13:1–10

1This will be my third visit to you. "Every matter must be established by the testimony of two or three witnesses." 2I already gave you a warning when I was with you the second time. I now repeat it while absent: On my return I will not spare those who sinned earlier or any of the others, 3since you are demanding proof that Christ is speaking through me. He is not weak in deal-

ing with you, but is powerful among you. [4]For to be sure, he was crucified in weakness, yet he lives by God's power. Likewise, we are weak in him, yet by God's power we will live with him to serve you.

Paul gave severe warnings to sinners on his second visit to Corinth (see 12:21). He is warning them again in this letter. His "third visit" would be a third witness against them if they did not repent. They knew the Scripture passages which state that everything must be established by two or three witnesses (cf. Num. 35:30; Deut. 17:6; 19:15; Matt. 18:16; 1 Tim. 5:19; Heb. 10:28; 1 John 5:8). He may be referring to three warnings previously given.[35]

Paul is definitely coming. He previously changed his plans to spare them a painful visit (1:23). This time he will not spare them. He does not want to be severe, but he will be if it is necessary.

They were demanding proof that Christ was speaking through him, that is, proof of his apostleship and authority (cf. 10:1–11). They knew from experience that Christ was powerful, not weak, in His dealings with them. Though He died in bodily weakness on the cross (Isa. 52:14; 53:5,7), in that weakness He paid the price for sin. Then He rose to life by God's resurrection power (cf. Rom. 6:4; Eph. 1:19–20). Paul humbled himself to be weak in Christ. He also lived in God by His resurrection power, not to serve himself or to accomplish his own purposes but to serve God's people.

[5]Examine yourselves to see whether you are in the faith; test yourselves. Do you not realize that Christ Jesus is in you—unless, of course, you fail the test? [6]And I trust that you will discover that we have not failed the test.

They demanded "proof" (Gk. *dokimēn*) that Christ was speaking through Paul (v. 3). Now, because Paul did not want to have to discipline them, he demands that they examine themselves and put themselves to the proof, "test" themselves (Gk. *dokimazete*) to see if they are in the faith. This may mean they must test themselves to see if they are in right relation to the faith, that is, to what the Bible teaches. It may also mean they should test themselves to see if their faith is genuine. They will not fail the test if Christ is living within them. Paul in irony uses a play on words here between *dokimazete* ("test yourselves")

---

[35]James Hernando, "2 Corinthians," in *Full Life Bible Commentary* (Grand Rapids: Zondervan Publishing House, in press).

and *adokimoi* ("ones who fail the test") a word used of false teachers who were on their way to hell and dragging others with them (used also in the Septuagint of Isa. 1:22 of dross). Then, if they are not disproved by failing the test, this will mean that Paul and his company have not failed the test either. This implies that the false apostles are wrong. Paul's detractors should realize this.

> **7Now we pray to God that you will not do anything wrong. Not that people will see that we have stood the test but that you will do what is right even though we may seem to have failed. 8For we cannot do anything against the truth, but only for the truth.**

Paul was more concerned about the Corinthians than about himself. He had expressed his concern over the possibility that some might not have repented. Now his prayer is for them that they will not do anything wrong or evil. He does not want to have to discipline them. Nor does he care whether people see that he has stood the test. He wants them to do right even if it seems that he has failed or been rejected.

Paul knows the truth will stand. No one has the ability to do anything against the truth.[36] If it is the truth, it will still be the truth no matter what people say or do against it. Ultimately, whatever is done will be for the truth. Thus the false apostles will eventually be shown to be false.

> **9We are glad whenever we are weak but you are strong; and our prayer is for your perfection. 10This is why I write these things when I am absent, that when I come I may not have to be harsh in my use of authority —the authority the Lord gave me for building you up, not for tearing you down.**

Paul is glad to be weak if that means the Corinthians are strong (cf. 12:7–10; Eph. 6:10). He had already said his goal was to edify them, to build them up (10:8). His prayer was for their perfection,[37] that is,

---

[36]Paul probably has the gospel in mind as "the truth." Victor Paul Furnish, *II Corinthians* (Garden City, N.Y.: Doubleday & Co., 1984), 573.

[37]Ibid., and Barnett prefer to translate "perfection" (Gk. *katartisin*) as "restoration." The corresponding verb does basically mean restore or put in proper condition. The Corinthians did need restoration. Paul Barnett, *The Second Epistle to the Corinthians* (Grand Rapids: Wm. B. Eerdmans, 1997), 612–13. (See the New Living Translation.)

that they may be made complete (through training, disciplined learning; cf. Eph. 4:12; Heb. 6:1).

Again Paul emphasizes that he writes these admonitions, so that he will not have to use his God-given apostolic authority harshly or with severity when he comes. God gave him that authority to build up believers, not to tear them down or destroy them.

F. Concluding Greeting 13:11–14

11Finally, brothers, good-by. Aim for perfection, listen to my appeal, be of one mind, live in peace. And the God of love and peace will be with you. 12Greet one another with a holy kiss. 13All the saints send their greetings.

Paul concludes by saying "good-by" to the brothers (including the sisters): *Chairete!* Literally it meant "rejoice," but it was used in those days to say good-by (though here he may actually mean "rejoice"). Then he reiterates his challenge to "aim for perfection" (by restoring themselves). Let them listen to the "appeal" in this letter (which could also be translated, "Be encouraged!" and thus do all Paul has encouraged them to do in this letter[38]). Let them forget their differences and be of one mind, "united in their understanding of 'the faith,'"[39] and be at peace. Then the God of love and peace will be with them. God is indeed a good God and wants them to enjoy the blessings of His love and His peace.

To show their love and peace, let them greet one another with a holy kiss, probably a kiss on the cheek—something that is still more common in Eastern and European churches today than a handshake.

The saints who sent greetings were the Macedonian believers where Paul was at the time.

14May the grace of the Lord Jesus Christ, and the love of God, and the fellowship of the Holy Spirit be with you all.

Paul concludes with a Trinitarian blessing. As Hernando says, it "remarkably agrees with and seems to condense Paul's understanding of God's salvation in Christ."[40] The grace (unmerited favor and mercy) of Jesus, the Anointed One who is our Lord, includes a gra-

---

[38]Barnett, 616.

[39]Ibid.

[40]Hernando, "2 Corinthians," in press.

ciousness that comes to believers because of His Calvary love, shown when He took our place on the cross. The "love of God" was also especially shown when He gave His Son that we who believe might not perish but have eternal life (John 3:16; cf. Rom. 5:1,7–8). The "fellowship of the Holy Spirit" includes our fellowship with the Father and the Son. It includes also fellowship with one another through the Spirit and all the blessings of the Spirit as well (1 John 1:3,7). It is experienced also through the gifts of the Spirit expressed in mutual love (1 Cor. 13).

Paul looked on the local assembly as a fellowship (Gk. *koinōnia*) of the Spirit. Paul wanted to see that fellowship restored among the Corinthians believers. This wonderful relationship is still available to all believers, a relationship with our Triune God and with each other.

Study questions for this section may be found in appendix B.

APPENDIXES

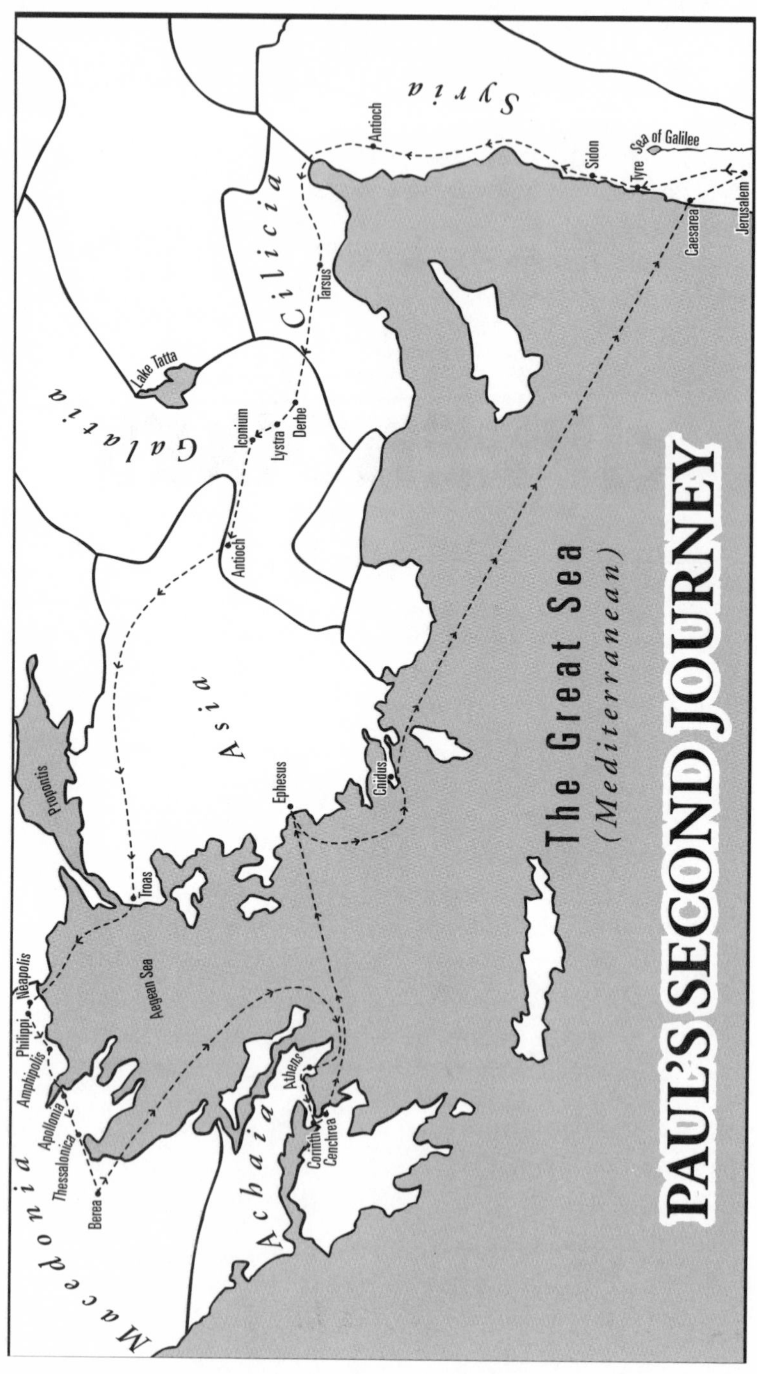
PAUL'S SECOND JOURNEY
The Great Sea
(Mediterranean)
Macedonia
Achaia
Asia
Galatia
Cilicia
Syria
Aegean Sea
Propontis
Lake Tatta
Sea of Galilee
Neapolis
Philippi
Amphipolis
Apollonia
Thessalonica
Berea
Athens
Corinth
Cenchrea
Troas
Ephesus
Cnidus
Antioch
Iconium
Lystra
Derbe
Tarsus
Antioch
Sidon
Tyre
Caesarea
Jerusalem

2 CORINTHIANS

I. Paul vindicates his conduct 1:1–2:11

1. What is the nature and purpose of the comfort that has its source in God?
2. How did the sufferings of Christ "flow over" into Paul's life? To what extent should we expect to experience this?
3. How did Paul show holiness and sincerity that come from God? How can we show the same kind of holiness and sincerity?
4. What is the significance of the "yes" and "amen" of God with respect to His promises?
5. What is the importance of the Spirit as a "seal" and as a "deposit," or first installment?
6. What caused the tears and broken heart of Paul (2:4)?
7. How can we keep Satan from outwitting us when we deal with the sin of a believer?

II. Paul's ministry under the new covenant 2:12–4:18

1. In what sense does God always lead us "in triumphal procession in Christ?"
2. How was Paul different from those who "peddle the word of God for profit"? How does this fit with 1 Timothy 5:17 where "double honor" means "double honorarium"?
3. Why does Paul call the body of believers in Corinth "a letter from Christ"?
4. Is there a sense in which we can be a letter from Christ?
5. Why does the letter of the new covenant kill?
6. How does Paul defend the ministry of the new covenant in Christ?
7. What kind of freedom is present "where the Spirit of the Lord is"?
8. How was Paul's ministry different from that of the false teachers in Corinth?
9. What is the treasure we have "in jars of clay"?
10. How was the resurrection life of Jesus revealed in Paul's body?
11. What is the secret of daily inward renewal as we grow older?
12. Why could Paul call his troubles "light and momentary"?
13. What can rob us of that "eternal glory" that far outweighs our troubles?

Paul's goals 5:1–6:13

Why does Paul use the conditional clause "if the earthly tent we live in is destroyed"?
What assurance does Paul give believers who die?
Why must believers appear "before the judgment seat of Christ"?
What did Christ's love compel Paul to do?
How can we keep from regarding believers from "a worldly point of view"?
What should be the chief message of Christ's ambassadors?
What does it mean to receive God's grace "in vain"?
How did Paul and his company show they were true servants of God?
How were the Corinthian believers responding to Paul's love for them?

STUDY QUESTIONS FOR 1 AND 2 CORINTHIANS

1 CORINTHIANS

I. Introduction 1:1–9

1. What good things about the Corinthian believers do you see in chapter 1?

II. Dissension in the Church 1:10–4:21

1. What divisions were beginning to develop in the local assembly and why?
2. Why did Paul personally baptize so few people?
3. What does the message of the Cross involve?
4. How is the gospel different from the wisdom of this world?
5. What was the attitude of the Jews and Gentiles to the preaching of Christ crucified and why?
6. What does God use to nullify the things unbelievers in this world highly esteem?
7. What in Christ Jesus is worthy of glory?
8. How was Paul's preaching different from the orations of the Greeks?
9. What was the secret wisdom Paul communicated to the mature believers?
10. Who knows the deep things of God and how does He communicate them to us?
11. What does Paul mean by "the spiritual man"?
12. What does it mean to have "the mind of Christ"?
13. What are the characteristics of a "worldly" Christian?
14. What attitudes were tending toward division in the local body of Christ?
15. What did Paul, Apollos, and God contribute to the growth of the local assembly?
16. Why is it important to be careful how we build the local assembly?
17. What does is mean to "suffer loss" (3:15)?
18. Why does Paul call the local assembly "God's temple," and what does this mean?
19. In what sense can we claim the statement "all are yours"?
20. Why does Paul care so little about how he is judged by his contemporaries or even by himself? Under what conditions is it unimportant what others think of us?
21. What were some of the Corinthian believers boasting about and why?
22. How does Paul explain what it means to be "made a spectacle"? What kind of example does this set for those who might claim apostolic ministry today?
23. How does the kingdom (rule) of God reveal itself?

III. Sinning Christians must be judged 5:1–6:19

1. Why is it important that Christians not tolerate sexual immorality?
2. What does it mean to "hand [someone] over to Satan"?
3. What does yeast symbolize in chapter 5?
4. How does Jesus fulfill the typology of the Old Testament Passover lamb?
5. If we are not to judge those outside the Church, how should we respond to those who want us to join marches, picket lines, etc.?
6. What kind of cases were Christians taking to pagan law courts?

7. Why does Paul want such cases to be decided within the local assembly?
8. What is necessary for a person to inherit the kingdom of God?
9. Why does the NIV enclose "Everything is permissible for me" in quotation marks?
10. Can we separate what our bodies do from what our spirits do or intend? Why is what we do in or with our bodies important?

IV. Questions answered 7:1–11:2

1. Why is 7:26 a key verse for understanding chapter 7?
2. Does Paul teach that sexual relations in marriage are only for procreation? Why or why not? How would you apply this to the matter of using anything to prevent conception?
3. Does Paul allow a believer to take the initiative in instituting a divorce? Why or why not?
4. What application can we make today of what Paul says about circumcision? About slavery?
5. Does 7:19 mean we should keep the Ten Commandments—or what does Paul have in mind?
6. Under what circumstances is it an advantage to remain unmarried?
7. How can we apply in today's world what Paul says about food sacrificed to idols?
8. Who are "the weak"?
9. What is meant by "a weak conscience"?
10. What principle should govern our activities so that we will not cause a weak believer to stumble or fall into sin?
11. How did Paul personally illustrate the principles taught in chapter 8?
12. What arguments show that those who teach the Word and spread the gospel should be supported?
13. Why did Paul give up his rights to such support?
14. What prize should all believers seek? How can it be obtained?
15. What will disqualify a person from obtaining the prize?
16. The Israelites were brought out of Egypt by grace through faith. In what ways was God faithful to them?
17. What caused some of them to die?
18. What is the significance of identifying "the spiritual rock" as Christ?
19. How does God show His faithfulness to us when we are tempted? Explain.
20. Why is pagan worship "the table of demons"?
21. How does doing "all for the glory of God" not cause anyone to stumble? Explain what is involved.
22. In what ways did Paul follow Christ, and how can we follow Paul's example?

V. Directions for worship 11:3–33

1. Does the fact God is Christ's Head mean that Christ is inferior or second-class? How does this apply to the relationship between husbands and wives?
2. How does Paul want male-female relationships to be reflected in public worship?
3. How should we apply today what Paul says about men's and women's hair?
4. What was the chief problem in the Corinthian believers' observance of the Lord's Supper and how did Paul want it corrected?

5. How does what Paul says about the Lord's Supper compare with the acco the Gospels?
6. What is necessary if we are to observe the Lord's Supper in a worthy m
7. Should servers withhold the elements of the Lord's Supper from unb From children?

VI. Spiritual gifts 12:1–14:40

1. In what ways do the Father, Son, and Holy Spirit cooperate in the a tion of spiritual gifts?
2. What examples of the nine gifts (12:8–10) can you give from the F experience?
3. Since the Holy Spirit administers the gifts "just as he determines," sibility does the individual believer have with respect to their opera
4. What interpretation of 12:12 seems best to you, and why?
5. How can the ministry of the gifts maintain both the unity and th the local body of believers?
6. What in chapter 12 shows that the gifts of the Spirit are for us to
7. Why is it possible for believers to minister spiritual gifts without
8. What are the most important characteristics and manifestations
9. When will gifts of prophecy, tongues, and knowledge no longer
10. In what ways will faith, hope, and love always continue?
11. Why is love the greatest?
12. What is involved in the gift of prophecy that makes it so valu body of believers?
13. What is the benefit of uninterpreted tongues?
14. When tongues are interpreted what benefits can the congrega
15. What limits does chapter 14 put on tongues? On prophecy?
16. What directions does Paul give for maintaining orderly wors

VII. Christ's resurrection and ours 15:1–58

1. What does Paul base his assurance of the truth of the gospe
2. Why is the promise of our resurrection so important?
3. What is the significance of calling Christ's resurrection "th
4. How should the assurance of our resurrection affect our w
5. How will our resurrection bodies be different from our pr
6. Why will it remain necessary for us to have bodies after J
7. For what purposes will God give us immortality in our r

VIII. Concluding instructions 16:1–24

1. What is the significance of asking the believers to set day of the week for the collection?
2. What does the Book of Acts tell about the "great do oppose" at Ephesus?
3. How can we apply the challenges and warnings Paul
4. Why does Paul call down a curse in 16:22?

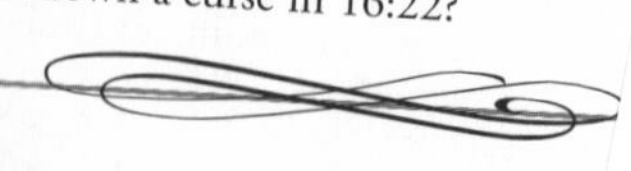

IV. Appealing to the Corinthians 6:14–7:16

1. In what ways could believers become "yoked together with unbelievers" and with what results?
2. What is involved in being separate?
3. What is necessary if we are to claim the promises of God?
4. What news did Titus bring that comforted Paul?
5. What is the difference between godly sorrow and worldly sorrow and what are the results of each?
6. Why was Paul able to say he had complete confidence in the Corinthian believers at this point?

V. Encouragement to give generously 8:1 to 9:15

1. What kind of example did the churches of Macedonia set?
2. In what ways did Jesus set an example?
3. What limits does Paul set on giving?
4. What did Paul do in order to avoid criticism of his administration of the liberal gift for the poor in Jerusalem?
5. How did Paul use the examples of the Greeks and Macedonians to challenge each other in giving?
6. What principles encourage generous giving?

VI. Paul's apostolic office and authority 10:1–13:14

1. Why did Paul appeal to the meekness and gentleness of Christ?
2. Why was it necessary for Paul to "wage war" and what did it involve?
3. What were Paul's weapons?
4. Why does Paul talk about boasting? Is he commending himself?
5. Why does Paul seem to do some foolish boasting?
6. What were the false apostles saying about Jesus?
7. What were the false apostles saying about Paul?
8. How can we detect false apostles?
9. Why does Paul describe his apostolic sufferings?
10. What did Paul learn when he was caught up to the third heaven?
11. Why was Paul given a thorn in his flesh and what did he learn from it?
12. What were the signs of a true apostle?
13. How did Paul show a spirit of dedicated love for the Corinthians?
14. What did Paul appeal to the Corinthians to repent of?
15. How did Paul promise to combine stern discipline with loving service?
16. Why did Paul challenge the Corinthian believers to examine themselves? How does this apply to us today?
17. Why can we do nothing "against the truth"?
18. What confidence does Paul show in his concluding exhortations and salutations?

SELECTED BIBLIOGRAPHY

Bruce, F. F. *1 and 2 Corinthians.* Grand Rapids: Wm. B. Eerdmans, 1983.

Carver, Frank G. "II Corinthians." In *The Beacon Bible Commentary.* Vol. 7. Kansas City, Mo.: Beacon Hill Press, 1968.

Clark, Gordon H. *First Corinthians: A Contemporary Commentary.* Nutley, N.J.: Presbyterian & Reformed Publishing Co., 1975.

Fee, Gordon D. *The First Epistle to the Corinthians.* Grand Rapids: Wm. B. Eerdmans, 1991.

Fisher, Fred. *Commentary on 1 and 2 Corinthians.* Waco, Tex.: Word Books, 1975.

Furnish, Victor Paul. *II Corinthians.* Anchor Bible Series, vol. 32A. Garden City, N.Y.: Doubleday & Co., 1984.

Hanson, R. P. C. *The Second Epistle to the Corinthians: Christ and Controversy.* London: SCM Press, 1967.

Hillyer, Norman. "1 and 2 Corinthians." In *The New Bible Commentary,* ed. D. Guthrie and J. A. Motyer. 3d ed. Grand Rapids: Wm. B. Eerdmans, 1970.

Hughes, Philip Edgcumbe. *Paul's Second Epistle to the Corinthians.* Grand Rapids: Wm. B. Eerdmans, 1973.

Lenski, R. C. H. *The Interpretation of St. Paul's First and Second Epistles to the Corinthians.* Minneapolis: Augsburg Publishing House, 1963.

Lias, J .J. *The Second Epistle to the Corinthians.* Cambridge, England: University Press, 1897.

Metz, Donald S. "I Corinthians." In *The Beacon Bible Commentary.* Vol. 7. Kansas City, Mo.: Beacon Hill Press, 1968.

Robertson, Archibald, and Alfred Plummer. *A Critical and Exegetical Commentary on the First Epistle of St. Paul to the Corinthians.* 2d ed. Edinburgh: T. & T. Clark, 1914.

Sumney, Jerry L. *Identifying Paul's Opponents.* Sheffield, England: Journal for the Study of the New Testament Press, 1990.

Thrall, Margaret E. *The First and Second Letters of Paul to the Corinthians.* Cambridge, England: University Press, 1965.

SCRIPTURE INDEX

OLD TESTAMENT

NEW TESTAMENT

SUBJECT INDEX

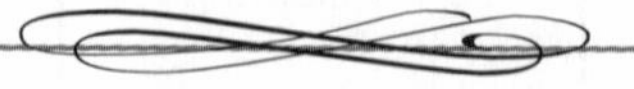